Shakespeare, Film, Fin de Siècle

Also by Mark Thornton Burnett

THE COMPLETE PLAYS OF CHRISTOPHER MARLOWE (*editor*)

NEW ESSAYS ON *HAMLET* (*co-editor with John Manning*)

* MASTERS AND SERVANTS IN ENGLISH RENAISSANCE DRAMA AND CULTURE: Authority and Obedience

* SHAKESPEARE AND IRELAND: History, Politics, Culture (*co-editor with Ramona Wray*)

Also by Ramona Wray

* SHAKESPEARE AND IRELAND: History, Politics, Culture (*co-editor with Mark Thornton Burnett*)

* *From the same publishers*

Shakespeare, Film, Fin de Siècle

Edited by

Mark Thornton Burnett
Reader in English
The Queen's University of Belfast

and

Ramona Wray
Lecturer in English
The Queen's University of Belfast

Foreword by Peter Holland

First published in Great Britain 2000 by
MACMILLAN PRESS LTD
Houndmills, Basingstoke, Hampshire RG21 6XS and London
Companies and representatives throughout the world

A catalogue record for this book is available from the British Library.

ISBN 0–333–77663–1 hardcover
ISBN 0–333–77664–X paperback

First published in the United States of America 2000 by
ST. MARTIN'S PRESS, INC.,
Scholarly and Reference Division,
175 Fifth Avenue, New York, N.Y. 10010

ISBN 0–312–23148–2

Library of Congress Cataloging-in-Publication Data
Shakespeare, film, fin de siècle / edited by Mark Thornton Burnett and Ramona
Wray.
p. cm.
Includes bibliographical references and index.
ISBN 0–312–23148–2
1. Shakespeare, William, 1564–1616—Film and video adaptations. 2. English
drama—Film and video adaptations. I. Burnett, Mark Thornton. II. Wray, Ramona,
1971–

PR3093 .S485 2000
791.43'6—dc21

99–059390

This book is printed on paper suitable for recycling and made from fully managed and sustained
forest sources.

10 9 8 7 6 5 4 3 2 1
09 08 07 06 05 04 03 02 01 00

Printed and bound in Great Britain by
Antony Rowe Ltd, Chippenham, Wiltshire

Contents

Acknowledgements

We are immeasurably grateful to Charmian Hearne, publisher at Macmillan, for supporting this project and encouraging its progress. As always, Charmian has been a model editor. We would also like to thank Kenneth Branagh for being able to squeeze in an interview during his busy shooting schedule. Thanks must go to Tamar Thomas for helping to set up the interview and to Phillip Rose for making available pre-shooting details of Kenneth Branagh's film version of *Love's Labour's Lost*. Sharon Lignier at Castle Rock negotiated the cover photograph, and Kenneth Branagh kindly allowed the image to be reproduced: to them both, thanks. At the Queen's University of Belfast, Jim McCluskey, Joan Rahilly and Tony Sheehan provided invaluable technical assistance – revealing the mysteries of audio equipment and translating seemingly unreadable computer disks. Finally, we thank the contributors for their efficiency in meeting deadlines and, when (sometimes copious!) rewritings and revisions were required, responding with brio and enthusiasm.

Notes on the Contributors

Douglas Bruster is an Assistant Professor of English at the University of Texas at Austin. He is the author of *Drama and the Market in the Age of Shakespeare* (Cambridge: Cambridge University Press, 1992), the inaugural title in the Cambridge University Press Studies in Renaissance Literature and Culture series. He is textual editor of *The Changeling* for *The Collected Works of Thomas Middleton* (Oxford University Press, forthcoming) and has published widely on Renaissance drama in such journals as *Renaissance Drama*, *Shakespeare Quarterly* and *Studies in English Literature*.

Judith Buchanan is a Senior Research Fellow at Worcester College, Oxford and lectures in Film Studies in the English Faculty at the University of Oxford. Since completing her doctorate on Shakespeare on film, she has published articles on Michael Powell's unmade film version of *The Tempest* (*Film Studies*, 1999) and on silent Shakespeare films for the journal of the *Maison Française* in Oxford (1999). She is currently writing two books – a general introduction to Shakespeare on film for the Longman/Pearson Inside Film Series and a historicized account of silent Shakespeare films.

Stephen M. Buhler is an Associate Professor of English at the University of Nebraska-Lincoln. His research interests range across philosophical backgrounds, performance histories and pedagogical practices. Recent publications include 'Counterpoint and Controversy: Milton and the Critiques of Polyphonic Music' (*Milton Studies*, 1998), 'Double Takes: Branagh Gets to *Hamlet*' (*Post Script*, 1997), 'No Spectre, No Sceptre: The Agon of Materialist Thought in *Julius Caesar*' (*English Literary Renaissance*, 1996, and *Shakespearean Criticism*, 1997), and 'Pre-Christian Apologetics in Spenser and Sidney' (*Spenser Studies*, 1999). He is completing a book about strategies of adaptation in Shakespeare films.

Mark Thornton Burnett is a Reader in English at the Queen's University of Belfast. He is the author of *Masters and Servants in English Renaissance Drama and Culture: Authority and Obedience* (London: Macmillan, 1997), the editor of *The Complete Plays of Christopher*

Marlowe (London: Everyman, 1999) and the co-editor of *New Essays on 'Hamlet'* (New York: AMS, 1994). He is currently editing the poems of Christopher Marlowe for Everyman and writing *Constructing 'Monsters' in Shakespearean Drama and Early Modern Culture* for the Macmillan Early Modern Literature in History series.

Richard Burt is Professor of English at the University of Massachusetts. He is the author of *Licensed by Authority: Ben Jonson and the Discourses of Censorship* (Ithaca and London: Cornell University Press, 1993), the co-editor of *Enclosure Acts: Sexuality, Property, and Culture in Early Modern England* (Ithaca and London: Cornell University Press, 1994), the editor of *The Administration of Aesthetics: Censorship, Political Criticism, and the Public Sphere* (Minneapolis and London: University of Minnesota Press, 1994), the co-editor of *Shakespeare, the Movie: Popularizing the Plays on Film, TV, and Video* (London and New York: Routledge, 1997) and the author of *Unspeakable ShaXXXspeares: Queer Theory and American Kiddie Culture* (New York: St. Martin's Press, 1998).

Peter Holland is Director of the Shakespeare Institute, Stratford-upon-Avon, and Professor of Shakespeare Studies at the University of Birmingham. Among his Shakespeare studies are an edition of *A Midsummer Night's Dream* for the Oxford Shakespeare (Oxford: Clarendon, 1994) and *English Shakespeares* (Cambridge: Cambridge University Press, 1997). He is currently writing his own study of Shakespeare and film.

Margaret Jane Kidnie is a Lecturer in English at South Bank University, London. She has published articles in the fields of gender performance and textual editing, and is currently publishing an old-spelling edition of Phillip Stubbes' *Anatomie of Abuses* with the Renaissance English Text Society. She is also completing an edition of four Ben Jonson plays for the World's Classics series (Oxford University Press).

James N. Loehlin is an Associate Professor of English and the Associate Director of the Shakespeare at Winedale Programme at the University of Texas at Austin. He is the author of *Henry V* (Manchester: Manchester University Press, 1996) in the Shakespeare in Performance series, as well as articles on teaching Shakespeare and Shakespeare and film. He is also a director and actor.

Amelia Marriette was a civil servant for twelve years, working as a Higher Executive Officer at the Defence Research Agency. Having completed her BA in History and Literature from the Open University in 1994, she resigned from her post and became a full-time student at the Shakespeare Institute (University of Birmingham). She completed her MA there in 1996 and is currently at the Institute completing her PhD. She lectures for the Open University and the Shakespeare Centre, Stratford-upon-Avon.

Andrew Murphy is a Lecturer in English at the University of St. Andrews. He is the author of *'But the Irish Sea Betwixt Us': Ireland, Colonialism, and Renaissance Literature* (Lexington: University Press of Kentucky, 1999) and the editor of *The Renaissance Text: Theory, Editing, Textuality* (Manchester: Manchester University Press, 2000). He is currently working on a book entitled *Shakespeare in Print: A History and Chronology of Shakespeare Publishing, 1590–2000*, to be published by Cambridge University Press.

Julie Sanders is a Lecturer in English at Keele University. She is the author of *Ben Jonson's Theatrical Republics* (London: Macmillan, 1998) and the co-editor (with Kate Chedgzoy and Sue Wiseman) of *Refashioning Ben Jonson: Gender, Politics and the Jonsonian Canon* (London: Macmillan, 1998). She has published articles in *English Literary Renaissance*, *Modern Language Review* and *Notes and Queries*, and is currently working on *Caroline Dramatists* for the Writers and their Work series as well as the *Oxford Book of Seventeenth-Century Women Poets*, for which she is a contributing editor.

Neil Sinyard is Head of the Department of English at the University of Hull. He is the author of numerous film studies, including *Filming Literature: The Art of Screen Adaptation* (London: Croom Helm, 1986) and *Children in the Movies* (London: Batsford, 1992). Currently he is writing *Graham Greene: A Literary Life* (Macmillan) and *Make It New: Modernism in the Arts, 1910–1914* (Camden House).

Emma Smith is a Fellow of Hertford College and a Lecturer in English at the University of Oxford. She has edited Thomas Kyd's *The Spanish Tragedy* (Harmondsworth: Penguin, 1998) and *Henry V* (Cambridge: Cambridge University Press, 2000) for the Shakespeare in Production series. Her current research is on ghosts in early modern English culture.

Ramona Wray is a Lecturer in English at the Queen's University of Belfast. She is the co-editor of *Shakespeare and Ireland: History, Politics, Culture* (London: Macmillan, 1997). She is currently completing *Women Writers of the Seventeenth Century* (Northcote House) and editing *Women, Writing, Revolution: An Anthology of Writing by Women, 1640–1660* (Blackwell).

Foreword

When, in *Troilus and Cressida*, Troilus tries to make desperate sense of the scene between Cressida and Diomedes, which he has just been watching, he reaches a position of absolute logical impasse in his attempt to reconcile the different Cressidas he has constructed out of his perception of her actions: 'This is, and is not, Cressid.'[1] The study of Shakespeare on film has often seemed intensely and agonizingly preoccupied with searching for answers to the self-imposed question of the films' relation to Shakespeare, and has usually triumphantly managed to come up with no better solution than that film is and is not Shakespeare.

Troilus watching Cressida and Diomedes is himself watched by Ulysses and Thersites. Without wishing to align myself too firmly with the cynicism of either of these bitter observers, I wonder whether it is time to seek for different questions to ask of the ever-increasing body of Shakespeare films. The amused detachment of Ulysses or Thersites in contemplating the agony of desire is still implicated in the fascination of the gaze itself on the revealed body; Thersites and Ulysses are as trapped in the scopophilic mechanism of the voyeur as Troilus is. Instead of gazing at the history of the study of Shakespeare films as versions of Shakespeare performance, we could now start to worry at the nature of the cultural circumstances that generate the object – Shakespeare films – which provides the material body for our gaze.

The last few years have witnessed the steady trickle of films turn into a flood. For the first time since the end of the era of silent film, Shakespeare films 'come not single spies, / But in battalions', bringing not so much the 'sorrows' Claudius was thinking of as an increasing awareness of the cultural pressures that have led film studios to turn so frequently now to their most prolific screenplay writer.[2] Film is the most expensive of art-forms. The scale of financial investment in film is so high and the possibility of financial return so large that this repeated and contagious turning towards Shakespeare, the iconic embodiment of élitist high culture, seems founded on a marketing assumption that 'Shakespeare' sells. Advertising a film is so costly that the expenditure on a film from the end of principal photography to distribution is now at least as large as the cost of filming itself.

But to whom does 'Shakespeare' sell its cultural cachet? The processes of film production mean that the product is endlessly sold and resold. It must be marketable to studio and backers, to stars and directors, to distributors and newspaper feature writers, to chat-show hosts and film reviewers long before it is ever sold directly to the cinema-going public. Thereafter it must be sold on to the video companies, to the film-buyers for television, to the supermarkets who sell the video and the publishers who will produce the book of the film. What drew Charlton Heston or Billy Crystal to appearing in Kenneth Branagh's *Hamlet* was just as much *Hamlet* as Branagh. What drew purchasers to buy a copy of *William Shakespeare's 'Romeo & Juliet': The Contemporary Film, the Classic Play* was not only the picture on the cover of Danes and DiCaprio about to kiss.[3] And I am quite sure that what led Sir Herbert Beerbohm Tree to take his theatre company out of the theatre in order to film a brief extract from *King John* in 1899 was as much the fortune that might come through the screening of the film and the fame of taking Shakespeare into the new era of cinematography as any idealistic notion of making Shakespeare more widely accessible.

One hundred years after Tree, perhaps little has changed. The parasitism of Shakespeare film on the theatre has weakened. The techniques of film have developed in complexity and possibility. The massiveness of the machinery of filming has increased gargantuanly. But at the *fin* of a rather different *siècle* the terms and conditions are still strikingly similar. Baz Luhrmann's *William Shakespeare's 'Romeo + Juliet'* is, I would argue, more culturally significant than Kenneth Branagh's *Hamlet*, not because of any judgement of film aesthetics or the critical values invoked by the scholarship of Shakespeare in performance, but simply because it is the first Shakespeare film to make a considerable return on its original investment, over sixty years after Warner Brothers put $1.5 million, double the original budget, into Reinhardt and Dieterle's *A Midsummer Night's Dream* in 1935 and lost most of it. Only by finding a new audience, an audience that has little or no interest in Shakespeare in the theatre (or indeed in Shakespeare *tout court*), can the investment be profitably returned.

By the time this foreword is published, three or four more Shakespeare films will be completed and distributed. Others now in pre-production will probably never be filmed. Remarkably, all will be generated by major studios. As a result of this interest, art-house Shakespeare is a rarity now, where for Orson Welles, Grigori Kozintsev or Akira Kurosawa it was the effective norm. Of the films with which the essays in this collection are concerned, only Mazursky's *Tempest* and Edzard's *As You Like It* fall in such a category. If art-house and video represent the extent of the distribution history of Adrian Noble's *A Midsummer Night's Dream*, it is an index of the film's commercial failure rather than a decision inherent in its conception. There is even space now for a mainstream release for a film about making a Shakespeare film, Al Pacino's *Looking for Richard*, the first Shakespeare metafilm.

Troilus cursed '[b]ifold authority' (V.ii.142) as a tension between reason and loss, but the multiple cultural authorities under which the commerce of Shakespearean commodification occurs represent reformulations of the rationality of profit. The line from the economics of the Globe theatre to those of the Sony Corporation is taut and strong. Shakespearean film can now be read against film rather than Shakespeare. But that is no great reach: playmaker and filmmakers would understand each other, and we can enjoy watching their gaze at each other.

Peter Holland

Notes

1   *Troilus and Cressida*, ed. Kenneth Muir (Oxford: Oxford University Press, 1994), V.ii.144. All further references appear in the text.
2   *Hamlet*, ed. G.R. Hibbard (Oxford: Oxford University Press, 1994), IV.v.74–5.
3   Baz Luhrmann, *William Shakespeare's 'Romeo & Juliet': The Contemporary Film, the Classic Play* (New York: Bantam Doubleday, 1996).

Introduction

Mark Thornton Burnett and Ramona Wray

To capture a sense of the distinctiveness of the film *Shakespeare in Love*, Jack Kroll in a *Newsweek* item offers a parody of Sonnet 18. In his rewriting, the sonnet's object of praise becomes cinematic artifact rather than mysterious lover:

> Shall I compare thee to an action flick?
> Thou art more witty, sexy, sweet and warm,
> No morphing monster, no karate kid,
> No drooling space-bug beats this movie's charm.[1]

With an intertextual gesture to the appropriation of the sonnet in the film itself, this new version of the verse sets up a dichotomy between established Hollywood genres – such as science fiction and action films – and the fresh-faced appeal of director John Madden's production.[2] Engineered here is a construction of *Shakespeare in Love* as a culturally superior work, one which casts into shade the (presumed) less demanding characteristics of other big-budget fare. From Kroll's revisioning, Shakespeare emerges as the implied repository of abiding qualities of intellect and sensibility: a joky imperialism is mobilized whereby Britishness wins out over the predictability of the American movie industry.

Itself a rewriting or reinventing of lacunae in Shakespeare's biographical record and the processes of his dramatic composition, *Shakespeare in Love*, however, can stand only partially as a British venture.[3] As a production featuring American performers and dependent upon US backing, the film, according to a recent newspaper analysis, lays claim to a 'contentious' '"Britishness"', and 'all that is is left is a vague idea of "cultural content"'.[4] *Shakespeare in Love* and Old

1

Blighty are not as close as it might initially appear. Furthermore, if Shakespeare acts as a guarantor for *Shakespeare in Love*'s cultural authority, he has not prevented the film from quickly being tarnished with the kind of mass-cultural association that a journalist such as Kroll is keen to denigrate. Almost as soon as an article appeared in the *The Daily Mail* about the film's possible borrowings from Caryl Brahms and S. J. Simon's novel, *No Bed for Bacon*, the *exposé*'s materials were being recycled in the same paper to advertise Danish bacon.[5]

Delightfully slanderous as such claims to indebtedness might be, more interesting is the way in which *Shakespeare in Love* owes its impact to, and builds upon the precedent of, two previous 'Shakespearean' films, Baz Luhrmann's *William Shakespeare's 'Romeo + Juliet'* and Shekhar Kapur's *Elizabeth*. It might be argued that *Shakespeare in Love*'s audacious conjuring with *Romeo and Juliet* was comprehensible only because of Luhrmann's commercial success, and that the film's choice of text consolidated a popular shift in Shakespearean protagonists (from Hamlet to Romeo) initiated by the earlier director. One might suggest, too, that the attention given to a reconceptualization of Elizabeth's early years in *Elizabeth* provides a legitimating force for a representation, in *Shakespeare in Love*, of the Queen in her decline.

Shakespeare in Love, in fact, has been generally facilitated by the rush of Shakespearean films that has overtaken cinemas over the course of the 1990s. Since the mid-1990s, there has been an explosion of filmic interpretations offering major reassessments of Shakespearean drama. In addition to Baz Luhrmann's *William Shakespeare's 'Romeo + Juliet'*, Kenneth Branagh's *Hamlet* and *Love's Labour's Lost*, Christine Edzard's *As You Like It*, Richard Loncraine's *Richard III*, Adrian Noble's *A Midsummer Night's Dream* and Oliver Parker's *Othello*, among others, have all attracted varying degrees of excitement, generating in the process considerable speculation about Shakespeare's marketability and cinematic appeal. To these can be added a plethora of films inspired by, or indebted to, the place of Shakespeare in the cultural imagination. *Shakespeare in Love* is perhaps the most obvious example of the fracturing of the dramatist into other narratives, but one must also mention Kenneth Branagh's *In the Bleak Midwinter*, Lloyd Kaufman's *Tromeo and Juliet*, Paul Mazursky's *Tempest* and Al Pacino's *Looking for Richard*. Such a revitalization of the Bard has had a two-fold effect. First, it has instituted as a crucial element of modern cinema culture an intertextual body of work with a Shakespearean theme. Second, it has allowed Shakespeare to take on a new prominence in the popular psyche. In a recent Radio 4 poll, Shakespeare was voted the 'Most Popular Personality of the Millennium', above Sir Winston Churchill (who was placed second) and Charles Darwin and Miss Piggy (who were placed runners-up).[6] The newspaper article about the poll featured a cartoon of a tearful Shakespeare accepting an Oscar-like statuette, a potent image of the links between cinematic appropriation and a public, media profile.

Nor does the Shakespearean cinematic deluge shows any signs of abating. Just out or in production as this book nears completion are film versions of *Hamlet* (with Ethan Hawke, Sam Shepard and Bill Murray), of *A Midsummer Night's Dream* (with Anna Friel, Calista Flockhart and Michelle Pfeiffer), of *Othello* (or *O*, as it is termed, with Mekhl Phifer, Josh Hartnett and Julia Styles) and of *Titus Andronicus* (with Anthony Hopkins, Jessica Lange and Alan Cumming).[7] Cinematic realizations with Shakespeare as their subtext continue, too, as is testified to by the films *Hear in Blood* (based on *Macbeth*), *Let the Devil Wear Black* (based on *Hamlet*) and *Ten Things I Hate about You* (based on *The Taming of the Shrew*), which are about to enjoy release.[8] Such has been the resurgence of Shakespeare in the cinema, moreover, that the Bard is being given a makeover for a whole host of related media appearances. A Shakespeare-inspired musical, *Play On!*, is on its way to Britain from the US, and the television station ITV has approved a £20 million plan to turn twenty of the Bard's 'greatest' plays into contemporary thrillers, police dramas and comedies to be broadcast on Sunday nights.[9] As the 1990s come to an end, it is Shakespeare, more than any other writer-artist, who is garnering an unprecedented representational attention.[10]

In 1999, as *Shakespeare, Film, Fin de Siècle* goes to press, all this seems a far cry from one hundred years ago, when, in the last few months of the nineteenth century, the first Shakespeare film, Herbert Beerbohm Tree's *King John*, unfolded at Her Majesty's Theatre in London. Yet, despite the technological, mass media and communication revolutions separating Tree and the glut of Shakespeare films of the 1990s, an end-of-century sensibility unites both cinematic endeavours. In a gesture characteristic of the twentieth century's final decade of Shakespearean filmmaking, *King John* embraces a poeticized version of the past (seen nowhere more obviously than in the interpolated scene of the signing of the Magna Carta), romantically recasting a history of Victorian social reform. This nostalgic movement finds its animating logic in the film's *fin-de-siècle* moment of production and links it to the latest crop of screen constructions of the Bard.[11] *In the Bleak*

Midwinter unfolds in an unspecified earlier moment of theatrical *bonhomie*; *Richard III* takes place in an imaginative rendering of the 1930s; *Hamlet* and *A Midsummer Night's Dream* evoke the world of the 1890s; and *Shakespeare in Love* invests in attempting to recover the so-called 'lost years' of Shakespeare's youth, the 1590s. To make cinematically pertinent a Shakespeare for the end of the twentieth century, it seems, is also to survey and represent a host of previous moments in which his transmission and circulation are implicated.

The essays gathered together in this volume argue that recent Shakespearean films are key instruments with which western culture confronts the anxieties attendant upon the transition from one century to another. In complementary ways, they confront the signif-icance of the *fin de siècle* and seek to address the relationship of the filmic Shakespeare to millennial themes and images. Far from promoting a 'dumbing down' of Shakespeare, the films, the contributors maintain, engage with some of the most pressing concerns of the present, apocalyptic condition – familial crisis, social estrangement, urban blight, cultural hybridity, literary authority, the role of reading and writing, the impact of technology and the end of history. In this sense, the films, which range from those which look forward to *fin-de-siècle* debates to those which are full participants in that ongoing discussion, glance to the future as much as they look back. On the cover of this book is reproduced a photograph of Kenneth Branagh as Hamlet. Meditating upon his image in one of the many mirrors that festoon the state hall of Elsinore, Branagh as Hamlet seems poised on the cusp of a liminal terrain, divided between two states of being. From the viewer's perspective, Branagh/Hamlet sees forward; from his own point of view, he contemplates in a backward direction his own reflection. It is a composition that neatly complicates the boundary between the 'real' and the 'imaginary' even as it splits and bifurcates Hamlet's perceived identity. In the same way that the Shakespeare films of the last decade have used a constructed 'now' to negotiate what is to come, so does the publicity still of Hamlet raise questions about things past and things still ahead.

Shakespeare, Film, Fin de Siècle opens with two essays which address, in a contrasting fashion, the relationship between Shakespearean filmmaking and postmodernity. For Andrew Murphy, whose interests cluster around the book, vexed intersections bind together Shakespeare, recent cinema and the text. Concentrating on the 'posterior' and 'rudimentary' textual aspirations of Branagh's *Hamlet* and the more emancipatory textual possibilities summoned up by Peter

Greenaway's *Prospero's Books*, Murphy offers a timely contribution to debates about the writer's authority and the stability of his/her work. His call for a millennial filmic intertextuality sits well with the post-modern interrogation of the supposed integrity and coherence of all textual announcements. With a comparable deployment of post-modernity comes Douglas Bruster's essay, which sees Mazursky's *Tempest* as an artistically self-conscious postmodern experiment. Although *Tempest* first appeared in 1982, it nevertheless demonstrates, as Bruster convincingly argues, a pronounced sensitivity to forms of visual experience, making it a telling commentary on the Shakespeare films of the 1990s that followed. Thus, through its characters (such as Phillip, who is both designer and filmmaker) and its properties (such as the aerial and the cave), the film offers a provocative allegory on the nature of art, on the tensions that feed rivalries between cinematic and televisual cultures.

Interrelated essays on the history play genre on film, which focus in particular on *Richard III*, ensue. In Stephen M. Buhler's essay, Loncraine's film, *Richard III*, constitutes a 'camp' statement which, in millennial mode, uses an eroticized irony, aestheticism, theatricality and humour to mock a gallery of movie genres from the 1930s onwards. Combining evocations of gangster and heritage film conven-tions and of Derek Jarman's *Edward II*, *Richard III* facilitates a voyeuristic representation of the sexual alienation and frustration of the central character. Similarly focused on the play *Richard III* is Neil Sinyard's discussion of Pacino's *Looking for Richard*. An appreciation of cinematic technique forms the backbone of this chapter, and Sinyard maps adroitly the Wellesian montage, dissolves, choreography and cross-cutting shifts of perspective through which the director communicates his filmic essay. Such a variety of styles, the chapter suggests, enables Pacino, at a transitional juncture characterized by canonical uncer-tainty and competing constructions of 'Shakespeare', to reveal the processes whereby he arrived at his unique interpretive vantage-point.

From the histories it is a short step to the comedies and to two more grouped essays. In Edzard's *As You Like It*, Amelia Marriette locates a distinctively *fin-de-siècle* creation, a filmic reflection upon a dystopian city divided into a corporate business world and an urban wasteland. Enlisting a Baudrillardian analysis, a reading of key movies from the 1980s and a specially commissioned interview with the director, Marriette presents *As You Like It* as a critique of post-Thatcherite urban policy. She also demonstrates how the film, despite its gloomy rework-ing of the play's pastoral elements, invests in open spaces, glass surfaces and liquid allusions to suggest a potential for psychological reformation. Where *As You Like It* centres upon one decade through which to view the play, Noble's *A Midsummer Night's Dream*, Mark Thornton Burnett contends in his contribution, favours three. The 1590s, the 1890s and the 1990s, Burnett argues, are all brought into play in Noble's production, in such a way as to sound variations on the drama's exploration of 'impressions', 'fantasies' and the 'imagination'. The director's particular concern is the untenability of the *fin-de-siècle* nuclear family, and the childhood reminiscences, literary allusions and sexual awakenings that pepper the action are instrumental in promoting this filmic focus. As Noble pursues his theme, moreover, he simultaneously provokes reflections upon rivalrous versions of history and modes of artistic enterprise.

Of course, the Shakespearean play that exercised the greatest imaginative engagement over the course of the 1990s was *Romeo and Juliet*, thanks, in part, to its reinvention in *Shakespeare in Love*. Both the play and its appropriations are attended to by Margaret Jane Kidnie and James N. Loehlin. *Tromeo and Juliet*, a generically amorphous, culturally diverse and violently oriented parody of Shakespeare's play, is considered by Kidnie from ecofeminist and Lyotardian positions. The film's emphasis on a 'risk society', encapsulated in its concern with ecological contamination and industrial capitalism, is seen by Kidnie as integrally related to its larger end-of-century critique of institutionalized systems of oppression. By simultaneously invoking 'high' and 'low' expressions of Shakespeare, Kidnie concludes, *Tromeo and Juliet* neither banishes nor privileges the dramatist: instead, it leaves him on both sides of the cultural divide. That mixture of 'high' and 'low' aesthetic features is also, Loehlin argues, central to the effect of Luhrmann's *William Shakespeare's 'Romeo + Juliet'*. The eclectic visual style, fashionable ironies and rock video flourishes are what preoccupy Loehlin in an essay that highlights the director's fascination with conspicuous consumption and civic breakdown. Invocations of 'teen films', such as *Rebel Without a Cause* and *West Side Story*, Loehlin maintains, represent a compendium of references to late twentieth-century popular culture, and they operate forcefully both as symptoms of the commercialization of young love and as signs of the media-saturated modes of the new millennium.

Arguably, the director who has stamped his presence most energetically on the Shakespeare films of the 1990s is Kenneth Branagh. To illuminate and contextualize Branagh's recent Shakespearean filmmaking is the task of the next three essays in the volume. Taking off from the thesis that Branagh's *In the Bleak Midwinter* is a *fin-de-siècle* scapegoat, Emma Smith argues that the film functions to reinforce the aspirations of the subsequent *Hamlet* to a classic cinema status. The film, she posits, both undoes and affirms the relevance of Shakespeare's *Hamlet*, addressing, at the same time, the problem of how to approach 'high art' in an age of ironic aesthetic detachment. Elaborating Smith's retrospective suggestions, Julie Sanders in her chapter approaches *Hamlet* by way of the death of Diana, Princess of Wales, and anxieties about the future of the monarchy in the twentieth century's final decade. Branagh's *Hamlet*, Sanders establishes, is tied up in contradictory ways with the iconography of monarchy inscribed on the British psyche. It is intimately associated, too, with the unsettled political climate that obtained at the close of the 1990s, hence its nostalgic but inconsistent yearnings for monarchical and communist forms of government. Concluding the Branagh triad of essays is Ramona Wray and Mark Thornton Burnett's interview with the director, which appears in this book for the first time. The interview, conducted in 1999, provided an opportunity for Branagh to reflect on all of his Shakespeare films thus far, and for him to respond to questions, several of which were stimulated by the essays themselves.

The *fin de siècle*, however, is only one framework within which Shakespearean filmmaking at the end of the 1990s might be appreciated. The final two essays in the collection, therefore, begin the project of opening out the films to accommodate other interpretative paradigms. While recognizing the pervasive influence of the millennium, these essays also acknowledge that there are related contexts shaping the filmic endeavour. In an extended disquisition on Parker's *Othello*, Judith Buchanan investigates the film's configuration of belonging and difference, and manipulation of the subjectivized gaze. The director's eroticization of the protagonist, and his utilization of hard objects, mirrors and diaphanous fabrics, work to consolidate a sense of Othello as a split, self-dramatizing misfit. Buchanan's concluding point is that the Christocentric assumptions underpinning the millennium make this moment in history of only partial relevance to discussions of racial alterity. In contrast, Richard Burt in his chapter extends the contexts shaping Shakespearean filmmaking by taking into account other mass-market narratives. He reads *Shakespeare in Love* alongside two popular novels to suggest that Shakespeare is being increasingly feminized, turned into a cultural effect of gender trouble, anxiety about sexual orientation and speculation about literary impotence. In *Shakespeare in Love*, in particular,

Burt argues, Shakespeare is represented as an artist who has to discard male collaborators to be creative. The resulting sense of an individuated artistic maturity fuels, in turn, an ironic treatment of the Hollywood industry which helped to produce the film in the first place. In recent years, thanks to both theatrical and ideological developments – landmark productions and theoretical shifts in English studies – Shakespeare has been reconstituted as a multicultural phenomenon, a site for argument over literary authority and an infinitely adaptable dramatic property. To these still unfolding versions of Shakespeare the films of the millennium are making a crucial contribution. They constitute not only a supplement to the newly reconstructed Bard in other media and representational systems, but also a significant stage in the process of remaking his works for the twenty-first century. Above all, Shakespeare films have been transformative, freeing up canonical notions, reconfiguring forms of performative attention, fostering productive tensions between the author and the *auteur*, and creating fresh links with other visual locations and technological venues. In that whirlwind of Shakespearean filmmaking that has left its imprint on the 1990s, we have witnessed a significant alteration in conceptions of Shakespeare and Shakespearean drama in the vernacular consciousness. The films have cross-fertilized, too, with academic constructions of, and approaches to, the dramatist, to the extent that distinctions between the various Shakespeares circulating in contemporary culture are increasingly difficult to maintain. For, even as the films raise questions about their own self-referential status, so is an increased interest being generated in the nature of the Shakespearean text, the modes of its transmission and its claims to authenticity. But if the films mark an end to one, twentieth-century, articulation of Shakespeare, they also announce another Bardic birth. The present generation of Shakespeare on film, and the one to come, promise to bring the karate kids, the morphing monsters and the space-bugs to the dramatist, and vice versa. Where one 'Shakespeare' ends and another begins only future filmic 'Shakespeares' will tell.

Notes

1. Jack Kroll, 'Close-Up on Will', *Newsweek*, 15 February (1999), p. 62.
2. See Marc Norman and Tom Stoppard's screenplay, *Shakespeare in Love* (London: Faber and Faber, 1999), p. 61. The sonnet is also reproduced in the collection inspired by the film, *Shakespeare in Love: The Love Poetry of William Shakespeare* (London: Faber and Faber, 1999), p. 49.
3. For reflections upon the background to the film, see Stephen Greenblatt,

'About that Romantic Sonnet', *New York Times*, 6 February (1999), section A29.

4. Andrew Pulver, 'Bard to Worse at the Multiplex', *The Guardian*, 5 February (1999), p. 19.

5. *The Mail on Sunday*, 7 February (1999), p. 32. On the borrowings, see Rhys Williams, '"Shakespeare" film script in copycat dispute', *The Independent*, 4 February (1999), p. 6.

6. *The Times: Mega*, 23 January (1999), p. 3.

7. 'All in love with Bard', *The Daily Mail*, 17 April (1998), p. 43; Jessica Shaw, 'Good Will Hunting', *Entertainment Weekly*, 12 February (1999), pp. 8–9.

8. *Flicks: Trailers*, June (1998), p. 7; Shaw, 'Good Will Hunting', pp. 8–9.

9. Maurice Chittenden, 'Wherefore art thou, Will?', *The Sunday Times: Focus*, 24 January (1999), p. 15; Nicholas Hellen, 'ITV gives Bard modern makeover', *The Sunday Times: News*, 19 July (1998), p. 10.

10. Bolstering this argument is the fact that *Hamlet* has recently been voted 'masterwork of the millennium'. See Anthony Clare, 'Simply the Best', *The Sunday Times: Culture*, 28 March (1999), pp. 12–13. One might also add that the Shakespeare Birthplace Trust, with the support of Shakespeare Link, Globe Education, the English Shakespeare Company, the Royal Shakespeare Company and Playbox Theatre, are planning the largest ever world-wide Shakespeare Performance Festival to celebrate the 'New Millennium' (announcement at the Shakespeare Association of America Conference, San Franciso, April 1999).

11. Drawing vast audiences during its substantial run, Tree's *King John*, a radically truncated version of the text, combined pageantry, artificial scenery, spectacular tableaux and stylish historical motifs in a bold interpretation of British imperial democracy. These and other details are taken from John Collick, *Shakespeare, Cinema and Society* (Manchester: Manchester University Press, 1989), pp. 35–7.

1
The Book on the Screen: Shakespeare Films and Textual Culture

Andrew Murphy

In a pivotal scene from Lloyd Kaufman's *Tromeo and Juliet*, Tromeo, having just stuffed tampons up Juliet's father's nostrils, reaches back to grab a hefty hardback volume from his lover's bed. As the father shouts, 'No, not Shakespeare!', Tromeo batters him across the head with the *Yale* text of the playwright's works. What is interesting here is not so much the role that the text plays in the assault, but rather an odd continuity failure. Close examination of the episode indicates that the film offers us an odd disjunction, owing to the way in which the individual sequences that make up the scene were filmed. Some segments of the scene were shot with the Shakespeare volume on Juliet's dressing table, some with the text on the bed, convenient for Tromeo to take it up as a weapon. Over the course of the scene, the book shifts in and out of view in the two locations, before finally ending up on the floor, spattered with Capulet's blood. The disjunction is perhaps emblematic of the relationship between Kaufman's film and Shakespeare's play: now you see the Shakespeare, now you don't (and mostly you don't, as you sit through scenes of masturbation, body piercing, incest and mutilation). Where the Shakespeare text does appear (in the occasional fragments of verse that are retained or in skeletal lineaments of plot), it is always dislocated and out of joint.

As Margaret Jane Kidnie notes elsewhere in this collection, Kaufman's movie folds the Shakespeare text – and Shakespearean cultural iconography – back upon itself in a series of parodic, knowing, self-conscious gestures. In a sense, we might say, the disjunct presence of the *Yale Shakespeare* within the film-frame serves to measure the parodic distance between Kaufman's film and the text which it spoofs and interrogates. Kaufman's gesture of putting a Shakespeare text on display within a Shakespeare film is not, however, wholly original.[1] A

10

number of critics have recently drawn attention to a 1916 silent film of *King Lear* which opens with the actor who will play Lear (Frederick Warde) dressed as a Victorian gentleman, seated in an armchair reading a book. As Douglas Lanier notes, '[i]n close-up that book is revealed to be *King Lear*, at which, via a camera trick, Warde dissolves into the character Lear and the narrative proper begins'.[2] If Kaufman uses the book to signal a kind of bravura self-consciousness, the Warde *Lear*, by contrast, seems to be endeavouring to negotiate, through the book, its own anxious relationship – as a severely attenuated, silent performance – with the text which is its source. The encounter with the book represents, in this instance, a kind of Bloomian moment, in which the film attempts to negotiate the fact of its own belatedness, and of its posterior, diminished status.[3]

Warde's early, condensed, silent *Lear* can usefully be contrasted in this regard with a more recent Shakespeare film – Kenneth Branagh's *Hamlet*. In Branagh's movie we find no self-conscious figuring of the text itself within the film-frame. Nevertheless, this *is* a peculiarly bibliocentric production. As Mark Thornton Burnett has noted, the movie is decidedly 'bookish' – 'a favourite retreat for Hamlet is his book-lined study: it is here, not accidentally, that he consults a treatise on demons before setting out to confront the ghost'.[4] The book-lined study is the central space associated with Hamlet in the film, and it is noteworthy that two of the entrances to the study consist of hinged bookcases.[5] The concealed doorways are wholly in keeping with Branagh's broader vision of Elsinore as a claustrophobic, secretive warren, but, by marking the primary entrances into Hamlet's own space in this way, we may also feel there is a subtle suggestion here that the central location at the heart of the narrative can only be accessed through the medium of text. Such centralizing of textuality is, of course, entirely consonant with the general tenor of Branagh's film. In contrast to Warde's attenuated, silent *Lear*, Branagh's *Hamlet* explicitly advertises itself as 'bring[ing] to the screen for the first time, the full unabridged text' of Shakespeare's play.[6] So Branagh's film purports to have overcome the central limitation which critics frequently register in relation to Shakespeare movies (the limitation which the Warde *Lear* begins by anxiously attempting to encounter), namely, the tendency of cinema to reduce the text in response to the technical or commercial limitations of the film medium.[7]

Branagh, then, in contrast to his predecessors, claims to offer the viewer the full text of Shakespeare's play.[8] But what, exactly, does that fullness consist in? What, in this instance, is meant by 'unabridged'?

Mark Thornton Burnett, in 'The "very cunning of the scene"', observes that the film is '[f]aithful to the 1623 First Folio [F1] version of the play'.[9] This is correct in the sense that pretty much all of the F1 text has been recorded in the film – including those passages that are unique to the Folio text. But the film offers us more than this, as it includes not just those passages that are unique to F1, but, for good measure (or extra measure), also incorporates all the passages unique to F1's predecessor text – the 1604/5 second quarto (Q2). Among these passages is the 'How all occasions do inform against me' soliloquy, which, though it does not appear in the F1 text, is (in one of the more bizarre moments in Branagh's film) centralized as a rhetorically and orchestrally bombastic set-piece in order to create an 'intermission' for the four-hour movie.

The exact nature of the relationship between F1 and Q2 *Hamlet* is complex and has given rise to a number of different theories. One conjecture which has found favour in recent years is that the changes made between Q2 and F1 represent a conscious decision to revise the text by cutting and refocusing, with minor additions to aid clarity. This was the position adopted by Stanley Wells and Gary Taylor when they chose F1 as their copy-text for the Oxford Shakespeare, relegating the Q2–only material to an appendix of 'Additional Passages'.[10] In this view, Q2 and F1 represent two coherently distinct and separate versions of the play, and the 'revisionists' and those who follow them would argue that to conflate the two versions – as editors traditionally did and as Branagh does in his movie – is to create a senseless hybrid.[11] To conflate the texts, in this view, is to ignore the specificities of Renaissance theatrical history, thereby producing a version of the text wholly alien to Shakespeare's own theatre.

Revisionism is just one line of thinking that has served to complicate our view of Renaissance textuality in recent years. Indeed, revisionism itself has been criticized for simply offering a multiplication of authorially sanctioned texts rather than advancing a more radical analysis of how Renaissance conceptions of textuality differ from our own.[12] Critiques of the concept of 'authorship' (and of the centrality of the author in the western tradition), which rely on seminal work by Barthes and Foucault (and, to a lesser extent, Derrida), have become rather hackneyed in recent years.[13] However, such critiques *do* have a particular force in a Renaissance context – especially in the theatrical realm.[14] A number of scholars have, for instance, stressed that the economics of the Renaissance theatre meant that playwrights had no further financial interest in – or control over – their work once it had been handed in to the commissioning theatre company and, indeed, that the notion of an author holding a proprietorial 'copyright' was entirely unknown in this period.[15] Other commentators have stressed the broadly 'collaborative' nature of Renaissance theatrical writing. At a purely literal level, for example, Jeffrey Masten has shown that collaborative composition was the norm rather than the exception among Renaissance playwrights.[16] But the issue is more complex than this. The Renaissance playtext can also, for instance, be characterized as 'collaborative' in the extent to which it combines and recycles materials derived from other textual sources. Thus, Timothy Murray has observed that 'Renaissance dramas were written as well as played according to the principle of theatrical plunder. To begin with, the Tudor/Stuart dramatists shared a vast information network of classical models, set pieces, and popular plots', and we might add to this, of course, the tendency of Renaissance dramatists to borrow from 'non-literary' sources as well.[17] Furthermore, as Paul Werstine has noted, such texts were also 'open to penetration and alteration' by a wide array of non-authorial functionaries, such as 'multiple theatrical and extra-theatrical scriveners ... theatrical annotators, adapters and revisers ... censors, and ... compositors'.[18] As a performance script, the play was also, of course, reliant on a larger-scale institutional structure – the theatre – for its very existence. The Renaissance playtext was thus, in the broadest and most complex sense, a collaborative, social entity, rather than the unique proprietorial product of a singular, isolated originator.

Peter Greenaway, commenting on the innate conservatism of mainstream film, has complained 'about cinema not reaching Cubism yet'.[19] Returning to Branagh's *Hamlet*, we might say that this is a production which, in terms of textual scholarship, has hardly yet reached beyond the bounds of a kind of crude version of New Bibliography.[20] Branagh's mission in presenting 'for the first time, the full unabridged text of Shakespeare's *Hamlet*' seems to have been to gather together every scrap of text which might conceivably be attributed to Shakespeare as author and to present this in all its copiousness as the most fully authentic version of the play. In the process, he ignores those revisionist arguments which suggest that we have inherited two distinct versions of *Hamlet*, each differently inflected by the revising playwright. He also ignores those more radical commentators who would lay stress on the complexity of the play as a social object, multiply fashioned and refashioned, and never securely locatable as the sole and exclusive product and property of a singular, centralized author.

Branagh thus works within a particular textual economy – an economy centred on the solitary, originary figure of the author. It is an economy, I would suggest, which does not square with the textual culture of the Renaissance itself. It is also, I will want to argue, an economy that does not quite fit with the nature of cinema either.[21] Before coming on to this, however, I want to return to Peter Greenaway and his comment about the retrogressive nature of mainstream cinema. Greenaway's own film, *Prospero's Books,* is, as its very title implies, like Branagh's *Hamlet,* a peculiarly bibliocentric production. Unlike Branagh's film, however, the status of the book in Greenaway's movie is perhaps a little more ambivalent, since, as Amy Fine Collins and Brad Collins have noted, in this film, '[b]ooks are handled caressingly but also desecrated violently – burned, soaked, pissed on and splattered with vomit'.[22]

Certainly, the textual universe that Greenaway presents in his film is enormously rich and complex. Just as the Renaissance book is openended, permeable to and traversed by other texts, so the twenty-four books which Greenaway includes in his film are very literally open, as they receive the world within their pages and disperse their contents outward beyond the boundaries of their covers ('There are rippling waves and slanting storms. Rivers and cataracts flow and bubble'; 'When the atlas is opened, the maps bubble with pitch. Avalanches of hot, loose gravel and molten sand fall out of the book to scorch the library floor').[23] In the conceit of Greenaway's film, it is from these books that the narrative of *The Tempest* is fashioned and, in this way, as Douglas Lanier argues, 'Greenaway makes visible *The Tempest*'s intertextuality, its status as a collection of discourses culled from a variety of prior sources rather than a unified, free-standing artwork'.[24] Likewise, the film opens with an image of textual circulation and generative bibliographic exchange. As Steven Marx has noted, in the credit sequence to the movie, Greenaway presents a kind of creation process:

> In the foreground of the marathon travelling shot, books are placed on tables and plinths and are passed from one naked spirit character to another. They open the books, read and reflect upon them briefly and then pass them on ... suggesting a transmission of texts across space and through time – the weave implied in the etymology of 'text' itself.[25]

One effect of the foregrounding of intertextuality in the film – its stressing of the textual weave – is that it serves to question traditional conceptions of authorship. The centrality of the author to the play is further interrogated by Greenaway's broader tendency within the film to disassemble and reconstitute the text. In this sense, the film's *Book of Languages* might be seen as providing a kind of self-conscious reference point for the movie's own opening up and dispersal of the structure of the play:

> This is a large, thick book with a blue-green cover that rainbow-hazes in the light. More a box than a book, it opens in unorthodox fashion, with a door in its front cover. Inside is a collection of eight smaller books arranged like bottles in a medicine case. Behind these eight books are another eight books, and so on. To open the smaller books is to let loose many languages. Words and sentences, paragraphs and chapters gather like tadpoles in a pond in April or starlings in a November evening sky.[26]

The generative centrality of the author is directly addressed in other segments of the film. For example, Greenaway himself has acknowledged that, in figuring Prospero as the 'writer' of *The Tempest*, he is playing on a particularly potent Shakespearean fantasy: 'Prospero is seen writing the text of *The Tempest* ... producing a longhand manuscript that – like all other Shakespearean manuscripts – has never been seen. The film's ending interferes with chronology and history and plays a game with this loss that is lamented by every Shakespearean enthusiast.'[27] Again, Greenaway seems to be interrogating conventional notions of authorship here, as the *faux* manuscript inscribed by Prospero as the play's figure for Shakespeare seems to present a kind of parody of the fetishistic object, which has long served as a locus of desire for orthodox Shakespeareans – the author's own 'foul papers'.[28]

What Greenaway offers us here, then, is a playful parodying of traditional desires for a particular form of Shakespearean textuality. We might note, however, that this ironic gesture is itself inhabited by another kind of authorial dream – one which has deep roots in conventional textual paradigms. In the western tradition, a profound split is conceived as existing between speech and writing, with speech being valorized as immediate, present and embodied, where writing is posterior, absent and disjunct. Derrida delineates the outlines of this mode of analysis as follows:

> speech being natural or at least the natural expression of

thought, the most natural form of institution or convention for signifying thought, writing is added to it, is adjoined, as an image or representation. In that sense, it is not natural. It diverts the immediate presence of thought to speech into representation and the imagination.[29]

The Shakespearean tradition has always dreamt of the possibility of bridging (or, perhaps more accurately, collapsing) this gap between speech and writing.[30] In the preliminary matter to the First Folio, Heminge and Condell observe of Shakespeare that 'His mind and hand went together: And what he thought, he vttered with that easinesse, that wee haue scarse receiued from him a blot in his papers'.[31] In this complex statement, we are offered a vision of the fusing of thought, speech, inscription and publication.[32] The unique value of Shakespeare, as Heminge and Condell see it, is that he manages to bring all of these things together in a single moment of synthesis: mind, voice, hand and the technology of reproduction all move together in absolute harmony.

For all its self-conscious irony, a similar vision, we might say, serves to motivate Greenaway's rendering of *The Tempest* in *Prospero's Books*. As Geoffrey Wall has noted, '[i]nsistently, at the thematic centre [of the film], there is an idealized Shakespearean calligraphy: a recurrent close-up of the (authorial) hand at work'.[33] Prospero, figuring the author, speaks and writes and calls the action of the play into existence in a single, simultaneous gesture. Greenaway, for all his bibliographic disjunctions, thus offers us an overarching vision of absolute textual harmony. The distillation of this act of textual perfection into the printed text is indicated at several moments in the film, such as when Gonzalo summarizes the action of the play following Prospero's direct encounter with the ship's party, where the image of the courtly gathering is overlaid with a scrolling image of the equivalent section of printed text from F1. Word is, as it were, instantaneously made text. Although, elsewhere in the film, we find Greenaway offering a broad and complex view of how textuality is constituted, here we witness the emergence of a kind of elevation of the printed text, which serves to mystify its status. Where Warde's *Lear* locates itself anxiously in the wake of the printed text, Greenaway's film seems to precipitate the text out from its own grand vision of the synthesis of speech, action and inscription.

Peter Donaldson has observed of *Prospero's Books* that '[t]hough [it] is a work in which books come apart, are dispersed, are seen to be written, [it] ends in a series of powerful images that remystify the book as the inscription of an originating discourse that is both artistic and magical'.[34] This process of 'remystification' is most clearly to be seen in the final segments of the movie. First, we might consider the moment when Prospero, prompted by his three Ariels, agrees to show mercy. As a token of his decision, he breaks his quill, and the snapping of the instrument of inscription signals a sequence of images of books being snapped shut. The scene operates as a kind of reversal of the opening credit sequence, where, as we have noted, a series of spirits, in a set of stylized movements, open various volumes and pass them from one to another. In the later sequence, to the accompaniment of equally stylized movements, a set of volumes is resoundingly slammed shut, one by one.[35] What we witness here is a complex moment of closure – the shutting of the books emblematizes the manner in which the narrative is being closed down upon itself in various ways. Where previously we were offered a vision of narrative as a woven, intertextual multiplicity, here the intertextual links are severed, so that only one text – isolated, complete and finite (since the instrument of inscription has been broken) – is allowed to remain active.

This narrowing both of the textual field, and of the conception of textuality itself, is confirmed by the scene in which Greenaway literalizes Prospero's decision to drown his books. It is here we discover that the twenty-fourth book is a version of F1, with nineteen pages reserved for the text of *The Tempest*, the manuscript copy of which is also discarded. Greenaway himself has described this scene as offering 'a typical postmodernist self-referential gesture', while Paul Washington has suggested that the scene registers a moment of 'undecidability' within the narrative.[36] Certainly, the scene has its own complexities, especially if viewed in a postcolonial context.[37] But what I want to stress here is, again, the fact that we are offered an image of textual narrowing and of the centralizing of a single, monumentalized object as a unique textual source.[38] Where previously we have witnessed the slamming shut of the 'source' books from which the text has been woven, here the volumes that make up Prospero's library are destroyed one by one, so that only the Shakespearean book remains. The fact that the F1 volume is oddly in need of an inscriptional 'supplement' in the form of the *Tempest* manuscript seems to pass unregistered in Greenaway's narrative. Rather, the combined volumes are united into a kind of textual object *sui generis*, which Greenaway himself credits as the unique source text on which the film itself depends: 'the last two [books] – a collection of Shakespeare's plays and *The Tempest* – are preserved. Otherwise, of course, I wouldn't have the wherewithal to make the film itself.'[39]

I would argue, then, that where, for most of the film, Greenaway operates within an economy of textual multiplicity and dispersal, in the end his concept of textuality radically narrows, as the single printed text is elevated out of the general textual field of which it is a part. Furthermore, I would agree with the argument set out by Peter Donaldson, who suggests that the concluding segment of the film, while it appears to offer a gesture of liberation, as the youngest Ariel leaps out over the top of the film frame, in fact provides a further closing down in reinstating the author at the centre of the narrative. As the film draws to a close, the image of Prospero, speaking the Epilogue, gradually shrinks into the centre of the screen, apparently making way for the 'relay race' of Ariels, which ultimately leads to the child figure's leap out of the confines of the picture frame. As Donaldson argues, however, the handling of the Epilogue works against such a liberatory reading. We can instead, Donaldson suggests, see the scene as signalling

> Prospero's continuing direction of the action, even in the absence of his moving form and voice; as the authorial sponsorship of a licensed enfranchisement over which Prospero and the canonical text of *The Tempest* retain authority. Instead of seeing Prospero as very small and immobile, we can see him as the originator of the film in an enhanced, permanent way ... [N]ow the image of Prospero remains fixed at the vanishing point, the implied origin of all that we see on the screen ... Prospero seems to suffuse the space; he has become one with the point of origin of the image, the point of convergence of a perspectival space that emanates from his unchanging simulacrum.[40]

What happens, I would suggest, at the end of Greenaway's fascinating and complex movie is that the film, far from breaking out of the cinematic frame, in fact collapses in on itself, sucked back into the vanishing point of the author and his singular, isolated text. Though Greenaway's image of the complete works appears at the conclusion of his film, whereas that of the Warde *Lear* appears at the beginning, both films in the end are equally circumscribed by the text.

*

Film has tended, then, over the course of the past century, to negotiate an anxious relationship with the Shakespeare text. In the process, film has often been locked into a particular view of textuality – a view that centralizes the author as the unique and isolated source of meaning and which sees the printed book as a sacrosanct ideal against which film must measure itself. I have been arguing here that this view of textuality is anachronistic when applied to the Renaissance and, indeed, we might say, when applied to the broader sweep of Shakespearean history. The Shakespeare text, far from being a stable, coherent, monumental object, is in fact a mutable and multiple entity. We have already noted of Branagh's monolithic *Hamlet* that it combines material from two distinct renderings of the narrative. But, of course, this is not the whole story, as there was also a third *Hamlet* published at the beginning of the seventeenth century – the 1603 first quarto, which provides a much shorter text conforming more closely to the conventions of the revenge tragedy genre.[41] Likewise, though the Warde *Lear* may have been anxious about its relationship to the standard text of the play, that text, in fact, was pretty much unknown in performance in England from the Restoration through to the early nineteenth century, as Nahum Tate's radical reworking of the play dominated the stage tradition. Tate's text is just one of an extensive array of adaptations which form an important element in Shakespearean textual history. These adaptations are variously motivated: often, as Michael Dobson has shown, they are driven by a desire to engage with contemporary politics; at other times, they seek to burlesque or parody the high cultural documents of the Shakespearean tradition.[42]

In closing, I would like to suggest that it is within this broader cultural and textual history that the Shakespeare film could more properly locate itself. Such films should be seen in the context of a cultural process rather than being measured against a particular static textual form (a form which is, in any case, in itself not stable, as the varied and complex history of Shakespeare editing amply demonstrates). Viewed in this light, we might see a film such as Gus van Sant's *My Own Private Idaho* as being perfectly well located within the broader Shakespearean tradition, in the sense that, just as the typical Shakespeare play provides an interweaving of materials drawn from other sources, so van Sant, in fashioning his narrative, draws from Orson Welles' *Chimes at Midnight*, which, in its turn, draws on Shakespeare's Falstaff material, supplemented by additional matter from Holinshed's *Chronicles*, on which Shakespeare also, of course, relies.[43] What van Sant offers, then, is a complex intertextual narrative in which the Shakespearean material operates within a elaborate and intertwined cultural referencing system.

Again, we might also see, for example, Zeffirelli's abridged and reordered *Hamlet* not as a travesty of the 'complete' text presented in Branagh's version of the play, but instead align it with the 1603 first quarto edition of the text, with which it shares a sense of fast-paced urgency and a clear generic focus. A telling observation in this regard is Ace Pilkington's perception that 'Zeffirelli's sudden inspiration as he watched Mel Gibson in *Lethal Weapon*, that here was a young actor who could play a new kind of Hamlet, had paid off in a return to the roots of Shakespeare's play – the revenge tragedy and *Hamlet* as thriller'.[44] Likewise, we might see filiations between the kind of political allegorizing we witness in such films as Richard Loncraine's *Richard III* or Olivier's *Henry V* and the narrative refocusing which Dobson has identified in Restoration adaptations, which turn the plays to explicit political ends, celebrating, for instance, the return to monarchy at the end of the republican era. Even so extravagant a parody as Kaufman's *Tromeo and Juliet* can be easily located within the context of a broader Shakespearean cultural history, as it has clear connections with the Shakespeare burlesque tradition. Thus, for example, Andrew Halliday's *Romeo and Juliet Travestie* of 1850 features a Juliet described in the *dramatis personae* as 'an uncommon nice Young Gal – the "One Daughter" of Capulet – a belle whom all the Young Fellows in Verona are anxious to ring'.[45] As in the case of Kaufman's film, Shakespeare himself ('in the attitude of Roubilliac's statue') puts in an appearance at the end of the piece, only to be dismissed by Romeo and the Nurse:

> ROMEO. Immortal bard – illustrious Swan of Avon,
>   Towards you, we own, we have not been behavin',
>   With that respect which we should like to pay,
>   But the fact is, if we essayed your play,
>   As you did write it – the boxes and the pit
>   Would say we could not act the play a bit,
>   And so that *with* us, not *at* us they may laugh,
>   We've winnowed your fine *corn* into *chaff*.
>   (SHAKSPERE *bows*)
> NURSE, (*going up*) Another thing you must remember, Poet,
>   You wrote burlesques yourself, and well you know it.
>   In 'The Midsummer Night's Dream'.
>   SHAKSPERE *descends*
>   I had him there. (pp. 38–9)

In addition to this, we can also connect Kaufman's film with a lively tradition of intersections between Shakespeare and pornographic publication. For example, the first ever 'Shakespearean' volume to appear in America was *Shakespeare's Jest* (1774) – 'a little volume of obscene jokes and indecent poems in the form of jests, riddles, and songs' – a number 'of the indecencies [being] specifically credited to Shakespeare through stories of their origin'.[46] And the intertwining of pornography and high culture in a Shakespearean cinematic context is also, of course, registered in the fact that in 1971 Playboy financed Roman Polanski's *Macbeth* and then, in the following year, produced the soft-porn *Playboy Twelfth Night*.[47]

The Shakespeare film has now reached the end of its first century. For much of that century, the book has been used, rather in the manner of Tromeo's *Yale Shakespeare*, as a weapon to attack the film, by registering the difference between what the film presents and the imagined ideal standard of the printed text. Perhaps, as we enter a new millennium, this may be a good time to abandon the tired old critical paradigms that have governed the study of filmed Shakespeare for the past several decades. It is time, I would argue, to reassess the relationship between the book and the film, and for film to take its place within the broader cultural formation that is Shakespearean textuality.[48]

Notes

1. For books on the stage, as opposed to the screen, see Frederick Kiefer, *Writing on the Renaissance Stage: Written Words, Printed Pages, Metaphoric Books* (Newark: University of Delaware Press, 1996).
2. Douglas Lanier, 'Drowning the Book: *Prospero's Books* and the Textual Shakespeare', in James C. Bulman (ed.), *Shakespeare, Theory, and Performance* (London: Routledge, 1996), p. 191.
3. Kenneth Rothwell has argued that '[p]age, stage and screen, the triad of Shakespearean incarnations, momentarily interface, though the tension generated among the three inevitably favours disconnection of the filmic from page and stage. To accomplish that, the book and the reader are figuratively and literally dissolved to make room for the movie' ('Representing *King Lear* on Screen: From Metatheatre to "Metacinema"', in Anthony Davies and Stanley Wells (eds), *Shakespeare and the Moving Image: The Plays on Film and Television* [Cambridge: Cambridge University Press, 1994], p. 213).
4. 'The "very cunning of the scene": Kenneth Branagh's *Hamlet*', *Literature/Film Quarterly*, 25 (1997), p. 81.
5. There are four entrances in total – the other two are never shown head-on in the film, so we never know what their doorways look like.
6. Quoted from the jacket of the video release of the film (Columbia Tristar Home Video, 1997).

7. The BBC/Time-Life videos also, of course, started out with the aim of providing unabridged performances, though subsequently the policy was abandoned.

8. As Emma Smith notes in her contribution to this volume, Branagh's *Hamlet* might usefully be contrasted with his *In the Bleak Midwinter* in this regard, in that, in the latter film, much is made of the necessity of cutting the text of *Hamlet* for performance.

9. Burnett, 'The "very cunning of the scene"', p. 81.

10. Wells and Taylor subsequently argued that they would ideally have liked to have treated *Hamlet* in the same way as they treated *King Lear*, by including in their edition two distinct texts of the play. See Wells and Taylor, 'The Oxford Shakespeare Re-viewed by the General Editors', *Analytical and Enumerative Bibliography*, 4 (1990), pp. 6–20. For the broader revisionist argument, see Grace Ioppolo, *Revising Shakespeare* (Cambridge, Mass.: Harvard University Press, 1991).

11. It isn't quite accurate to suggest that all editors before Wells and Taylor insisted on producing conflated texts. For example, in 1885, George MacDonald published an edition of *Hamlet* based on F1, with the Q2-only passages printed in smaller type at the foot of the page.

12. I am thinking here, in particular, of the critique of revisionism offered in Margreta de Grazia and Peter Stallybrass, 'The Materiality of the Shakespearean Text', *Shakespeare Quarterly*, 44 (1993), pp. 255–83.

13. See, in particular, Michel Foucault, 'What is an Author?', in Paul Rabinow (ed.), *The Foucault Reader* (Harmondsworth: Penguin, 1991), pp. 101–20; Roland Barthes, 'The Death of the Author', and 'From Work to Text' in *Image/Music/Text* (London: Fontana, 1977), pp. 142–8, 155–64. For a counterview, see, for example, Gary Taylor, 'What is an Author [Not]', *Critical Survey*, 7 (1995), pp. 241–54.

14. Much of what follows in this paragraph is a condensed version of an argument I set out at greater length in my own chapter ('Texts and Textualities: A Shakespearean History') in my edited collection, *The Renaissance Text: Theory, Editing, Textuality* (Manchester: Manchester University Press, 2000).

15. On the economics of the Renaissance theatre, see Peter W. M. Blayney, 'The Publication of Playbooks', and Kathleen E. McLuskie and Felicity Dunsworth, 'Patronage and the Economics of Theater', in John D. Cox and David Scott Kastan (eds), *A New History of Early English Drama* (New York: Columbia University Press, 1997), pp. 383–422 and pp. 423–40. The concept of copyright did not fully come into being until the late eighteenth century. See Mark Rose, 'The Author as Proprietor: *Donaldson v. Becket* and the Genealogy of Modern Authorship', *Representations*, 23 (1988), pp. 51–85, and the work of John Feather, especially 'The Publishers and the Pirates: British Copyright Law in Theory and Practice, 1710–1755', *Publishing History*, 22 (1987), pp. 5–32.

16. See his *Textual Intercourse: Collaboration, Authorship, and Sexualities in Renaissance Drama* (Cambridge: Cambridge University Press, 1997).

17. Timothy Murray, 'From Foul Sheets to Legitimate Model: Antitheatre, Text, Ben Jonson', *New Literary History*, 14 (1983), pp. 641–64.

18. 'Narratives About Printed Shakespeare Texts: "Foul Papers" and "Bad"

Quartos', *Shakespeare Quarterly*, 41 (1990), p. 86.

19. Marlene Rodgers, 'Prospero's Books – Word and Spectacle: An Interview with Peter Greenaway', *Film Quarterly*, 45:2 (1991), p. 13. Greenaway's comment is, of course, an overstatement – see, for example, Richard Abel, *French Cinema: The First Wave, 1915–1929* (Princeton: Princeton University Press, 1984).

20. To say this is, however, to be rather unfair to the New Bibliographers who, after all, did at least seek to honour what they assumed to be the author's 'intentions'. In this sense, 'revisionism' is effectively an outgrowth of New Bibliography.

21. One might think here of the '*auteur*' tradition in cinema studies, though this, perhaps predictably, has had little impact within the Shakespeare film tradition.

22. Amy Fine Collins and Brad Collins, 'Drowning the Text', *Art in America*, 80, June (1992), p. 54.

23. From, respectively, *The Book of Water* and *An Atlas Belonging to Orpheus*, quoted from *'Prospero's Books': A Film of Shakespeare's 'The Tempest'* (New York: Four Walls/Eight Windows, 1991), pp. 17, 20. Further quotations relevant to the screenplay are taken from this source.

24. Lanier, 'Drowning the Book', p. 197.

25. Steven Marx, 'Progeny: *Prospero's Books*, Genesis and *The Tempest*', *Renaissance Forum*, 1:2 (1996), p. 6. This electronic journal may be found at: http://www.hull.ac.uk/Hull/EL_Web/renforum/v1no2/marx.htm.

26. Greenaway, *'Prospero's Books'*, p. 21. There is an interesting similarity between Greenaway's *Book of Languages* and Michael Warren's *The Complete 'King Lear'* (Berkeley: University of California Press, 1989). Warren's 'edition' consists of a folder containing two Quarto texts and one Folio text, presented in an unbound, loose-leaf format, together with a bound parallel text of F1 and Q1. The unbound sheets enable the reader to disassemble and recombine the text of *Lear* just as *Prospero's Books* disassembles and recombines the text of *The Tempest*.

27. Greenaway, *'Prospero's Books'*, p. 32.

28. See, for instance, the debates surrounding the passages of *The Book of Sir Thomas More*, which some scholars consider to be in Shakespeare's hand. For representative early material, see A. W. Pollard (ed.), *Shakespeare's Hand in the Play of 'Sir Thomas More'* (Cambridge: Cambridge University Press, 1923). For an analysis of the whole issue of attribution relative to *More*, see Scott McMillan, *The Elizabethan Theatre and 'The Book of Sir Thomas More'* (Ithaca: Cornell University Press, 1987). For an excellent critique of the very notion of 'foul papers', see Werstine, 'Narratives'.

29. Jacques Derrida, *Of Grammatology*, trans. Gayatri Chakravorty Spivak (Baltimore: Johns Hopkins University Press, 1976), p. 144.

30. I have taken up this issue in greater detail in '"Came Errour Here by Mysse of Man": Editing and the Metaphysics of Presence', *Yearbook of English Studies*, 29 (1999), pp. 118–37.

31. *Mr. William Shakespeares Comedies, Histories, & Tragedies. Published According to the True Originall Copies* (London, 1623), sig. A3r.

32. One of the meanings of 'utter' in the Renaissance was 'To issue by way of publication; to publish' (*The Compact Edition of the Oxford English*

Dictionary, 2 vols [London: Book Club Associates, 1979], II, p. 488).

33. 'Greenaway Filming *The Tempest*', *Shakespeare Yearbook*, 4, Spring (1994), p. 336.

34. 'Shakespeare in the Age of Post-mechanical Reproduction: Sexual and Electronic Magic in *Prospero's Books*', in Lynda E. Boose and Richard Burt (eds), *Shakespeare, the Movie: Popularizing the Plays on Film, TV, and Video* (London and New York: Routledge, 1997), p. 175.

35. See also Marx, 'Progeny', p. 50. Marx reaches a completely different conclusion, arguing that 'Greenaway may be expressing an impulse to break free from the constraints of bookish scholarship and filmmaking in favour of organic procreation or live theatre'.

36. Rodgers, '*Prospero's Books*', p. 239; Paul Washington, '"This Last *Tempest*": Shakespeare, Postmodernity, and *Prospero's Books*', in Heather Kerr, Robin Eaden and Madge Mitton (eds), *Shakespeare: World Views* (Newark: University of Delaware Press, 1996), p. 239.

37. On the significance of *Caliban's* retrieving the books from the water, see Marx, 'Progeny', p. 51.

38. To see F1 in these terms is, of course, to fail to understand the particularities of its history, since F1 is not a single, static textual entity. F1 was likely published in three distinct states: lacking *Troilus and Cressida*; including *Troilus and Cressida*, opening with a crossed-out blank page; and including *Troilus and Cressida*, but with a 'Prologue' substituted for the crossed-out page. In addition, the process of 'stop press' correction means that all copies of F1 contain a mixture of corrected and uncorrected sheets, such that Peter Blayney has argued that 'no two copies have yet been found to contain exactly the same mixture of early and late pages'. See his *The First Folio of Shakespeare* (Washington: Folger Shakespeare Library, 1991), pp. 24, 15.

39. Rodgers, '*Prospero's Books*', p. 16.

40. Donaldson, 'Shakespeare in the Age of Post-mechanical Reproduction', p. 175.

41. Q1 contains some 2,200 lines of text, Q2 about 3,800 lines and F1 around 3,570.

42. See Dobson's *The Making of the National Poet: Shakespeare, Adaptation and Authorship, 1660–1769* (Oxford: Clarendon, 1992).

43. 'The "narrative voice" in *Chimes* presents a commentary upon action and character, and has a vigorous new dimension to it, for the commentary passages are taken from Holinshed's *Chronicles*, the source material for Shakespeare's histories' (Anthony Davies, *Filming Shakespeare's Plays: The Adaptations of Laurence Olivier, Orson Welles, Peter Brook and Akira Kurosawa* [Cambridge: Cambridge University Press, 1988], pp. 141–2).

44. 'Zeffirelli's Shakespeare', in Davies and Wells (eds), *Shakespeare and the Moving Image*, p. 174. A number of the essays included in Thomas Clayton (ed.), *The 'Hamlet' First Published (Q1, 1603)* (Newark: University of Delaware Press, 1992) discuss the characteristics of Q1 in performance.

45. Andrew Halliday, *Romeo and Juliet Travestie: or, The Cup of Cold Poison. A Burlesque in One Act* (London: Thomas Hailes Lacy, 1850), p. 2. All further references appear in the text.

46. Alfred Van Rensselaer Westfall, *American Shakespearean Criticism 1607–1865* (New York: H. W. Wilson, 1939), p. 80.

47. On this aspect of Shakespeare culture more generally, see Richard Burt, *Unspeakable ShaXXXspeares: Queer Theory and American Kiddie Culture* (New York: St. Martin's Press, 1998).
48. My thanks to Mark Thornton Burnett and Ramona Wray for providing the occasion for this piece and for their helpful comments, and to Barbara Hodgdon and Neil Rhodes for their advice and feedback. My thinking on many of these issues has been considerably sharpened by participating in Bruce Smith's 'Shakespeare and Visual Culture' seminar at the Folger Institute.

2
The Postmodern Theatre of Paul Mazursky's *Tempest*

Douglas Bruster

The director Paul Mazursky's *Tempest* received mixed notices when it opened during the late summer of 1982. While the film struck David Denby as 'startlingly fresh and beautiful' and 'one of the liveliest movies of the year', others, especially those reviewing the film for more select outlets, described *Tempest* in ways that set it off invidiously from its model. John Simon, for example, saw Mazursky as 'tearing Shakespeare to rags', and Stanley Kauffmann felt the film an 'affront to us'.[1] These last assessments were echoed by Pauline Kael's sharp remark in *The New Yorker*: 'It takes a high degree of civilization to produce something so hollow.'[2] Because its director's career had itself been so uneven – successes and failures coming in close rotation – this controversial film was quickly relegated to the growing list of Mazursky's commercial disappointments, and largely forgotten. Yet such neglect is both unmerited and unhelpful, for Mazursky's *Tempest* remains not only an aesthetically satisfying work, but one which meaningfully charts the status of the aesthetic in the globalized culture of the late twentieth century. Indeed, in its focus on the increasingly private visuality which has accompanied our 'high degree of civilization', *Tempest* is arguably the first postmodern Shakespeare film, a prologue to, even an explanation of, the many Shakespeare adaptations that followed.

Much of this function evolves from contradictions surrounding *Tempest*, for the film often works against its director's immediate intentions. Setting out to make a film about personal crisis, Mazursky succeeds in illustrating cultural change; paying reverence to the idea of the theatre, he demonstrates why, in our time, theatre must be more revered than realized. The importance of such contradictions to our understanding of *Tempest* hinges on their origin as well as their effect, as they both derive from the resistance, of Shakespeare's play, to a certain filmic myth endorsed by Mazursky. By 'myth' here is meant a patterned story which, recurring across individual films, argues for a particular vision of life. Since the late 1960s, this myth, and the collaborative mode of production it relates, have coalesced into a style that personalizes Mazursky's films.

To grasp this myth, and the form it takes in *Tempest*, we might begin by observing that Mazursky rarely works with original material. Some of his films adapt other works outright – as, for example, *Willie and Phil* (1980) with François Truffaut's *Jules and Jim* (1961), and *Down and Out in Beverly Hills* (1986) with Jean Renoir's *Boudu Sauvé des Eaux* (1932). Many other of his films advertise the influence of the more obvious European filmmakers taken up by the American intelligentsia during the 1950s and 1960s. Renoir, Fellini, Truffaut and Antonioni are the directors around whom Mazursky's personal canon has formed. Not surprisingly, *Tempest* virtually catalogues allusions to such films as Antonioni's *L'Avventura* (1960), and Fellini's *La Dolce Vita* (1960) and *8¹/₂* (1963). In his remakes and homages alike, Mazursky can be seen as attempting to collaborate with these film-makers – to acknowledge their achievements while extending their visions into another time, language and idiom. His films reveal him, accordingly, as much *collaborateur* as *auteur*.

Mazursky's desire to collaborate with European icons has a structural precedent in the stories which several of their films tell. These narratives involve upper middle-class figures discovering a partner's infidelity, then accommodating themselves to that infidelity in ways which depart from the typical morality of their social group. *Jules and Jim*, *Boudu Sauvé* and Antonioni's *La Notte* (1961), for example, all feature characters struggling to reorient themselves to a lifestyle traditionally not middle-class but aristocratic at base. Their eventual acceptance or toleration of an 'open' marriage (the acquisition of what *The Awful Truth* [1937] memorably calls 'a Continental mind') stands as the narrative version of the *complaisance* which collaboration entails for Mazursky: the willingness to share amiably, to compromise, to deny one's proprietary claims over the world and those in it. These European source-films explore what human relations look like when possessiveness is turned on its head, when sharing is taken to its extreme. Mazursky attempts to insert himself into these relations by replicating their triangles with the directors of the films. Into the mediating position taken by a character in the European models are placed the films themselves; hence *Jules and Jim* appears not only as *Willie and Phil* but as the figure of desire in *François and Paul*.

More than a few of Mazursky's films allegorize this myth of collaboration through the relation of two 'worlds'. The first of these worlds typically consists of a single individual. Such Mazursky films as *Bob & Carol & Ted & Alice* and *Down and Out in Beverly Hills* unapologetically devote their attention to the mid-life crises of newly successful yet alienated men: *Bob & Carol*'s Bob Sanders and Ted Henderson, *Down and Out*'s Dave Whiteman. These men anxiously search for meaning, and in the end their crises involve abandoning sexual possessiveness. In fact, their stories might be called dramas of marital impotence, for the general 'solution' their films imagine consists of a potent friend or colleague who sleeps with each man's wife. Rather than being a betrayal, this infidelity appears to be necessary experimentation, and the maritally impotent man (he typically has an affair outside the marriage) accepts a sexual relation otherwise repugnant to the possessive American bourgeois.

Accepting their wives' sexual freedom gives these men *entrée* to the fluid and festive society of difference which makes up the second, and larger, of Mazursky's worlds. This world is sometimes characterized through harmonious arrangements of figures in group scenes: the extended family welcoming back Jerry Baskin into the fold in *Down and Out*; the dozens of strangers mingling in the casino carpark in *Bob & Carol* while '(What the World Needs Now is) Love Sweet Love' plays. Entering this larger world hinges on a mental reorientation. The world itself bears a physical diversity: each of its multitude of persons has a different appearance and set of desires. When they mingle, in one of the films' dance-like, group conclusions, the viewer as well as the main character is asked to imagine a challenging variety of possible lifestyles.

Such is the basic pattern which Mazursky's *Tempest* follows, and it seems clear that what drew him to Shakespeare's play was its apparent openness to the psychological and aesthetic allegory that he had deployed in previous films (and which he would return to in the years following *Tempest*). In the Shakespearean text Mazursky found a focus on the nature of art, a dispossessed, anxious artist figure, potent companions and rivals related to that figure, a large cast of supporting characters from whom an alternative world might be fashioned, and an emphasis on forgiveness. All these appear to coincide with the story Mazursky likes to tell with his films. For several reasons, however, Shakespeare's *Tempest* resists Mazursky's translation, and it is in this resistance that much of the film's value lies.

Its story unfolds as follows. Mazursky's Prospero is named Phillip Dimitrious, a celebrated New York architect of Greek heritage. The film opens with the remote Greek island to which Phillip has come with his daughter, Miranda, and his companion, an American woman named Aretha (Shakespeare's Ariel). There they live in the company of Kalibanos, an islander. We learn in a series of flashbacks that this trio of Americans has fled to the island to avoid Phillip's wife, Antonia, as well as her lover (and Phillip's former employer), Alonzo. Alonzo, a gangster who has hired Phillip to design a casino, wishes to hold Phillip to his contract even as Antonia desires to regain Miranda. Together with Alonzo's unlikely entourage – which includes Alonzo's son, Freddy (representing Ferdinand), Trinc (a comic representing Trinculo), a doctor named Sebastian, and a starlet named Dolores (representing Gonzalo) – they arrive at the island and are surprised by a sudden storm which leaves them wet and relatively helpless at Phillip's feet.[3] Following a ritualistic sacrifice, and during a group celebration characteristic of Mazursky's work, these figures reconcile themselves to one another in new ways. The film closes, after Phillip and family return triumphantly to the island of Manhattan, with its cast taking a curtain call at the house on the Greek island.

As this summary might make clear, Mazursky attempts to make Shakespeare's romance realistic and possible. So tranquillizing is Don McAlpine's expansive cinematography, in fact, that one realizes only in retrospect the basic smallness of Mazursky's ambitions. To be sure, Mazursky's storytelling has always shown the influence of his early work in television as actor and writer. The mixed tenor of his films derives in large part from the yoking of his filmic models (such as Renoir and Truffaut) to a sensibility shaped by American television – a union perfectly articulated by the Jill Clayburgh character in *An Unmarried Woman* (1978) when she describes the spirit of her friends as 'part *Mary Hartman* and part Ingmar Bergman'. Mazursky's taste in actors has shown the pull of television as well: from Elliott Gould and Dyan Cannon to Margot Kidder and Michael Ontkean, Mazursky's players are invariably overextended by the ambitious scope of film. This is true for such *Tempest* actors as John Cassavetes (Phillip), Gena Rowlands (Antonia) and Molly Ringwald (Miranda), whose performances cohere primarily in their failure to match the broad demands of the medium. Likewise, *Tempest* can be said to tell Shakespeare's large story in a small way. In place of Shakespeare's focus on Machiavellian politics, dynastic marriages and the issues of mercy and grace, Mazursky gives us the repertory of pop psychology: mid-life crises, self-fulfilment, dropping out.[4] The odd result is a text sometimes like, sometimes quite unlike, its source. In the words of Judith

Buchanan, '*Tempest* emerges by turns minutely attentive to, and extravagantly negligent of, its Shakespearean precursor'.[5]

This is necessarily the case because much in Shakespeare's work resists Mazursky's habits of thought. For instance, Prospero's punishment of Caliban is too central to the *Tempest* story for Mazursky to cut it. But its inclusion means that, however sympathetically Mazursky wishes to present him, Phillip remains jealous and controlling. Further, neither Prospero nor Phillip enjoys the moral licence which so many of the characters in Mazursky's twentieth-century sources display, and which would seem even less natural to John Cassavetes than to a younger generation of actors that includes, among others, Natalie Wood and Richard Dreyfuss. As the Nick Nolte character says in *Down and Out*: 'Hey, you gotta be what you gotta be.' And certainly one of the most significant changes to the drama that the film makes is its transformation of the magic in Shakespeare's play. Mazursky replaces Prospero's occult power with the visual range of cinema – particularly, with the special effects of the American tradition in popular film. Transposing, to the conclusion of his film, the storm which gives the works their name (a move, to be sure, entirely in keeping with the classical Hollywood narrative), Mazursky lends the tempest an importance which diminishes our interest in the film's characters.

If Phillip's controlling character does not accord with the *complaisance* which Mazursky sees as integral to artistic collaboration, neither does *Tempest*'s emphasis on the apparatus of film itself – its visual splendour and special effects – allow the director to convince us of the interest in the theatre which the film professes. In each of these instances, *Tempest* betrays the shapes of the source narrative which lead the film to work differently from many of Mazursky's other films. *Tempest* thus tells a story which exceeds its director's control, a situation which the film seems conscious of in the flashback sequence in which a drunken Phillip bursts into a party and dances with a reluctant Broadway producer played by Mazursky himself. Although *Tempest* stages more harmonious dances (the film is full of dancing and dance music), this awkward encounter, and a later sequence in which Phillip attempts to force Miranda to tango, remain apt metaphors for the potentially frustrating relations of power in any joint endeavour. The two forced dances can be seen, more particularly, as confessions of the difficulties which Mazursky had in accommodating a play from the 1600s to a philosophy of accommodation which unfolded, in America, primarily during and after the late 1960s. These difficulties make *Tempest* more complicated, and more interesting, than the story that Mazursky is used to telling, for they prevent the film's immersion in the *clichés* of psychological well-being which characterize so much of his work.[6]

What replaces pop psychology in *Tempest* is a virtual catalogue of representational modes, devices and spaces. That is, *Tempest* continually refers to various kinds of art, and to places in which spectators are entertained. The organizing centre of these references is, of course, Phillip Dimitrious, who seems an architect less of buildings than of open spaces for seeing: the loft and its views, a casino, a theatre. And it is his attempt to control the spectacles in such spaces that reminds us of architecture's *doppelgänger*, the twin occupation which sparks our deepest cultural fantasies of godlike creative powers – that of filmmaker. For, even if we repress our knowledge of Cassavetes' career as a director, it is difficult to avoid seeing Phillip as a figure of the filmmaker in *Tempest*. Mazursky, it should be pointed out, prefers filmmakers as characters. One thinks immediately of the documentarian Bob Sanders in *Bob & Carol*; of the title character of *Alex in Wonderland* (1970), a young director; of Phil D'Amico, the cameraman in *Willie and Phil*; and of Max, the video-artist son in *Down and Out*. Like these characters, Phillip is continually associated with the 'camera eye' of film. Instead of Prospero's magic staff, for instance, Phillip's instrument of power is a cherished telescope which he keeps by him throughout the film. Just what kind of power the telescope provides becomes clear by the film's final sequences, when Phillip peers through it to watch the boat bearing Antonia, Alonzo and their entourage to the island. The isolation of Phillip's view here obviously doubles that of a film director peering into an eyepiece to approve a shot. Immediately preceding the storm which answers Phillip's repeated mantra, 'Show me the magic', the camera-eye voyeurism assures us that the ensuing magic is a filmic special effect.

This is actually the second time we hear Phillip speak this line. We first hear it in a flashback, where – after drunkenly ending the party at the Dimitrious apartment – Phillip says 'Show me the magic' to a thunderstorm which parallels the chaos of his mind and marriage. What makes this instance especially telling for *Tempest*'s allegory of filmmaking is its *mise-en-scène*, which has Phillip standing before a rectangular bank of windows and looking into the fierce illumination of the lightning. The allusion to the apparatus of cinema is unavoidable; seeing Phillip behind this symbolic screen, we recall earlier meditations on cinematic technology and reality in a variety of classical Hollywood films. But where *Tempest* differs from Keaton's *Sherlock,*

Jr (1924), as well as from Woody Allen's homage piece, *The Purple Rose of Cairo* (1985), and from a similar concern with the vitality of the illuminated image at the beginnings of *Citizen Kane* (1941) and *Sullivan's Travels* (1941), is in its pointed juxtaposition of this meta-filmic moment with various other forms of aesthetic representation. In this scene and elsewhere, *Tempest* contrasts its interest in film with ancillary modes of art. Although it shares these earlier films' awe of projected light (Phillip's relation to these electrical storms is almost religious in nature), *Tempest* goes on to consider film in relation to drama, television, dance and the plastic arts.

When Phillip stands behind the screen-like bank of windows, staring out into the eye of the storm and its blinding, projected light, he does so from within the context of a resonant 'space' in *Tempest*. This is the apartment which he designed, as he takes pains to inform his visitors: 'I did it. I did the whole thing.' But, in the culture of marital separation which the film explores, it is no longer his space. Throughout *Tempest*, this apartment is associated with Antonia, his wife, and with the theatrical career she wishes to resume. Several shots here include a framed theatrical poster advertising a production in which she has starred: Antonia Dimitrious in *Such Sweet Sorrow*, an allusion, of course, to Shakespeare's *Romeo and Juliet* (the joke is continued when we read that the director of this play is Don McAlpine, the film's cinematographer). This large, wooden-floored space feels like a modern theatre (perhaps the first theatre Phillip has built), a thematic strengthened by a Broadway party which Antonia hosts, and during which the guests, along with Miranda, engage in conversation about *Macbeth*, Pirandello and Pinter, and spontaneously break into song. The theatrical aura of this space is punctured by Phillip's arrival, however, and although he picks up the logic of the stage in his drunken improvisation ('I enjoyed your entrance', the Broadway director tells him as the guests leave, 'But I felt the scene was a little overplayed'), his true element is the filmic spectacle allegorized by the lightning show at the sequence's end.

The differences between drama and film here become clearer when we realize that Phillip's refusal to collaborate with Alonzo (either in building the latter his casino, or in acquiescing to Alonzo's affair with Antonia) marks Phillip as an independent, controlling artist. He could not differ more from the accommodating ideal of Mazursky's other films. Appropriately, three of the four primary 'places' in *Tempest* – the Dimitrious' apartment, the unfinished casino and the unfinished island theatre – are designed by Phillip, and the fourth place –

Kalibanos' cave – remains outside Phillip's control. Along with Phillip's connection to film, these places set out a sequence of entertainment venues in the West: the 'Greek' theatre which Phillip and the others work to construct; the Broadway stage, represented by its personnel in the Dimitrious' apartment; film, represented by Phillip and his telescope; and, finally, the casino under construction – a place where pleasure is to be enjoyed nakedly, without the formalities of plot that encumber theatre and cinema alike.

Yet nowhere does the film more consciously allegorize the history of art than in Kalibanos' cave, for it is here that *Tempest* displays a variety of representational forms. Even the dialogue seems conscious of cultural sequence, as, upon meeting Kalibanos, Trinc and Sebastian recite a mixed list of Greek achievements: 'Acropolis … *Never on Sunday* … Democracy … Telly Savalas'. The place's symbolic heritage – a Greek cave concerned with art – was noted by at least one of the film's reviewers, who called it 'a modern substitute for Plato's Cave'.[7] To the extent that their voyage to the island functions, for the visiting Americans, as a kind of journey back in time, Kalibanos' cave appears to be the birthplace of their culture. Among the forms which the film's viewers encounter there are ithyphallic statuary (in the final revised draft of the screenplay, the cave walls were to feature pornographic drawings); the music of Kalibanos' clarinet; the dancing of Phillip to Kalibanos' music; and drama – the 'drag' costume of Kalibanos following the storm, his wardrobe (which hangs on a line, recalling Prospero's bait-like garments in *The Tempest*), and the vaudevillean *schtick* of Trinc and Sebastian as they back into the cave and crack jokes about their predicament. While Kalibanos' cave offers Platonic resonances in its focus on art, then, it does so through an Aristotelian catalogue.

But the cave *is* modern, and what makes it especially so is Kalibanos' embrace and mastery of modern life. To begin with, Kalibanos has commercial designs upon those who enter his cave. He keeps the pornographic statuary under a curtain, for instance, which he raises as he offers the lewd figures for sale. The camera's voyeurism at this point reminds us how frequently *Tempest* connects vision with sex – more precisely, with spectacles of a potentially erotic nature. Its gaze at the statuary parallels that of Kalibanos at the beginning of the film, when he peeps at a swimming Miranda from behind a bush on a cliff – the steep gradient of which, like the bush, imperfectly hides its resemblance to a theatre's concave seating area. It also recalls an unintended moment of voyeurism shown in flashback, when Phillip and Miranda accidentally observe, from an overpass, Antonia climbing into a limousine with Alonzo. The latter's priapism not only accords with the potent interloper of Mazursky's collaborative myth, but is symbolically frozen in the statues that Kalibanos peddles to his visitors.

The most forceful commentary on the relation of vision to sexuality in *Tempest*, however, comes with the film's interest in television. Whereas the allegory of *Tempest* identifies Phillip with film, and Antonia with the stage, it consistently shows Miranda to be a child of television. Kalibanos uses the promise of a 'Sony Trinitron' to lure Miranda to his cave, where he attempts to seduce her. This television and its programmes, of course, nearly complete the sequence of entertainment forms articulated in *Tempest*; in what is surely a pun on the nature of the cave's interest in western culture, the programme Miranda watches is a dubbed episode of *Gunsmoke*. The final revised screenplay describes the moment: '[Kalibanos] runs to the set and clicks it on. Miranda is goggle-eyed.' As the television distracts Miranda, Kalibanos begins stroking and kissing her, until she rouses from her virtual trance and punches him, leaving the cave in anger. News of this attempted seduction enrages Phillip. This is the second instance in which we see him angry; the first occurs during the party sequence in the Dimitrious' apartment, where he upbraids Miranda and Antonia because Miranda is watching television at such a late hour (as well as joining the Broadway party). In each instance, a filmic storm follows an episode of television viewing – viewing which, because it offers a world outside the nuclear family, *Tempest* analogizes to unlicensed sexual experience. When Phillip confronts Kalibanos, for instance, he temporarily misunderstands Kalibanos' confession – 'I show her my TV' – as having a bodily reference. Yet we realize that this is not entirely a misunderstanding. For, however much Mazursky's own creative faculty has been shaped by the medium, however much *Tempest*'s Miranda can therefore be said to be Mazursky's own daughter, his film tells the story of Phillip's antagonism towards the medium and the almost magical manner in which it challenges his authority.

Throughout *Tempest*, both story and characters work to show Phillip's importance: he must be begged to return Miranda to Antonia; the casino cannot be completed without his efforts; strangers recognize his name as betokening 'the famous architect, Phillip Dimitrious'; he educates Kalibanos. His authority as a creative artist manifests itself also in the construction of the outdoor amphitheatre on the island, a task in which he aids and directs Miranda, Aretha and Kalibanos. This

still unfinished theatre is used twice in the film, each time for a spontaneous, danced celebration: first, by the crew of humans constructing
the theatre, then by Kalibanos' goats, who appear to leap through the
air as Kalibanos plays 'New York, New York' on his clarinet. Like the
impromptu singing during the Broadway party, these moments
testify to the unscripted nature of theatre in Mazursky's imagination:
actors are simply creatures with theatricality in them, who might
break into song or dance at any moment. But although Phillip joins
in during this first celebration, he is also at pains to interpret it, to
identify its meaning for the group; ensuring, in short, that the others
learn its lesson. Phillip is a teacher. But he is also, like Alonzo, a
'boss' and owner. In contrast to the classical Greek theatres, the
island arena is *his* theatre: he has imagined it, and it is constructed
according to his vision. As he says to Aretha in a pensive moment:
'I'm worried about my theatre.' It is never clear why he is worried
about his theatre, whether he is building or rebuilding it, or who will
watch performances there. Significantly, the only audience *Tempest*
offers (in a long shot that cannot avoid being at least partly ironic)
is Nino, the dog.

If the theatre has become, in Mazursky's argument, a relic whose
primary function is to support the spontaneous behaviour of actors,
Phillip's allegorical medium – that of film – is also finding itself
replaced by a newer mode of entertainment. However powerful the
architect/filmmaker appears to be (indeed, Mazursky envisages Phillip's
authority more in terms of earlier directors – such as a Griffith,
Eisenstein or Blassetti – than of the postwar *registi*), he finds that this
importance does not give him control over his career or family: his wife
has an affair with his employer; his daughter eventually declares her
independence; his 'friend', Kalibanos, attempts to seduce his daughter.
Where Alonzo and Kalibanos figure as the companion/rivals of Phillip
in Mazursky's allegory of amiable collaboration, then, television functions as a potent medium which threatens the dominion of film and
filmmaker alike. *Tempest* suggests that, should drama survive, it will
survive on television. As Miranda declares, while watching the Johnny
Carson Show during the Broadway party, 'I saw something by Pinter on
TV. It was really boring.'

Miranda is, however, instantly absorbed by the Italian-language
episode of *Gunsmoke*, and this absorption in a television programme
whose language she does not appear to know is *Tempest*'s way of
calling our attention to the manner in which television has tran-
scended, even obliterated, the boundaries of various languages and

cultures. Relevant here is a visual pun, for although Mazursky renames Shakespeare's Ariel, *Tempest* 'remembers' the spirit's name in at least two sequences. This first occurs when Phillip, Aretha and Miranda discuss their flight while on a rooftop surrounded by television antennae (we are reminded of Phillip's connection to a different form of visuality as they gather around his telescope to do so). A second instance transpires when Kalibanos hastens to erect a hidden antenna in order to bring television into his island cave. As he says to Miranda: 'Have a seat while I fixa the aerial.' The camera admires the ingenuity of Kalibanos' improvised aerial: it creaks out of the island's underbrush in a manner appropriate to the comedy of his desire. But, like a weed growing in what Phillip has called a 'paradise', the aerial prefigures, even produces, the latter's wrath, and hence the subsequent storm which shipwrecks Alonzo, Antonia and their companions. Shakespeare's Ariel occupies our memory as a creature of invisibility and extension; *Tempest* locates these qualities not in the physical being of Aretha, but in the omnipresence of television signals. Even as Mazursky transforms Plato's Cave into a tourist trap, so does he exchange Ariel for aerials.

Mazursky is able to make such a punning translation significant for us precisely because, like the characters in his films, he routinely sees the outside of things. This devotee of canonical European cinema is at his best, in fact, when observing the changing surfaces of American life. His films particularly chronicle emergent themes and lifestyles, less the way his audiences live than the way they will live. Scattered details, viewed years later, add up to a kind of prophetic insight into cultural shifts. Watching *Tempest* again, after nearly two decades, for instance, we might note Mazursky's respect for the new presence of Japan in world trade, something which emerges not only in his use of a brand name here ('Sony Trinitron'), but also in the 'Honda' jacket which Kalibanos puts on during his seduction attempt, and in the tables of Japanese tourists in the Greek restaurant. Such moments strike us as invigoratingly *authentic*, conveyors of a shared quiddity of existence. *Tempest* is so full of these exterior details in part because it is Mazursky's habit to see them, and in part because the myth he likes to relate continually glances off his source text; confronted with intransigent material, Mazursky was left to ruminate on the process of his art and on the distance between his source and himself. What he omits from the core of Shakespeare's story is replaced with the outside textures of contemporary life and art.

This dedication to the surface explains why *Tempest* joins, even exceeds, so many of his films in its emphasis on the gaze. To watch Mazursky's *oeuvre* is to follow the history of the camera in American life. Beginning with the documentary filmmaker in *Bob & Carol* (whose working visits to San Francisco, of course, call up not only the culturally prominent energies of the 1960s, but also the role of the portable camera in framing them), his cameraman gradually gives way, through a sequence including Alex, Phil and Phillip, to Max in *Down and Out*, who uses video to capture his dysfunctional family life. The date of this film – 1986 – testifies to Mazursky's sensitivity concerning cultural movements, for this was just prior to the time when countless American households would possess video cameras which came to shape, even produce, the events they sought to record. But reviewing *Bob & Carol* brings us an anticipation of such *tableaux*, as Bob perches atop a vantage-point with his movie camera to record a family birthday party, obnoxiously 'directing' Carol so as to improve his shot. The technology used for Bob's San Franciscan documentary alters their family life in the process of chronicling it. This is Mazursky seeing the way that we would see, and hence the way we would come to live.

It is this sensitivity to the forms of visual experience, coupled with a stubbornly foreign source text, that makes *Tempest* such an acute commentary on the many Shakespeare films that followed its release. *Tempest* anticipates the conditions that made these Shakespeare films possible through its emphasis on the sequence of aesthetic forms which has seen the replacement of theatre by screen, of three-dimensional public spaces by the flat surfaces of film and television. While much about Mazursky's film celebrates, in Phillip, a godlike director figure, *Tempest* remains too faithful to its moment of production to aver that such is more than a nostalgic fantasy. The film's uncertainty about Phillip's relation to the storms (it is never clear, for instance, whether he produces them or merely capitalizes on them) confesses to the distance between contemporary filmmakers and the special effects that drive their films. Like such filmmakers, Phillip admires the force of these effects but has little, if any, knowledge of how to create them.

Tempest finds the spectacular to be narcotic as well as mysterious. For *Tempest*, in fact, the condition of postmodernity is a descent into an exhaustive, fetishized visuality. Towards the end of its long sequence of forms lies a bright television screen; completing the fall into pure entertainment is the still unfinished casino with its equally purposeless, and equally draining, pleasures. *Tempest* defines such experience as emergent by chronicling, with Miranda and Freddy, the rise of a generation to whom public spaces are all but a memory, for whom drama exists as only one of a large number of offerings on television, and with whom even spectacles are increasingly experienced in private. Thus while *Tempest* lacks the stylistic self-consciousness of some of the Shakespeare films of the 1990s, it meditates on the cultural conditions which, in preparing for these films, have changed how we experience Shakespeare. For example, when a well-known reviewer suggested that one could appreciate *Prospero's Books* (1991) only when scrutinizing it frame by frame (and, in fact, urged viewers to do so), he doubtless meant this as a compliment to the film's visual richness.[8] But the experience this would suggest – a single person stopping and starting a film at will – is an intensively private, even fetishistic one, and closer to that provided by a casino's montage of attractions than to the communal experience of the Greek theatre.

'Humans go to the movies.' So, at least, observes Miranda when pointing out the island's deprivations. And although we may initially agree with her interested definition, contrasting the modernity of the cinema with the Greek island's classical amphitheatre, *Tempest* asks us to see a continuity between these venues based on their public nature. Both have been followed, even supplanted, by a decidedly less public way of experiencing drama. Where much of Phillip's role is invested in articulating the difference between film and television, his daughter's seduction by the latter suggests that television has not only displaced its forerunners, but absorbed both film and theatre within its smaller but luminous scope. What has succeeded going to the theatre, and going to the movies, is watching drama on television at home, in virtual solitude. The accessible Shakespeare that comes to us this way is small, flat and private – bright figurines speaking poetry. Such a reduction of Shakespeare – productions commodified for perpetual reviewing – is part and parcel of our high degree of civilization. In recording the stages by which we came to this juncture, *Tempest* remains a film to think with as well as about.

Notes

1. David Denby, 'Such Stuff as Dreams are Made On', *New York*, 15, 16 August (1982), p. 42; John Simon, 'Dishonored Bones', *The National Review*, 34, 17 September (1982), p. 1162; Stanley Kauffmann, 'Variations on Two Themes', *The New Republic*, 187, 20–7 September (1982), p. 28. For other positive notices, see, for example, Stephen Farber, 'A Whiz Brews an Ill Wind that Blows Well', *The New York Times*, 131, section 2, 29 August

(1982), pp. 13–14; Lawrence O'Toole, 'A Potent Toast to Life', *Maclean's*, 27 September (1982), p. 61 ('The movie is an extraordinarily original flight of the imagination from a director just reaching the prime of his powers'); and Jack Kroll, 'A Switch on the Bard', *Newsweek*, 100, 16 August (1982), p. 59 ('[Mazursky's] *Tempest* is a tenderly amusing celebration of the rueful pleasures of mortality').

2. Pauline Kael, 'Buzzers: The Current Cinema', *The New Yorker*, 58, 20 September (1982), p. 128.

3. On Dolores' correspondences to Gonzalo, see Judith R. Buchanan, 'Visions of the Island: *The Tempest* on Film, 1905–1991', unpublished D.Phil. thesis, University of Oxford (1997), p. 168. I am grateful to Buchanan for sharing her work with me.

4. The film's immersion in this thematic can be seen in the following sequence of lines from Antonia and Phillip, respectively: 'Are you happy?'; 'Are you having a good time?'; 'Are you okay?'; 'I want to quit'; 'I want to get out'; 'I've had enough'. Compare also Phillip's 'We're all nervous'; '[I'm] generally feeling tense'; 'These bore me'; 'The money and the power don't mean a thing'; 'My life is very complicated right now'; 'Most of the time I don't give a shit about anything'. Understandably, the majority of the reviews of *Tempest* employ the phrase 'mid-life crisis', although it does not occur in the film itself.

5. Buchanan, 'Visions of the Island', p. 165.

6. *Clichés* take on the status of philosophy to Mazursky's characters, retaining a truth value only occasionally called into question by the films themselves. As the psychiatrist relates to the Jill Clayburgh character in *An Unmarried Woman*: 'They're your feelings: just feel 'em'; so does the Nick Nolte character in *Down and Out* advise the confused son: 'Hey, you gotta be what you gotta be'; and Phillip in *Tempest*: 'You know what Lao Tse said, don't you? "Nature. And it speaks true, why not man?".'

7. O'Toole, 'A Potent Toast to Life', p. 61.

8. '*Prospero's Books* would be an ideal film to watch on laserdisc, where with a hand-held remote you could freeze any frame and study its subtleties.' Roger Ebert, '*Prospero's Books*', *Chicago Sun-Times*, 27 November (1991), section 2, p. 37.

3
Camp *Richard III* and the Burdens of (Stage/Film) History

Stephen M. Buhler

As the twentieth century concludes, the burdens of its history – and of what was made of its historical inheritances – have been more and more overtly thematized in several art-forms. One hallmark of post-modernism is a detached playfulness with history: wry quotations of the past appear as isolated architectural elements, as recontextualized figures in visual works, as characters haunted by lost (but tantalizingly 'present') connections with source-texts in narrative. The enormities of this century provide sufficient rationale for such detachment; if the earnestness of high art is no longer conceivable in the West after the Holocaust, then understated disengagement offers a welcome refuge. An alternative path, though, is a heady immersion into the unsettling stuff of history, a wilful involvement with the passions as well as the trappings of the past. Such a passionate approach may still entertain ideas of performativity as well as sincerity; Shakespeare's historical tragedies regularly depend upon both. In his dispute with readings that ignore this volatile mixture, Jonathan Dollimore has argued that a Shakespearean playtext such as *Antony and Cleopatra* is predicated upon what he calls 'the profound truth of camp, the "deep" truth of the superficial: if it's worth doing, it's worth overdoing'.[1]

Ian McKellen and Richard Loncraine, in adapting *Richard III* for the motion picture screen, have detected in that play and its stage history the same injunction to overdo. The resulting film certainly revels – as Dollimore reminds us about camp – 'in a desire it simultaneously deconstructs, becoming a form of theatrical excess which both cele-brates and undermines what it mimics'. We have in their film of *Richard III* not only theatrical but cinematic excess, as an array of movie conventions from the 1930s onward are gleefully and some-times wickedly invoked. Among these conventions are some of the richest materials associated with the camp sensibility: these include the production values of the Hollywood musical, which rely on the ephemera of art deco styles and fashions, and the elusive, arbitrary signs that mark the matinée idol. At the same time, their *Richard III* exploits the more recent conventions of the 'heritage' film (most strongly associated with Ismail Merchant and James Ivory) in order to interrogate a more unsettling aspect of both the camp sensibility and reactions to it: the frequently alleged connection between homoeroticism and fascism. By engaging with such materials in such a manner, McKellen and Loncraine have alienated not a few observers. But they have risked – even invited – such alienation in order to explore the sexual politics within the playtext and its performance traditions.

The film effectively interweaves reassurance and danger, echoing camp's problematization of 'safe' categories and markers; the supposed safety of what is historical and therefore settled (as is often the case in 'heritage' filmmaking) provokes camp's irreverent response and revision. McKellen and Loncraine reject the argument advanced by Shakespeare's Richard, when he tries desperately to consolidate his power via marriage, that 'what is done cannot be now amended' (IV.iv.291).[2] As a result, they resist several received notions about the nature of Richard's villainy and his appeal to audiences. The idea that Richard *must be* attractive because of his powerfully 'malign sexuality' (which is how more than one critic has described Laurence Olivier's influential performance) warrants closer investigation and invites mockery, which is where camp may enter. As Jack Babuscio notes, the four features 'basic to camp [are] irony, aestheticism, theatricality, and humour'.[3] All four are clearly at work in McKellen and Loncraine's *Richard III*, but an often disturbing comedy is regularly foregrounded. For Babuscio, humour

> constitutes the strategy of camp: a means of dealing with a hostile environment and, in the process, of defining a positive identity.[4]

The film considers how Richard has been configured both in hostile and positive lights, both within the play and in its historical and theatrical contexts. Humour helps in confronting, if not bearing, the multiple burdens of the past.

The film directly connects with the theatrical history of *Richard III* in acknowledging its origins in a celebrated Royal National Theatre production that opened in 1990 and continued, on tour, for over two years. Directed by Richard Eyre, this production realized an analogy that Ian McKellen had asserted for years in his one-man show, *Acting Shakespeare*: that the Richard of the *Henry VI* plays and *Richard III* fore-shadows the totalitarian leaders of the twentieth century. Drawing upon British flirtations with fascism in the 1930s, as well as later revivals of the National Front, the production repeatedly evoked that time and place: 'Victoria Station', for example, was the imagined site of the Prince of Wales' return in III.i, since 'the royals always arrive[d] in London by rail' at that time.[5] The triumphal poster that unfurled upon Richard's accession deliberately imitated the idealizing kitsch that rendered the Führer both hero and exemplar. Richard himself (and therefore McKellen himself) appeared on the poster naked – a youthful, Aryan warrior, healed of deformities by virtue of his charisma, his power, his office. As Lois Potter observes in her review of the stage production, Richard's poster 'hint[ed] perhaps at the fantasy that motivates his cult of war'.[6]

From early on in the process of adapting the play – and the 1930s' era production – for the screen, McKellen was thinking in terms of sexuality and in terms of jolting his audience with outrageous humour. One example that did not survive successive rewrites is reproduced in McKellen's introduction to the published screenplay:

26   INT. CATESBY'S OFFICE
     Sir William Catesby, the King's private secretary, is on the phone to Lord Hastings, the Prime Minister.
          CATESBY
     The King's physicians fear him mightily.
     Prime Minister, the King doth call for you.
27   INT. HASTINGS' PRIVATE APARTMENT AT 10, DOWNING STREET
     Hastings, 60 years old, is answering the phone, as his teenage mistress massages his fat body towards orgasm.
          HASTINGS
     Catesby, I come!

McKellen shrugs this off as one of the early draft's 'infelicities', but the principle at work here, of outrageously eroticizing lines and scenes, remains in force in the completed film.[7] Perhaps the most notorious example is the assassination of Rivers, which the play does not depict but which McKellen thought important to include. Loncraine is cred-ited (at least by McKellen) with the macabre scene of Rivers first being coaxed toward orgasm by the air hostess he met on his transatlantic flight to London – the Woodvilles are marked as American *arrivistes* –

and then impaled upon a sword, which is thrust from beneath the mattress by Tyrrell. McKellen's *Carry On, Catesby* approach in his version of Hastings' scene survives in this more outrageous episode. The camp effect of the scene is heightened by its link to what follows: the screams of the air hostess blend with the shriek of a train whistle, in conscious imitation of a similar device in Alfred Hitchcock's film of *The Thirty-Nine Steps*.[8] The campiness, though, is not entirely a matter of McKellen and Loncraine's related strategies; as Dollimore suggests, much of the extravagance in performance is implicit in the text.

From the film's outset, McKellen and Loncraine ground their introduction of camp sensibility in Richard's status as an outsider from his own family; we soon discover that they envisage Richard specifically as a sexual outsider. His alienation is, first and last, physical – a matter of distance and incapacity. Though he briefly greets his family for a group portrait and attends, as he must, the celebratory dance in honour of the Yorkist victory, Richard stays at a remove from his mother, his brothers, and the circle of his brother Edward's now royal family. The camera pays special attention to the children of the court: along with the doomed Princes, we see Lord Stanley's son, who will be held hostage at Bosworth Field. Richard's ultimate rival in all such matters, Richmond, is shown dancing with his eventual bride, Princess Elizabeth. It is not only Clarence and Edward, nor even Edward's heirs, who occasion Richard's envy.

The transformation of the first lines of the play's opening soliloquy into a public encomium for Edward is presented almost as an interruption of the 'merry meetings and delightful measures' from which Richard is excluded. On the soundtrack we hear a big-band setting for Marlowe's 'The Passionate Shepherd to His Nymph'; the lyrics also incorporate lines from Ralegh's poem, 'The Nymph's Reply', which suggest Richard's own resistance to the developing dynastic myth. In addition, the line that registers doubt that there is 'truth in every shepherd's tongue' may signal that people could have remained sceptical towards Richard's blandishments. At one point, Richard and Edward face each other – Richard on the bandstand, Edward seated amongst his family in the place of honour across the hall. They are adversaries upon a symbolic field of battle, but only Richard knows this. In the playtext, Richard initially shares with us, his audience, what he 'should' feel in response to Edward's accession. In the film, Richard persuasively *performs* the emotions of brotherly love, family pride and humane relief that peace, after years of civil unrest, has finally broken out; he conceals the internecine enmity he bears. While he acknowledges that 'Grim-visaged war has smoothed his wrinkled front', his own visage is anything but smooth: under his left eye are exaggerated bags, and his left jaw is similarly underscored. As McKellen informs us, both the stage and film productions have built upon the idea that Richard is indeed 'half made-up', with a 'good' side (the right) and a 'bad' (the left, or sinister, of course).[9] Here, close-ups of his ravaged face already signal his resistance towards maintaining the present, peaceful order. He merely mouths the sentiments, as the camera focuses strictly on Richard's mouth, its accompanying moustache, and discoloured, uneven teeth: 'And now, instead of mounting barbed steeds, / To fright the souls of fearful adversaries, / He ...' (and in mid-phrase the scene changes).

We move abruptly from the Great Hall to the Water Closet. As the speech continues, the personified War 'capers nimbly in a lady's chamber / To the lascivious pleasing of a lute', while Richard himself limps hurriedly to a urinal. Richard's contempt for all that might occur in 'a lady's chamber' is all the stronger for being expressed in the men's room. As Samuel Crowl has observed, Richard relieves both spleen and bladder; as Robert F. Willson, Jr, also suggests, he enacts his disenchantment with his family's celebration.[10] Still more is going on, though: Richard looks down at his urinating penis and comments on an important reason for being not only disenchanted with the dynastic triumph but estranged from it. He looks up and says, 'But I, that am not shaped for sportive tricks, / Nor made to court an amorous looking-glass', before glancing down again and continuing:

> I, that am rudely stamped –
> Deformed, unfinished, sent before my time
> Into this breathing world, scarce half made up ...

At this point, he has finished, zipped up and turned to adjust his military collar while looking in the mirror.

> And that so lamely and unfashionable
> That dogs bark at me, as I halt by them ...

He washes and dries his right hand, continuing to consider himself in the mirror.

> Why, I, in this weak piping time of peace,
> Have no delight to pass away the time,

> Unless to spy my shadow in the sun,
> And descant on my own deformity.
> (I.i.14–16, 20–7)

At this point, he notices us in the mirror. Before he turns around to face us – cinematic voyeurs all – we have already been drawn into seeing Richard as he sees himself. The film presents him as alienated from his family because of his incapacity to continue the York line in any form. He is separated from the physical processes of patriarchy and cannot fully share in its triumphs.

Sexual frustration is a major component of McKellen's interpretation of the role. He had appeared as Iago shortly before tackling Richard III for the National Theatre production and – as is often the case with actors – saw a connection between the characters. McKellen, having 'delved into the jealous psychology of a sexually frustrated husband ... was prepared to explore Richard's humanity rather than reducing him to an emblem of wickedness'.[11] His Richard, then, is sinned against as well as sinning; the hostile environment Babuscio sees as a precondition for camp is palpable in the Yorkists' own view of Richard. He may sin against himself, as the desperate, conscience-stricken soliloquy after dreaming of his victims indicates. He also has considerable help in developing self-contempt, notably from his mother, the Duchess of York. McKellen is explicit on this point: Richard has suffered from his mother 'verbal and emotional abuse which from infancy has formed her youngest son's character and behaviour'.[12] To establish this, though, McKellen has to transform the Duchess' character – with the help of the Shakespearean playtext, as several of Queen Margaret's bitterest lines are assigned to the Duchess herself. In the film, Maggie Smith does her utmost to sustain McKellen and Loncraine's view of the character as pitiless and 'rock-like', most clearly towards her youngest son.[13] She is beyond Niobe, past tears. Instead, she sustains an icy rage against the child whose very body mocks her maternity, whose incapacity prevents him from sharing in the family's continuation. McKellen's interpretation suggests that Richard seeks a kind of vengeance against her in his murderous attempts to extinguish the line utterly and in his (often successful) attempts to make such villainy comic.

Despite this, McKellen ignores the potential for comedy that many performers have found in Richard's conquest of Lady Anne. As many commentators have observed, the film's presentation of this encounter is considerably muted from that offered by Eyre's stage version. This indicates a certain conflict within the psychosexual reading of the character of Richard that McKellen intends: even as his Richard overplays the role of screen lover, the same self-doubts that can inspire extravagance can also introduce a note of sombre desperation. One supremely theatrical effect from the stage production, though, has been intensified in the film: Richard's offering Anne a ring – again from his 'good' hand – as a kind of betrothal between them:

> *He slowly lifts his right hand to his mouth and, with his teeth, pulls off his family signet-ring.*
>   RICHARD
>   Vouchsafe to wear this ring.
> *RICHARD slides the ring, wet with saliva, onto her engagement finger.*[14]

The erotic charge of the scene, which was considerable on stage, is heightened by the use of close-ups here. Kristen Scott Thomas' Anne quietly gasps as the ring actually slides onto her finger. She can barely utter her next line, a last gesture towards resistance: 'To take is not to give.' The sexuality, though, is to a great extent autoerotic – as Richard initially performs a kind of fellatio on himself – and this feeds the self-regarding exuberance of Richard's own commentary on what has transpired between Anne and himself:

> Upon my life she finds, although I cannot,
> Myself to be a marvellous proper man.
> I'll entertain some score or two of tailors
> To study fashions to adorn my body
> [And then return lamenting to my love].[15]
>   [*Half-singing*]
> Shine out, fair sun, till I have bought a glass,
> That I may see my shadow as I pass.
>   (Adapted from I.ii.258–9, 251–62, 266–8)

The couplet is intoned brightly, sounding something like the 1930s' tagline, 'Is everybody happy?' Now that he is nearly alone (although still with us, the audience), the irony in his circumstances inspires elation: 'a marvellous proper man', indeed! Richard's manner with assorted victims of the recent war waiting in the hospital's corridors is solipsistically merry. He then dances his way upstairs, as a song that might befit a Fred Astaire musical (perhaps *Top Hat*) blares on the soundtrack; we realize that it is a reprise of 'The Passionate Shepherd'. The camp sensibility triumphs along with Richard, who strikes a hammy pose as the music ends. The pose, however, turns inward rather than out: Richard turns away from the camera.

As McKellen tells it, Richard with Anne 'inspires himself by playing the fantasy role of romantic lover', as embodied by a panoply of 'screen heroes': he mentions Clark Gable, Clifton Webb, David Niven and Douglas Fairbanks by virtue, in part, of the stylized moustache they wear and that this Richard wears by McKellen's own choice.[16] On screen, Richard appears far more inspired in the contemplation of his success than in the performance of his courtship. The role of roman- tic lover is not fantastic only for Richard, but for anyone: the role is part of a fantasy aggressively mounted, marketed and naturalized in the 1930s for consumption in the communal isolation of a darkened theatre. (McKellen and Loncraine later suggest this dynamic when Richard, nearly oblivious to his entourage, savours newsreel footage of his coronation.) What identifies a man as a certain type of lover, beyond the requisite 'score or two of tailors', is his romantic regalia – a moustache, perhaps a cigarette casually dangling from his lips. The arbitrariness of such marks of the screen hero, though, underscores the constructed quality of the role itself and invites the detached mirth of camp. One vivid illustration of the process is the pencil-line moustache that has now become an emblem for film director John Waters, perhaps today's shrewdest student and *auteur* of camp sensi- bility. McKellen's reasons for avoiding campiness in the actual dialogue between Richard and Anne include his conviction that 'Richard has had little success with sex, because he doubts anyone could find him physically attractive and has devoted himself exclu- sively to his career as a full-time soldier'.[17] There is profound bitterness in McKellen's view of the character, as seen in the actor's suggestion that, when Richard casts doubts upon the legitimacy of Edward's children, he acts out of envy towards the easy heterosexual potency of his brother Edward. According to McKellen, the slander derives from 'Richard's bitterness that he feels unattractive to women'.[18] There is a lovely ambiguity in that phrase: is Richard bitter because of the unattractiveness or – a situation interrogated by camp send-ups of norms of beauty – is he bitter because of being made to *feel* unattractive?

Not only is Richard described as 'sexually frustrated', not only is there the sardonic comment (in this version) on how ill-'shaped' is his sexual organ, there is also a reference in the published screenplay to

Richard and Anne's forgoing sex after their 'first unsuccessful attempt'.[19] The lack of success would seem a foregone conclusion here. An essay by Ian Frederick Moulton, written before the release of the film, substantially supports the idea. Along with other explanations for Richard's hypermasculinity and militarism (including, in this case, the impact of his father's death), Moulton offers an idea drawn from Francis Bacon, who in his essay 'Of Deformity'

> also contends that, if the genitals do not function properly, erotic energy will circulate in other channels. Bacon cites the eunuch as an example of how 'deformity is an advantage to rising [in social standing]'. That which is unable to raise itself physically may rise socially instead. Clearly, this is the social dynamic of Richard's deformity.[20]

Moulton goes on to argue that since Shakespeare's Richard – unlike his historical model, who fathered children both legitimate and illegitimate – is 'detached from patriarchal economies of reproduction', the phallic power he can so effectively wield, and 'on which patriarchal order depends', itself becomes a threat to that order. The 'proper patriarchal proportion is reintroduced' only by Richmond's accession to the throne.[21]

Moulton's essay, then, suggests that the interpretation in itself is textually and culturally sustainable. As we have seen, McKellen and Loncraine not only sustain it, but run with it. Richard's inability to penetrate procreatively is repeatedly hinted at, and the film makes explicit his satisfaction in cutting life short. When Richard later urges Edward's widow, Queen Elizabeth, to 'acquaint the Princess / With the sweet, silent hours of marriage joys' (IV.iv.329–30), the implied promises ring preternaturally hollow. Since this Richard knows that he is incapable of continuing the Yorkist line, how crass indeed are the lines that promise Queen Elizabeth that she will be, if no longer the mother of kings, at least a grandmother thereof.[22] All she need do is give Richard her daughter's hand in marriage:

> *Eliz.* But you did kill my children.
> *K. Rich.* But in your daughter's womb, I bury them,
>   Where, in that nest of spicery, they will breed.
>   (Adapted from IV.iv.422–4)

In the stage production, that last line had been cut. McKellen recalls that one critic – left unnamed – found in the deletion a key to a problem with his interpretation of the role: the stage Richard simply was not 'sexy enough'.[23] For the film, McKellen and Loncraine restore the 'sexy' line, but not because they agree with the critical assessment. In the published screenplay, McKellen observes that here 'Richard's sense of the erotic owes more to barrack-room boasting than to the bedroom'.[24] Beyond the braggart-soldier tone, though, the playtext's language introduces uncontrollably morbid images along with the claim to productive patriarchy and dynastic resurrection. The decidedly non-erotic clumsiness of the scene continues, in the film, with Richard's brutal kiss of farewell.

This Elizabeth, though, draws upon her own resources to counter Richard's misogyny and dysfunction. This is trumpeted in the film through an audacious rearrangement of the playtext – and further revision of history – by having Richmond marry Princess Elizabeth before the battle of Bosworth Field. The marriage remains Queen Elizabeth's doing: in the role, Annette Bening registers relief and joy at the ceremony. She also enjoys this strategic triumph over Richard and his desperate (and humiliating) attempt to seduce her into consenting to an alliance. She is not content with telegraphing her intentions to Richard's rival; the Queen has apparently marched young Elizabeth straight to Richmond's camp and expectant embrace.

We hear the Archbishop's closing prayer after solemnizing the marriage – a full nuptial mass, it appears. His devotions are taken from the final speech of the playtext, which is there assigned to Richmond himself:

> O Lord, let Richmond and Elizabeth
> By Your fair ordinance be joined together,
> And let their heirs – God, if thy will be so –
> Enrich the time to come with smooth-faced peace.
> (Adapted from V.v.29, 31–3)

The words are set in direct conflict with Richard's opening image of 'grim-faced War' smoothing his countenance into a simulacrum of peace. In addition, the words propose actual progeny from this political union. Before preparing himself for war, Richmond kisses his bride and offers a truncated version of his prayer in V.iii. He also, we discover soon after, leads Elizabeth to his tent, where they happily consummate the marriage.

Instead of being visited in the night by the same ghosts that so terrify his adversary, Richmond enjoys 'fairest-boding dreams' that are here inspired by the woman with whom he has spent the night. It is Princess Elizabeth, and not an attendant lord, who asks him: 'How have you slept, my Lord?' The scene self-consciously echoes Franco Zeffirelli's cinematic rendering of Romeo's and Juliet's aubade. This idyllic 'Morning in England' provides an eroticized analogue for the portrait of Britain depicted on Richmond's iconic poster in the stage production. Richard's idealized figure had trumpeted a fantastic, restorative process upon his own person; in contrast, Richmond's poster announced the revitalization of the land itself – green hills, fertile soil, an end to the barrenness of Richard's monstrous *régime*. Where the stage production had literally laid bare the fiction of Richard's imagined renewal and then replaced that myth with yet another, the film presents the image of the loving couple themselves as England's hope. Peter Holland indicates his discomfort with the stage Richmond's emblematic backdrop in his review of the National Theatre production. Richmond's arrival

> was heralded by a new backcloth, a chocolate-box saccharine depiction of the English countryside, a rural idyll of everything Richmond is fighting for. I desperately wanted to see this vision as ironic but the production left no space for such a reading.[25]

The iconized English landscape seemed to call for some kind of ironization – and the reasons for irony are strongly suggested in the complete closing speech as well as by early Tudor history. The film's idealized presentation of easy, comfortable sexual love on the eve (and the morn) of a portentous battle not only allows but demands an ironic response. The sense of irony intensifies when one recalls the playtext's version of spectral visitors to the two military leaders; their promises of victory or defeat, not the messengers themselves, constitute what is fair or ill to these dreamers. What follows in the film – the staging of the battle and the transfer of power to Richmond – enlists irony in the service of camp.

In the published screenplay, McKellen relates the story of the original idealization of Richard for the stage and describes its replacements for the US performances and for the film. The scene is the Lord Protector's office:

> Behind his chair, there is a full-length oil-painting of Richard looking every inch a leader, with two perfectly formed hands, his leather greatcoat around his shoulders. For the RNT, Bob Crowley

designed a massive backcloth similarly celebrating Richard's heroism. From a quick polaroid, I was painted naked, the left arm wholly restored and held aloft, in the manner of the Third Reich's monumental symbols of manhood. Richard Eyre believed that the penis (though a copy of my own) was ill-proportioned and had it slightly painted over. For the USA, the portrait was again exhibited but modestly clad in a full suit of armour.[26]

For the film, as for US stage audiences, Richard's sexuality is obscured by the trappings of Nazi hero-worship. The armour that McKellen anachronistically wore for the play's battle scenes was inspired by 'The Standard-Bearer': this painting of Hitler by Hubert Lanzinger was reproduced in the production's programme, which informs us that the portrait was Hitler's own choice as 'the official painting of the Führer for the Great German Art Exhibition, 1938'.[27] The film's blackshirt-style uniform, leather coat and riding crop engage not only with the historical phenomena comprising fascism but also with past attempts to 'explain' fascism psychosexually.

In *Political Inversions: Homosexuality, Fascism, and the Modernist Imaginary*, Andrew Hewitt traces persistent cultural associations involving homosexual desire (and its repression), 'feminine' surrender to a totalitarian cult, militarism and hypermasculinity. Theodor Adorno, among others, filtered a view of fascism through Freud's theories of mass political behaviour, lending a kind of legitimacy to those cultural associations. Hewitt observes that

> Adorno's binary construction of homo-fascism [consists of] narcissism and effeminization ... for Adorno, even as the homosexual surrenders his desire, he in fact acts it out – as a desire *to* surrender .... Thus, while Adorno seems to argue that it is the repression and false sublation of homosexual desire that is dangerous, he inevitably argues at other points that it is *un*repressed desire (homosexual desire for surrender) that is dangerous. The homosexual is a fascist because he is repressed – and a fascist because he is not repressed enough![28]

Much of McKellen's and Loncraine's *Richard III* explores the 'obvious' links that Hewitt effectively problematizes. The very same camp sensibility that might reinforce the cultural associations between fascism and homosexuality helps to undermine them. Neither Richard's repression (apparently sublimated into dreams of martial force and political power) nor his lack of repression (his misogyny, his 'weakness' both in striking the messenger with news of Buckingham's capture and in caressing him while asking pardon, and his weeping into Ratcliffe's arms) survives as explanation under the pressure of cinematic extravagance.

The film goes to extremes in marking Richard and Richmond as polar opposites, and this continues in the final battle. While Richard abandons the wounded Ratcliffe and executes Tyrrell for even suggesting retreat, Richmond waves off his men to pursue Richard alone. Such *clichés* of the action-adventure movie are accompanied by auditory and visual overstatements. The music for this final chase is a melodramatic rewrite of Isaac Albeniz's virtuoso guitar composition, 'Asturias'. Looming over Richard as he tries to elude Richmond, we see an impressively phallic smokestack which has survived the barrage of artillery. Although meant to be part of 'a massive abandoned factory', the location, it turns out, is the old Battersea Power Station – which earlier in the film serves as the Tower. The contrast between Richard's presumption and Richmond's potency in several arenas of conflict and conjunction could not be clearer.

Nevertheless, the film concludes by calling their differences into question. When cornered by Richmond on the girders of the ruined factory, Richard reaches out with his 'good' hand and invites his enemy to join him. He uses words that in the playtext appear as the couplet prefacing Richard's oration to his troops: 'Let's to it pell-mell, / If not to Heaven, then hand-in-hand to Hell!' (V.iii.313–14). He falls backward, while Richmond fires his revolver superfluously after him. Richmond then looks directly at the camera – as no one else in the film has done, other than Richard – and smiles quietly, a bit smugly, as we hear Al Jolson's version of 'Sittin' on Top of the World'. A transaction has occurred by which *both* pretenders to the throne feel, as McKellen says, 'that they are sitting on top of the world'.[29] At this point, we see Richard's body plummet from the girders, with the massive tower again in the background. We then see Richard grinning as he falls into flames. The song's lyrics apply in several uncanny ways, including an echo of James Cagney's character in *White Heat* bellowing 'Top of the world!' to his deceased mother as fiery explosions surround him.[30] There are also verses that aver that 'A bundle of money don't make me feel gay, / My sweet little honey is makin' me say: / I'm sittin' on top of the world'.

While considerable commentary on this film glances back at the National Theatre production in which McKellen starred, there are

other chapters in stage history that also provide analogues and predecessors. Looming behind all recent productions is Olivier's approach
to the role, seen by Hugh Richmond as the culmination and even
distillation of the Colley Cibber tradition.[31] Olivier's Richard, like
Cibber's, is a charming, complete villain; in his film, there are but few
traces extant of the stirrings of conscience that Shakespeare's Richard
has to shake off vigorously. As in Shakespeare's playtext, Richard is
visited by the ghosts of his many victims, but, in Olivier's film, they
seem to emanate from Richmond's camp; they assault Richard from
without, not within. Richard is disturbed by them; he cries out in his
sleep. But even as he exclaims, 'Ratcliffe, I fear, *I* fear', his very emphasis indicates surprise at being moved: it is simply not his nature.
Olivier, outdoing Cibber, has completely excised Richard's troubled
soliloquy and therefore has smoothed the way for the character's
rebound from this 'uncharacteristic' uncertainty. One of Cibber's
most famous interpolations is delivered with quiet relish: 'Richard's
himself again', we are told in a confident, intimate aside, as Olivier
mounts his horse.

McKellen has set his and Loncraine's film of *Richard III* in contrast to
the Cibber tradition and specifically to Olivier. In its parodic reconstruction of the play's stage history, the film intends a very different
reading of its principal character. The interpretation McKellen most
resists is that of Richard as 'psychopath': instead, the actor wishes
(partly, we have seen, as a result of playing Iago beforehand) 'to explore
Richard's humanity', retaining the revelation of 'a troubled conscience
in his final, alarming soliloquy'.[32] Instead of being visited by ghosts
(much less spirits hailing from the enemy camp), Richard is haunted by
the memory of living voices: those of his victims and their survivors.
Rather than elide Richard's sense of his own guilt, McKellen provides a
corruscating, deliberately compressed reading of the soliloquy:

> I did but dream! O coward conscience.
> What do I fear? Myself? There's none else by –
> Richard loves Richard; that is, I am I.
> (Adapted from V.iii.179–80, 183–4)

In his own commentary on the scene, McKellen observes that the
words of this last line ('the most remarkable' of the whole 'remarkable
speech', he says, even in full-text versions) are 'as modern and as bleak
as Samuel Beckett's'.[33] His on-screen performance underscores the
affinities with Beckett's disjunctive, affectless world. But there is a

moral core here, as well, which places into curious balance both the nihilistic beauty of Beckett and the sentimentality of a psychological approach to character. While, in one sense, this line 'explains every- thing' (Richard is 'Unloved from birth by even his mother'), it is followed by lines that devastatingly bring Richard to account 'For hateful deeds committed by myself'. McKellen's delivery of the solilo- quy makes clear that self-pity cannot assert itself against both Richard's despair and his acuity: 'There is no creature loves me', including himself. Even so, he invites and accepts the comfort offered by Bill Paterson's Ratcliffe. McKellen's emphasis is not, as with Olivier, on the character's agency ('*I* fear') but on the unfamiliar passion he admits: 'Ratcliffe, I fear ... I *fear*.'

McKellen and Loncraine want to reveal Richard's 'newfound conscience' without minimizing either the tragedy he has visited 'on his victims and their survivors' or the 'tragic sense of waste' that attends Shakespeare's account of these quasi-historical events.[34] They apparently hope that the film allows the character his moments of vulnerability without making him yet another victim. Both his villainy and his passion – agency and otherness, vulnerability and iden- tity – are alternately communicated and ironized. Similar strategies with Elizabethan and Jacobean playtexts were employed by Derek Jarman, first with his *The Tempest* and then with an 'improvement' (his own, semi-jesting term) of Marlowe's *Edward II*. In the published version of the screenplay for the latter film, Jarman notes how he insisted on letting the homosexual characters be unsympathetic; he records that Andrew Tiernan 'is not playing Gaveston in a way that will endear me to "Gay Times"'.[35] He also comments, though, on McKellen's public avowal of being gay and his subsequent receiving of honours from the government of John Major:

> McKellen's knighthood is ... shocking: wining and dining in the erroneous belief that his honour improves our situation. There are many gay men with Tory hearts who believe in this honour. I don't. It was brave of Ian to come out – but that is all he had to do.[36]

Jarman's own experiments with classic texts and recent history, with tragedy and camp, have clearly impressed both McKellen and Loncraine. His use of the song 'Stormy Weather' in *The Tempest* and 'Every Time We Say Goodbye' in *Edward II* provides a striking prece- dent for the ending of *Richard III*. Other echoes of Jarman occur in the later film. For example, the same actor, Roger Hammond, largely represents the Church in both films: in *Edward II*, he is the Bishop of York, representing political alarm at the King's sexual politics and coercing Edward into approval of his favourite's banishment; in *Richard III*, he is 'the Archbishop' who is Richard's first principal defector and who later presides over Richmond's marriage to Princess Elizabeth. The differences between the films, however, are profound: Jarman worked with dramatic characters whose sexuality is discussed directly in the play; McKellen and Loncraine work both with a text that is less direct and a stage tradition that interacts and interferes with that text. Just as Shakespeare's sexuality is less certain than Marlowe's, so sexuality in *Richard III* is more elusive than in *Edward II*. McKellen and Loncraine's camp *Richard III* is to some extent a response to Jarman's *Queer Edward II* (the title of the published screenplay) and to Jarman's critique of McKellen's less adversarial, more accommodating public persona as 'A Knight, Out'.

Resisting the impulse to 'out' Richard, McKellen and Loncraine examine the possible dynamics of a closeted sexuality in the character. Generations of actors and audiences have determined – and over-determined – Richard, especially in the Cibber tradition. Much of that 'stage history' Richard is present in the film: he is the charismatic villain at the centre of a play about the sexiness of power politics. But in addition to that Richard is another, whose stage history involves questions of theatrical (and actors') sexuality. Along with 'sexy' power politics (Dr Kissinger's ultimate aphrodisiac), this film of *Richard III* also explores the power of sexual politics. In the film, realm holds sway over governments; even unruly sceptres, such as Edward IV's, seem preferable to barren ones. This can affect the reputation of actors, as in Olivier's ascendancy and, in the US, Barrymore's; Neil Sinyard's essay on Al Pacino and *Looking for Richard* suggests continuing associations between what (and who) controls by violence and what (and who) allures as a result.

Camp, Dollimore asserts, 'thrives on bathos', and few scenes can be as thrillingly and intentionally bathetic as the depiction of McKellen's Richard literally descending from the heights (of tragic hubris or of melodramatic excess?) into the welcoming flames.[37] In itself, though, bathos seems a woefully inadequate response to the stories implicit in the film's visual echoes of 1930s' political and military history; if this *Richard III* offers refractions on the sexual politics of fascism – and sexual politics more generally – only to dismiss them as insignificant, it could be accused of using mockery as a refuge from the burdens of historical suffering. But neither the film nor camp itself precludes a concomitant, if sometimes disorienting, seriousness from registering with the bathos. A character in Christopher Isherwood's novel, *The World in the Evening*, captures that aspect of camp succinctly and, well, elegantly: 'You're expressing what's basically serious to you in terms of fun and artifice and elegance.'[38] All four elements – earnestness and vulgarity, intelligence and style – jostle against each other in McKellen and Loncraine's *Richard III*.

Notes

1. Jonathan Dollimore, 'Shakespeare Understudies: the Sodomite, the Prostitute, the Transvestite, and Their Critics', in Jonathan Dollimore and Alan Sinfield (eds), *Political Shakespeare: New Essays in Cultural Materialism* (Ithaca and London: Cornell University Press, 1994), p. 147.
2. All references from Shakespeare's play are taken from *Richard III*, ed. Antony Hammond (London: Methuen, 1981). McKellen, in the published screenplay, mentions only 'standard editions' as his textual sources: see Ian McKellen, *William Shakespeare's 'Richard III': A Screenplay* (New York: Doubleday, 1996), p. 39.
3. Jack Babuscio, 'Camp and the Gay Sensibility', in Richard Dyer (ed.), *Gays and Film* (New York: Zoetrope, 1984), p. 41.
4. Babuscio, 'Camp', p. 47.
5. McKellen, *'Richard III'*, p. 12.
6. Lois Potter, 'A Country of the Mind', *Times Literary Supplement*, 4557, 3–9 August (1990), p. 825.
7. McKellen, *'Richard III'*, p. 14.
8. McKellen, *'Richard III'*, p. 150.
9. McKellen, *'Richard III'*, pp. 29–30.
10. Samuel Crowl, *'Richard III'*, *Shakespeare Bulletin*, 14:2 (1996), p. 38; Robert F. Willson, Jr, 'Hunchbacked Führer: Loncraine's *Richard III* as Postmodern Pastiche', unpublished paper presented at the 1997 meeting of the Shakespeare Association of America, p. 4.
11. McKellen, *'Richard III'*, pp. 22–3.
12. McKellen, *'Richard III'*, p. 22.
13. McKellen, *'Richard III'*, p. 155.
14. McKellen, *'Richard III'*, p. 85.
15. Lines in brackets indicate restorations of the playtext that do not appear in the published screenplay.
16. McKellen, *'Richard III'*, p. 80.
17. McKellen, *'Richard III'*, p. 64.
18. McKellen, *'Richard III'*, p. 184.
19. McKellen, *'Richard III'*, p. 198.
20. Ian Frederick Moulton, '"A Monster Great Deformed": The Unruly Masculinity of Richard III', *Shakespeare Quarterly*, 47 (1996), p. 265.
21. Moulton, '"A Monster"', p. 255.
22. Moulton ('"A Monster"', p. 265) argues that Shakespeare's Richard, 'despite his concern to buttress his rule with dynastic marriages ... gives no

thought to progeny'. We see in this passage that Richard does consider offspring, if only as rhetorical capital.

23. McKellen, *'Richard III'*, p. 254.
24. McKellen, *'Richard III'*, p. 254.
25. Peter Holland, 'Shakespeare Performances in England, 1989–90', *Shakespeare Survey*, 44 (1991), pp. 189–90.
26. McKellen, *'Richard III'*, p. 182.
27. Royal National Theatre, programme for *King Lear* and *Richard III*, Summer (1990), p. 14.
28. Andrew Hewitt, *Political Inversions: Homosexuality, Fascism, and the Modernist Imaginary* (Stanford: Stanford University Press, 1996), pp. 66–7.
29. McKellen, *'Richard III'*, p. 286.
30. James N. Loehlin, '"Top of the World, Ma": *Richard III* and Cinematic Convention', in Lynda E. Boose and Richard Burt (eds), *Shakespeare, the Movie: Popularizing the Plays on Film, TV, and Video* (London and New York: Routledge, 1997), p. 75.
31. Hugh M. Richmond, *Shakespeare in Performance: 'King Richard III'* (Manchester: Manchester University Press, 1989), p. 58.
32. McKellen, *'Richard III'*, p. 23.
33. McKellen, *'Richard III'*, p. 274.
34. McKellen, *'Richard III'*, p. 274.
35. Derek Jarman, *Queer Edward II* (London: BFI Publishing, 1991), p. 20.
36. Jarman, *Queer Edward II*, p. 106.
37. Dollimore, 'Shakespeare Understudies', p. 148.
38. Quoted in Babuscio, 'Camp', p. 49.

4

Shakespeare Meets *The Godfather*: The Postmodern Populism of Al Pacino's *Looking for Richard*

Neil Sinyard

'It has always been a dream of mine to communicate how I feel about Shakespeare to other people.' So says Al Pacino at an early stage of *Looking for Richard* in a remark which clearly posits this film as the culmination of that dream. What is unusual is the way he has gone about it. Unlike traditionalists such as Laurence Olivier and, more recently, Kenneth Branagh, whose desire to communicate their love of Shakespeare on film has resulted in a handsomely mounted production of a selected play (in which they both direct and star), Pacino's approach is altogether looser, more open, less grandiose. True, he directs and plays the leading role, but *Looking for Richard* is not simply an adaptation of *Richard III* but a meditation on what Shakespeare means at the end of the twentieth century.

To this end, Pacino employs a wide variety of styles. Filmed extracts from the play and from rehearsals are intercut with discussions with actors and academics and *ciné-verité* interviews with people on the street. In addition to the textual complications and ambiguities of the play itself, the topics raised through this method include the different traditions of performing Shakespeare in Britain and America, the contrast between an academic's and an actor's approach to a theatrical text, and the difference between acting Shakespeare on film and on stage. In the process, the title of the film takes on a new meaning. The ostensible subject of 'King Richard' is enlarged (in a neat visual conceit in the opening titles) to '*Looking for Richard*'. One concept/title becomes the other – one starts with *King Richard* but ends with *Looking for Richard*. As such, the visual conceit stands as a metaphor for the film as a whole. Pacino is documenting not so much his final, finished interpretation of the role as the stage-by-stage process by which an actor arrives at an interpretation through his quest for the core of the character.

The film's quest for Richard is simultaneously a means of raising questions about the modern relevance of Shakespeare and suggesting ways of interpreting, and making accessible, Shakespeare for future generations. It is here, I think, that the method and the millennium merge, because it is hard to conceive of a film of Shakespeare being mounted in quite this way in an earlier decade. Quite simply, the method constitutes an alert attempt to deal with a late twentieth-century cultural situation, which is seeing the decline of the book and literacy against the competition of global media; which is experiencing an undermining of the literary canon, with its attendant cultural/ideological implications and assumptions; and which is witnessing an increasing hostility to what might be called aesthetic élitism, of which Shakespeare stands as a supremely significant example. How, then, can Shakespeare's plays be made to seem exciting and attractive when the dramatist seems symptomatic of an intimidating, incomprehensible and even irrelevant tradition that many parts of society, academia and education are rejecting? *Looking for Richard* is an attempt to answer that question, and Pacino couches his response in a manner that is openly personal and implicitly postmodern.

How can the eclectic, elusive style of *Looking for Richard* be characterized? The adjective the film calls to mind is 'Wellesian'. The film's mesmerizing montage has something of the stylistic panache of that most audacious of screen adapters of Shakespeare, Orson Welles. Welles would undoubtedly have empathized with Pacino's obsession in bringing this project to the screen. It is well known that Welles made his celebrated film of *Othello* in bits and pieces over a period of years when he could raise enough money from his screen performances to continue filming.[1] Pacino, similarly, made *Looking for Richard* over a period of three-and-a-half years, shooting bits and pieces between his lucrative acting assignments on such Hollywood blockbusters as *City Hall* (1994) and *Heat* (1995), which were helping to finance the venture, and enticing his cast with the offer of 40 dollars a day and as many doughnuts as they could eat. However, the most important Wellesian connection is not so much the Shakespearean mania as the stylistic manner. What Pacino achieves in *Looking for Richard* is something that Welles had attempted twenty years before, though not in one of his Shakespeare films but in *F for Fake* (1976): namely, a new cinematic form of the filmed essay.

As Welles tried to elaborate it, the filmed essay takes a theme and then explores and embroiders it in cinematic terms, using whatever style or visual conceit that seems most appropriate at the time – documentary, dramatic fragment, still photography, captions, hand-held interview, parallel editing or whatever. To recognize *Looking for Richard* as an essay on what one might call appreciating Shakespeare – what he means to us, how one breaks through the barriers of prejudice and incomprehension – gives a different perception of the film's form. Simply taken as an adaptation or interpretation of *Richard III*, it is obviously fragmented, incomplete. But taken as a whole as an illustrated essay on Shakespeare, the modern actor and the modern audience, the film is 'organic' (to borrow a word Pacino uses about the play): it is all of a piece. This is experimental, educational, egalitarian cinema under the guise of enquiry and entertainment.

Some more detailed description of and commentary on the film's form and texture are necessary to understand Pacino's strategy. If Pacino's great aim is to communicate his passion for Shakespeare, his first task is to discover to whom this passion is being communicated, whom he needs to convert. Who comprises the audience for a Shakespeare film nowadays? If the words of the great Elizabethan playwright can touch the soul of a New Yorker of humble origins and Sicilian parentage, then potentially Shakespeare can reach anyone. But how do you reach those people for whom the very name of Shakespeare is culturally intimidating or, at the very least, a bad school memory? In street interviews that begin the film, Pacino and his co-writer and producer, the actor director Frederic Kimball, find that people either know nothing of Shakespeare or profess themselves baffled by his language. The finding is underlined in interviews with the actors Kevin Kline and Kenneth Branagh, who relate childhood memories of boring teaching and incomprehensible productions. Pacino's first problem, then, is how to communicate his passion for a playwright who is feared and barely understood through a play which, in addition to its complex language, ideally requires some knowledge of the Wars of the Roses. The significant issue here is that Pacino's audience research, as it were, will bear some influence on the shape the film will take: for example, the film will include – necessarily, Pacino would argue, if he is to reach the audience he wants to reach – explanatory commentary as well as filmed extracts.[2] Moreover, one feels that Pacino is including these interviews as a yardstick against which his film can be measured. By the end, will his film have made Shakespeare more accessible to such people, without condescending to the text or the audience?

This is a delicate task, and how effectively or otherwise Pacino opens up access to Shakespeare without trivializing or vulgarizing his source is open to individual judgement. It is worth noting, though, that, as the film goes on, the extracts become longer, as Pacino's confidence in his interpretation and, implicitly, in the audience's understanding grows. This is a different strategy from that adopted by Mel Gibson and Franco Zeffirelli for their 1990 version of *Hamlet*, for example, where Gibson appeared in a special 54–minute *Hamlet* video made for American schools entitled *Mel Gibson Goes Back to School* in order to explain and illustrate the excitement of the play. Pacino does not separate this problematic from his film but builds it into the structure, invites an audience to come complete with their prejudices and preconceptions, and encourages spectators to see what he can do with their views.

One interviewee, a black American, clearly gives Pacino hope. Not only does he know about Shakespeare; he says: 'We should all speak like Shakespeare 'cos then the kids would have feelings.' The barrier to understanding Shakespeare, the man claims, is the spiritual malaise of modern society where people have no feelings or lack the words to express them. Shakespeare, who, in the man's words, 'not only helped us, he instructed us', can function to overcome that barrier. The black American actor, James Earl Jones, similarly recalls the impact of Shakespeare on him when working with his uncle in the fields of Michigan and hearing, in his uncle's quotation from Shakespeare, language of a resonance that Jones had thought resided only in the Bible. That there is an *emotional* core to Shakespeare's dramatic poetry – in other words, not so much a meaning to be unravelled but a *feeling* to be disclosed – is an intuition that will be developed later in the film by the theatre director, Peter Brook, who argues that, if the actors know what every moment is about in emotional and psychological terms, then the language will take care of itself. (It was Brook, it might be remembered, who attempted to deal with this language difficulty by commissioning Ted Hughes to write a modern blank verse version of *King Lear* but found himself inexorably drawn back to the original through the sheer power and eloquence of the poetry.)

This approach informs many of the rehearsal scenes in *Looking for Richard*. They are often a combination of read-through and discussion, where the dialogue sometimes slips between modern paraphrase and textual fidelity as the actors struggle to get a handle on the Shakespearean verse through a modern, colloquial definition of their characters' emotional states. Penelope Allen as the Queen is particularly good at this: in some ways, she is stronger in the rehearsal scenes (where she fluctuates between passionate paraphrase and actual quotation) than in the extracts from the play. Yet it is all an attempt to reveal what Pacino sees as the psychological truth and universality of emotion in Shakespeare's text through the actors' own explorations and discoveries. By following the process, Pacino aims to clarify the product.

As an example of this kind of dramatic exploration, Pacino examines and enacts Richard's opening speech. He tries it on a student audience, who have difficulty in following the opening two lines because of the imagery and the reference to the Wars of the Roses: 'Now is the winter of our discontent / Made glorious summer by this sun of York.' So Pacino burrows away at this opening speech to make its intentions clear. As is revealed elsewhere in the film, one of his characteristics as an actor/interpreter is to bear down on a single line or phrase in a speech as a means of giving a key to the whole passage. To begin with, the film focuses on the single word 'Now'. As the actress Rosemary Harris remarks, it is exciting to start a play with 'Now' – an imperative to the audience to wake up and take heed. It is not only a clarion call to the audience: for Pacino, Richard, too, is clearly preoccupied with the 'now-ness' of the situation.

Elaborating this idea of the 'now', Pacino cues in the academic Barbara Everett for a fuller description of Richard's situation at the beginning of the play. Everett highlights the dilemma facing Richard, who, now that peace has been established, must translate his masculine aggression into amatory pursuit. Peter Brook takes the point a step further: he suggests that the key word of the opening speech is 'discontent'. It is the clue to Richard's state of mind (the use of the royal plural in '*our* discontent' might even be a subconscious disclosure of his designs on the throne) even as he says that this period of discontent is over. The significance of this for the actor is that it means that the opening dozen lines of the speech must be played against their ostensible meaning – in short, ironically. From the first, then, irony is revealed as a significant feature of Richard's discourse.

Barbara Everett has a nice phrase for 'irony' in the film: 'hypocrisy with style'. There will later be a good example of this when Richard is affecting reluctant ambition and a religious demeanour as Buckingham is offering him the crown before a clamorous crowd. For Vanessa Redgrave, what is being shown here is the quintessence of the modern politician – hypocrisy not honesty, show without substance. Later in the opening speech, Pacino introduces an echo on the word 'deformed' to suggest the way it reverberates in Richard's mind as a spur to motivation, and the way the play will offer Richard's physical deformity as a visual/metaphorical analogue to his psychological corruption. But again what is important here is Pacino's insistence on showing us not simply an interpretation of the speech but the actor's journey towards reaching that interpretation. Visually this is suggested through cutting between the informal rehearsal of the speech and the full costume delivery, to give the sense of a performance, as it were, taking shape. Feeling his way into the role, Pacino invites an audience to join the sense of exploration – an actor prepares – and explication.

If part of the strategy of the film is to debate and remove some of the barriers that afflict American audiences when confronting Shakespeare, a related issue is raised and incorporated into Pacino's film essay: namely, the feeling of inhibition and inferiority that afflict American *actors* when confronting the Bard. What are the reasons for this, and how can they be overcome? One reason is clearly the daunting tradition and achievement of American performers' British contemporaries and forbears. Another explanation raised has to do with an ingrained, naturalistic style of American acting, particularly derived from the 'method', which is antithetical to Shakespearean acting.[3] Even when performing Hamlet on screen, Mel Gibson commented that he had become careless in the enunciation of consonants – a bad habit, he said, picked up from acting in American films, where naturalism is emphasized to the nth degree.[4]

The problem, though, is not so much applying an inappropriate naturalism to Shakespeare. It is more that American actors in Shakespeare become self-conscious when, as Derek Jacobi suggests, the great strength of American acting, particularly film acting, is the very opposite of this kind of self-consciousness – ease, reality, seeming spontaneity. It is a bold practice for Pacino to discuss this problem in the body of the film. It both anticipates and in a way disarms a predicted critical response to the film (Pacino would no doubt remember the critical mauling of his 1979 production of *Richard III* on Broadway, particularly of his diction, which Walter Kerr had dismissed as '*Richard of Third Avenue*').[5] It also consciously invites an audience, when seeing the extended extracts, to make a personal judgement on how successfully the problem is being solved. Only Aidan Quinn's Richmond jars: the ponderous delivery sounds uncomfortably like a young John Wayne. Pacino, Kevin Spacey as Buckingham, Alec Baldwin as Clarence, Kevin Conway as Hastings, Harris Yulin as the King, and Penelope Allen as the Queen deliver the poetry with vigour and an alertness to its rhythm and sense.

In his interview, Sir John Gielgud offers a somewhat different explanation for the problems encountered by American actors in
Shakespeare. He suggests somewhat darkly that they never think to
get a sense of the style of the Elizabethan period by looking at paint-
ings or reading books. Pacino's attempts to immerse himself in
Shakespeare's world are seen in slightly farcical visits to the playwright's birthplace and to the Globe Theatre, but curiously the topic
of books is something that recurs in the film.[6] One of the sub-texts of
Looking for Richard, as it must be in any contemporary Shakespearean
production for the modern media, is its relation to the printed text in
a context of a new technology that is overwhelming print culture. (A
more extended discussion of this issue is to be found in Andrew
Murphy's chapter at the start of this volume.) How the film addresses
and discusses this relationship is, in a sense, the *leitmotif* of this
chapter, and the significance and implications of the method as an
aspect of interpretation will be discussed in the conclusion. However,
there is one particularly suggestive detail when, at one stage, Pacino
finds the bound copy of the text he is working from, with all its
sources and footnotes, literally too heavy – he can hardly lift it. He is
next seen in rehearsal, having exchanged this mighty volume for a
more malleable paperback. In some ways, this detail is a metaphor for
Pacino's whole approach to filming Shakespeare and making him
accessible – reducing this heavy burdensome cultural artefact that
overpowers the individual to something one can confidently hold in
one's hands. The visual motif of riffling through pages that seem as
light as air, as thin air, reinforces that feeling. That issue of size and
scale, and the translation of theatrical text to modern media, is picked
up later in a somewhat different context by Peter Brook, who dwells
on one advantage film has over the theatre in Shakespeare: the close-
up. Shakespeare's language, Brook argues, is the 'language of thought',
and, the quieter a character speaks (which a close-up permits), the
closer he or she can be to himself. It is a perception that is not lost on
Pacino, who whispers his lines in close-up when Richard is self-
communing but who adopts a more declamatory delivery when
Richard is consciously 'playing a role'. It is also an example of the way
the film takes us through the process of Pacino learning how to play
his part: Peter Brook is clearly an important signpost on the way.

With the casting, Pacino has allowed the performers to find the part
rather than to match the parts with the performers. But one match, he
confesses, is very hard to make: the casting of Lady Anne. The film's
solution (Winona Ryder) was not entirely successful: the sound

quality of her scenes was so poor that her vocal performance had to be re-dubbed at a later stage by Kate Burton. (Perhaps out of deference, Pacino does not actually show this but does cite Burton on the end credits.) Clearly, the problem of casting is exacerbated by the difficulty many commentators have had in reading the scene's motivation. Why does Richard wish to woo and marry Lady Anne? Pacino is seen wrestling with various interpretations, as if wanting to give a sense both of a production's inevitable evolving problems and a text's multiple possibilities. It would be useful to Richard's cause if he can be seen to have won over a potential enemy. It would be a challenge to his powers of persuasion and deceit. 'Was ever woman in this humour won?' If Richard can win over Anne, with the disadvantages of his deformity and the monstrosity of his behaviour to her husband and father-in-law, who can he not win over? The scene is superbly filmed, with sinister dissolves that suggest a swooning into an abyss, an expressive use of shadow to correlate to the duplicity and darkness of human motive, and a hypnotically choreographed series of movements, which are matched by the choral contributions of Howard Shore's score. 'I'll have her – but I'll not keep her long.' For Laurence Olivier, this was a cheeky sardonic aside, as if his mind was already racing on to bigger challenges. For Pacino, it is the core of the speech in terms of its strategy and its villainy: he will have Anne, but only for as long as it suits his purposes. He twirls his sword like a cane in delight at his rhetorical triumph, for, if he can surmount a hurdle so formidable, what can stand in his way?

Richard's motivation seems clear enough. What about Lady Anne's, however? She will not murder him and duplicate his crimes, but why does she succumb to his wooing? There is an interesting moment during the rehearsal of this scene when everyone seems momentarily blocked by the psychological obscurities. Is it the fascination of the abomination? Is Anne's heart more mysterious at this point than Richard's? Frederic Kimball ventures a suggestion. What if Anne set out deliberately seeking Richard, expecting to meet him? The cast seems to stare at him in some amusement and disbelief, and Pacino's response is to suggest consultation with a literary professor for guidance, as if the issue needs an expertise beyond that of mere theatrical practitioners. Kimball promptly explodes in what seems momentarily like genuine anger, insisting that it is actors, not academics, who can uncover the truth about Shakespeare. It is a curious moment in the film which raises a number of questions. To whom does Shakespeare belong – the actors, the academics or the audience? Does some person, or community, hold the key to understanding Shakespeare? Pacino deftly defuses the situation through humour, playfully anointing Kimball with his sword and awarding him a PhD, and suggesting that it is just another opinion. Cut to a shot of the scholar Professor Emrys Jones, who says he 'really doesn't know' why Anne behaves as she does in this scene or why, historically, Richard needed to marry her at all. Cut back to close-up of Kimball, seeming to stare at this evidence of academic incomprehension in simultaneous disbelief and self-justification.

Arguably, *Looking for Richard* sends up academia in the way in which it films the academic contributions. It is not entirely clear what an audience is expected to make of the husband and wife team of Emrys Jones and Barbara Everett, who, in this film, stand for the English intellectual tradition in Shakespearean interpretation. Well-spoken, intense, bespectacled and upper middle-class English academics framed against their bookshelves: are they being offered up as an example of those who teach as distinct from those who do, or as evidence of the kind of ivory tower, intellectual obfuscation that has put people off Shakespeare? Emrys Jones seems to have been cast not so much because of his impressive credentials as a Shakespearean scholar but because he looks the part.[7] For much of the time he is scarcely allowed to articulate a coherent sentence, a reminder that a film performance, even in documentary, is very much in the hands of the editor. For Kimball, people like these seem to be the enemy, reflecting the kind of approach to Shakespearean drama that *Looking for Richard* is attempting to surmount. This might be the reason why he seemed so sensitive to Pacino's suggestion that they consult a literary professor, as if academics are the higher law. Pacino is more circumspect, and other aspects of the film suggest that the contributions of academics such as Everett and Jones are not simply comic relief. If there is an element of send-up in the film, it is not confined to the presentation of the academics: Kevin Kline's facetiousness about Shakespeare or Vanessa Redgrave's pomposity about iambic pentameter seem no less comical. There is an element of self-parody in Pacino's visit to the Globe when preparing for Richard's nightmare before battle, in the hope that ghosts will appear to him – doing, as he says, that 'method-acting-type stuff'. Pacino wants to include as many voices on Shakespeare as possible, from the ignorant to the informed, from the exploratory to the educational, and the professional academics should not be excluded from this dialogue. Indeed, he does seem to assimilate into his production some of the astute interpretative points as offered by Barbara Everett in particular.

Moreover, when Professor Jones exclaims that Shakespeare saw Richard and Buckingham as 'gangsters, as ... upper-class thugs', it strikes a chord. It connects with the visual design of the film; with the star persona of Al Pacino; and with the relation of *Richard III* to film genre. It has sometimes been suggested that the narrative paradigm of the classic gangster film, from *Little Caesar* (1930) and *Public Enemy* (1931) to Francis Ford Coppola's *Godfather* movies, is *Richard III*.[8] One similarity between both is the distinctive rise/fall structure: a ruthless hero eliminates rivals to ascend to the top, only to find himself isolated, vulnerable, friendless, ready for a fall. Another has to do with the audacity of its hero, towards whom an audience develops ambivalent feelings, being simultaneously required to deplore him for his cruelty and corruption yet admire him for his diabolical cunning and daring. (The feeling is particularly acute in *Richard III*, since Richard so often takes an audience into his confidence, making them, in a sense, his accomplices.) There are some gangster movies that seem consciously to court this parallel. For example, Richard Wilson's bio-pic, *Al Capone* (1958), has a scene straight out of *Richard III*: Capone (Rod Steiger) succeeds in courting the widow (Fay Spain) of a man he has killed. She is both disgusted and fascinated by his love for her, while he is both awed and disoriented by her attraction to him. For the most powerful modern equivalent of Richard III's behavioural strategies – the chilling hypocrisy yet dazzling chutzpah – one need look no further than the celebrated baptism scene of Francis Ford Coppola's *The Godfather* (1972), where Michael Corleone's (Pacino) renunciation of sin during the baptism service of his godchild is impiously crosscut with the murderous elimination of his Mafia rivals by Michael's cohorts, acting on his instructions. Indeed, I would suggest that this scene is consciously echoed in *Looking for Richard* in the virtuoso cross-cutting between a scene of potential reconciliation between King, Queen, Hastings and other rival factions, and the brutal murder of Clarence, calculatedly contrived by Richard to blow apart this fragile harmony as part of his strategy of divide and conquer.

The execution of Hastings is another scene that has an echo in *The Godfather*. In the rehearsal discussion, Kevin Conway as Hastings has likened this council meeting scene to a Mafia 'gathering of dons', and the scene plays like that in *The Godfather* where a guilty conspirator falls into the trap laid by Pacino's hero, and a room full of his erstwhile friends empties to leave the man to his fate.[9] To a modern audience, *Richard III* at moments like this looks more like a topical than a Tudor tragedy, and, because of his screen associations, Al

Pacino brings all the appropriate resonances. For all his versatility, Pacino has always excelled in roles with criminal connections, whether as Corleone or Carlito, Scarface or Donnie Brasco. In screen acting terms, one could not have a better guide across the character contours of Richard III than Al Pacino, nor one who can so effectively exploit his screen persona to make a remote Shakespearean hero seem so modern and living and 'real'.

By exploiting its similarities with Shakespearean narrative and characterization, Pacino can argue for Shakespeare's modernity and accessibility. But the film also gives Pacino a point of reference in terms of dramatic texture, visual style. For example, like *The Godfather*, Pacino's staging of *Richard III* is full of false declarations of love and whispered conspiracies in another's ear. In contrast to the *ciné-verité* style of the documentary sections, Pacino's filming of the play extracts are lit like *The Godfather*, with faces in shadow (leading an audience to reflect upon secret thought processes and potential untrustworthiness) and pools of darkness sometimes irradiated by flashes of blood-red. It is as if Pacino asked his cameraman, Robert Leacock, for these sections to imitate the style of Gordon Willis, who is famously known as the 'Prince of Darkness' to his cinematographic peers for his distinctive use of shadow and dark, seen not only in the *Godfather* movies but in Alan J. Pakula's paranoid conspiracy thrillers such as *The Parallax View* (1974) and *All the President's Men* (1976).

This photographic style is effectively carried through into Pacino's rendering of the final part of the play. He makes a visual feast out of Richard's nightmares before battle, with subliminal flashes of accusing faces and voices filmed through red filters. A hero whose very shadow could cast a chill before he himself appeared now finds himself afraid of shadows. How do you kill him off? What should be the visual conception behind Richard's death? This is posed by the film as a final interpretative problem. Barbara Everett gives a clue: think of it as a boar hunt, where a man of animalistic instincts is now himself the prey. The real battle, anyway, says Emrys Jones, has been the ghost scene, Richard fighting a losing struggle against his inner demons which will leave him exhausted for the Bosworth conflict. The insights of Everett and Jones seem to feed into Pacino's interpretation of 'My kingdom for a horse', which is a line delivered finally not as a rousing shout but as a resigned aside, as if to say: 'After all the struggle and sin to gain the throne, it has come to this.' Ambition has ended in anti-climax and isolation, as with Pacino's other gangster heroes like Michael Corleone: it is perhaps the melancholy behind the megalomaniac that attracts him. Looking for Richard: has he been found? Or does the search go on? 'If I told him about that other ten rolls of film', says the cameraman in a confidential aside to a colleague, 'he'd want to use it.' The implication is that, for Pacino, the quest for the core of a character like Richard is endless.

In coming to some conclusion about the nature and extent of Al Pacino's achievement in *Looking for Richard*, one might see the film in the context of a number of interrelated questions. What is the significance of the film at this historical juncture? How do its political underpinnings relate to anxieties about the millennium? Does it take Shakespeare in new directions as we enter a new century?

At the time of Pacino's film, there seemed to be three main ways of doing Shakespeare on film. The first might usefully be seen as a continuation of the Olivier tradition, most recently represented by Kenneth Branagh's full-length *Hamlet* (1997). It has visual spectacle in its 70 mm format, and its all-star cast is an attempt to entice a mass audience. But it is basically conservative and traditional: an exciting, comprehensive rendering of the text that nevertheless remains, as it were, caviare to the general and leaves the problems of language, comprehension and Shakespeare as cultural icon untouched. The emphasis is on reverence for the text, not relevance: it preaches to the converted, not to a new audience. A second way is the Richard Loncraine/Ian McKellen version of *Richard III* (1995), which attempts to emphasize the text's modern relevance by updating the setting to the 1930s. The problem there, though, is an incongruity between text and context (the two can jar) and the vexed and unsolved question of the comprehension of the text for a mass audience. The third way is the most radical: the complete appropriation of Shakespearean narrative and poetry and its total translation and transformation into the modes of modern media. Baz Luhrmann's *William Shakespeare's 'Romeo + Juliet'* (1997) is a stunning reconceptualization of the play in the visual language and forms of today. As James N. Loehlin argues elsewhere in this collection, here visual flair cancels out the cast's vocal shortcomings. I would go further, however. The film's visual flair cancels out Shakespeare, to the extent that an audience might be forgiven for not being able to recall one line of dialogue.

What Al Pacino has come up with in *Looking for Richard* is an innovative fourth way, and it may be the most radical and far-reaching strategy of them all. Like Branagh's *Hamlet*, his film has the appeal of a starry cast, but not the oppressive reverence and fidelity to the text. Like Loncraine/McKellen, Pacino points up the contemporary resonances but avoids the stylistic clash. Like Luhrmann, he aims to lure a young audience, but he wants them to embrace Shakespeare's poetry not bypass it.

Like the other modern directors, Pacino wants to reconnect people with Shakespeare, but his programme to this end is more imaginative. Making the dramatist comprehensible and accessible through the methods described is one way. Pointing up the play's modernity is another, either through alluding to likenesses with *The Godfather* or handling scenes such as that involving the uneasy reconciliation and unlikely friendship between former sworn enemies in such a manner that audiences might even be put in mind of modern events (such as the Northern Ireland peace agreement).

What Pacino is doing, then, in *Looking for Richard* is not simply modernizing Shakespeare for popular consumption but postmodernizing him for popular consumption – by no means an easy task. He does this through a classical mixture of 'high' and 'low' cultural traditions, a mixture that is essentially one of *forms*: dramatic extracts intercut with what Pacino calls the 'doc-drama type of thing', and soundbite Shakespeare (the bites getting bigger as the film progresses) intercut with documentary footage involving actors, academics and the public. Ostensibly this is a similar postmodern perspective to that described elsewhere in this collection by Mark Thornton Burnett in his chapter on Adrian Noble's *A Midsummer Night's Dream* (1997): that is, an approach characterized by irony, explicit allusions to modes of production, a mixture of 'reality' and fantasy and so on. But Pacino wears his intellectual credentials lightly. He is a playful postmodernist. *Looking for Richard* demystifies and deconstructs Shakespeare whilst at the same time offering a thesis on acting – as fun, discovery, exploration, research, communication, community – based around a character who also loved acting.

The film is unfinished and the performance unfinished of a character who describes himself in his opening speech as 'unfinished'. The film embraces fragmentation, enhanced by a montage that leaps about in time and place with a mobility that only cinema can manage (like that subliminal memory flash of Queen Margaret's dire prophecy that occurs to Buckingham after his rejection by Richard – a striking moment since, as Emrys Jones has argued, Margaret essentially stands for memory in the play). What Pacino acknowledges in the film is something that has recently been informing Shakespeare teaching in schools in this country: that one cannot gain the interest of an audience sceptical of Shakespeare by focusing *exclusively* on the text.

Moreover, Pacino has constructed in cinematic form the equivalent of what has been described as the central task of late twentieth-century criticism, where 'we consider the play as a dynamic interaction between artist and audience and learn to talk about the process of our involvement rather than our considered view after the aesthetic event.'[10] It seems to me that Pacino's film, in its exploratory nature, and in the virtue it makes of its very incompleteness, is following the same intuition. It could be the style of the future.

Notes

1. The privations have been amusingly documented in Michael MacLiammoir's book about the making of the film, *Put Money in thy Purse: The Filming of Orson Welles' 'Othello'* (London: Eyre Methuen, 1952).
2. In an interview with the critic, Geoff Andrew, Pacino elaborated on the reason why he had approached the film in the way he did. 'I did consider filming the play straight', he said, 'but I wondered how I could do that when the great Olivier had done it and taken it as far as you can. So I had to think of a different concept, and I thought back to how I'd toured colleges fifteen, twenty years ago: I'd read poetry and picked things from plays, and when I spoke to students they were resistant to Shakespeare every time I brought him up. And I remembered that when I explained the story and led them in a bit with a language they felt comfortable with, and then slipped into Shakespeare, it was easier for them to grasp his work; they needed that preamble. So I thought for the film I'd mesh that with doing bits of the play' ('To Play the King', *Time Out*, 15–22 January [1997], pp. 22–4).
3. The film and theatre director, Elia Kazan, who co-founded the Actors' Studio and was closely associated with the 'method', has some interesting observations on this in his autobiography, *A Life* (London: Pan Books, 1989). 'We don't have a Shakespeare, and our actors were not and are not now prepared to play Shakespeare. Nor were they truly interested. The Group Spirit was born in the thirties. We were gathered to do plays that "said something" about our lives. Our spirit was contemporary' (p. 157). He later tended to confirm a criticism that has often been made of Lee Strasberg's training of actors – that it equipped them to evoke contemporary reality but it left them at sea with the classics. (The assault by London critics on the Actors' Studio's infamous production of Chekhov's *Three Sisters* is generally held to be the definitive example of this.) Kazan comments: 'Lee would talk about the wonderful Shakespeare scenes he'd seen in his classes, but what I saw there did not impress me. We never really succeeded in wedding the necessary vocal force, clarity of speech, dexterity with words and love of the language to the emotional techniques of the Stanislavski-Strasberg method' (p. 654).
4. See Neil Sinyard, *Mel Gibson* (London: Bison Books, 1992), pp. 68–71.
5. Quoted in Andrew Yule's *Al Pacino: Life on the Wire* (London: MacDonald & Co., 1991), p. 200.

6. Setting is used expressively, but also sometimes ironically and comically in *Looking for Richard*. When Pacino and Kimball visit Shakespeare's birth-place in Stratford-upon-Avon to pay dutiful homage, Kimball is disappointed – even as a tourist spectacle, it leaves a lot to be desired – and Pacino, while claiming to be having an epiphany, admits that he is just not showing it. Moreover, the lights from the camera activate the fire alarm so that the actor's epiphany is interrupted by the Stratford-upon-Avon Fire Brigade. It is a vignette that undercuts the solemnity of the occasion and is a reminder of another aspect of Shakespeare that Pacino has to take on board: not only the great dramatist but the great tourist attraction too.

7. See particularly his book, *The Origins of Shakespeare* (Oxford: Oxford University Press, 1977), which has an illuminating chapter detailing the influences on *Richard III*.

8. Some similarities between the characteristics of the archetypal movie gang-ster and those of the Shakespearean tragic hero are explored, for example, in Robert Warshow's essay, 'The Gangster as Tragic Hero', in his collection of essays, *The Immediate Experience* (New York: Atheneum, 1970), pp. 127–33, and in Stuart M. Kaminsky's *American Film Genres: Approaches to a Critical Theory of Popular Film* (New York: Dell Publishing, 1974).

9. I am thinking particularly of the scene towards the end of *The Godfather*, in which the informer, Sallozzo (Al Lettieri), previously thinking himself secure, suddenly finds himself amongst erstwhile friends who, on Michael Corleone's instructions, are to become his executioners. His appeal for help or clemency, like that of Hastings, falls on deaf ears.

10. Norman Rabkin, *Shakespeare and the Problem of Meaning* (Chicago: University of Chicago Press, 1981), p. 27.

5
Urban Dystopias: Reapproaching Christine Edzard's *As You Like It*

Amelia Marriette

When Christine Edzard released her film version of *As You Like It* in October 1992, the pressure to be successful at the box office was not an overridingly important concern. The director's independent working conditions, her tight budget (£800,000), limited filming period (only five weeks) and art-house distribution suggested that her film would be artisanal in nature.[1] Refusing to sit easily alongside other major Shakespearean cinematic productions, Edzard's *As You Like It*, in fact, reveals greater affinities with the avant-garde genre, a 'personal mode ... made by individuals or very small groups of collaborators' and unmarked by 'commercial imperatives, corporate hierarchies and a high degree of specialization and division of labour'.[2] Viewed in such terms, *As You Like It* emerges as experimental and challenging, a work by a relatively emancipated filmmaker which dispenses with convention and tradition to create a unique Shakespearean utterance. Concentrating on its distinctive relocations, its utopian aspirations and its doubling arrangements, and using insights gained from a specially commissioned interview with the director herself, this essay argues that the film can only be fully appreciated when assessed in its own avant-garde terms as a postmodern experiment attendant upon, and sensitive to, a *fin-de-siècle* moment.

Determining Locations

Edzard's best known work prior to *As You Like It* was a BBC adaptation of Charles Dickens' *Little Dorrit* (1987). The similarities between this six-hour epic and Edzard's film are telling. Both highlight the city as a metaphor; both consider the complexities of viewing circumstances from double perspectives; and both centre upon observing societies at work. In approaching Shakespeare's play, Edzard drew directly on her experience of adapting Dickens' novel. As she explained in interview:

> in the case of Dickens, the truth of the character is in the nine-teenth century, and the truth does not materialize until you start putting in all the detail. The issue with *As You Like It* is completely different. First of all, I don't believe that you can reach the sixteenth century in that sort of way. It's too remote: it would become an archaeological dig. The nineteenth century has a close-ness to us in reproduction terms. The intention of the play is that it is a play and that it is meant to be rethought every time you do it. A film has to be as tightly rooted to its origins as is feasible, and it has to carry the message that the past has changed to us.[3]

Because Edzard's *As You Like It* relocates the play to a contemporary, urban environment of the 1990s, it might be suggested, then, that the director's agenda is to update seemingly remote Shakespearean preoc-cupations. Thus the court becomes a corporate business emporium and the forest a wasteland. This urban relocation is given a further twist in that both imagined worlds are envisaged as urban dystopias: the corporate world, though architecturally grand, is corrupt and shallow, while the wasteland is shabby, containing no permanent buildings. Such is the visual logic of Edzard's film, moreover, that a *frisson* of meaning is created between the 1590s and the 1990s: the contemporary London of modernity is connected to its early modern predecessor through a transcendent vision of national blight. As the historian Asa Briggs notes, 'the difference between relative and absolute poverty continues to shape all discussions on social stratifi-cation'. Today's 'buskers, beggars, sleepers-out and squatters generate conflicting reactions that would have been familiar at the end of the pre-industrial sixteenth century'.[4] By directing attention to economic parallels which recur at salient historical junctures, Edzard establishes a recognizable world which is not too distant from a modern audi-ence's experience.

Elaborating this link is the use of contemporary dress: *As You Like It* is the first modern dress Shakespeare film of recent times. Costume supplies the characters with a background, an identity and a past. For example, the film follows the banishment of Rosalind (Emma Croft) with a contrived scene, which places her and Celia (Celia Bannerman) in a large closet. Celia hectically rummages through her clothes while arguing that she and Rosalind should seek Duke Senior in the Forest.

Discarding evening-dresses and gorgeous robes, Celia finally selects sensible, walking shoes and a headscarf – the characteristic garb of a middle-class urbanite planning a trip to the country. In contrast, Rosalind chooses jeans, a stocking cap, boots and an oversized jacket – a choice which visually differentiates her from Celia. The contemporary unisex nature of the costume makes Rosalind a convincingly androgynous figure. The historical transference staged by the film, and made immediately apparent through costume, is further heightened by the urban context.

Despite the modern setting, Edzard retains the play's original language and, indeed, includes much more than either the 1936 Paul Czinner or the 1979 Basil Coleman Time Life/BBC versions.[5] When her *As You Like It* is placed alongside these two earlier filmic interpretations, Edzard's decisions take on a positively inspirational aspect. Neither Czinner nor Coleman appreciate that the 'past has changed to us'. Both faithfully adhere to the conventions and restrictions of the pastoral in directorial emphases which have been criticized as artificial, irrelevant and lacking in imagination. Critics especially took exception to Czinner's fabricated forest, which took up 300 feet and filled two stages. A contemporary review stated that the 'camera' had brought no new advantages to the interpretation of the play, highlighting the 'settings' as the worst features: 'The exterior of Duke Frederick's palace looks as if it had been designed by Gunter; the interior resembles the foyer and corridors of a Super Cinema De Luxe. The Forest scenes are less vulgar but more insipid.'[6] If this 1936 version proved unpopular, so, too, did the later BBC film. In Jack Jorgens' words, its 'actors seem reluctant to move for fear of tripping over a branch or disappearing from the shot ... The blocking and framing are often awkward, the compositions ungainly and the cutting poorly timed'.[7] Against such uniformly adverse views, the distinctiveness of Edzard's film takes on a particular cultural resonance.

Instead of avoiding the complexities of the conditions of history which inform it, Edzard's *As You Like It* celebrates a sense of its own time. It is therefore unfortunate not only that the film was poorly received on release but that, contrary to judgements on earlier cinematic realizations of the play, Edzard should have been criticized for avoiding forest scenes, for her rejection of the pastoral. H. R. Coursen's response is typical. Commenting on the film's use of 'modern dress' and the 'placement of "Arden" on the concrete of a construction site', he finds 'disquieting' the references to 'trees and a forest' and the 'allusions to curtal axes and a doublet and hose'.[8]

Attacking the disjunction between setting and language, Coursen fails to appreciate that Edzard, running counter to her filmic predecessors, delights in calling into question the whole notion of verisimilitude. Following Coursen, Russell Jackson sounds a similar note. His objection is that the 'film is a poor representative of the vigour that "modern dress" can bring'. 'In the wasteland', he writes, 'the references to trees, streams and deer are allowed to stand, and the contemporary social focus is hopelessly vague ... The play's mixture of pastoral vagueness and social precision is lost, to be replaced with modern pieties rather than analysis and argument.' While Jackson appreciates Edzard's purposefully worked linguistic and contextual discrepancies, he rejects the film for falling between 'old-fashioned' and 'modern' interpretative structures.[9] As I go on to argue, however, Edzard's film can, in fact, be seen as a forerunner of the more effectively radical Shakespearean films of the late 1990s, such as Loncraine's *Richard III* and even Luhrmann's *William Shakespeare's 'Romeo + Juliet'*.

The director's recognition that, as a Renaissance literary trope, the pastoral is unfamiliar to a modern (even an art-house) audience, allows the film to refract *fin-de-siècle* fears in a century marked by a determined will to mechanize and urbanize. In inner cities, particularly, scrappy, barren pieces of land have already become the only 'green' stretches of ground that afford any notion of 'pastoral' escape. As has recently been noted, 'urban sprawl has swallowed up almost two million acres of countryside since 1945'.[10] In Edzard's film, then, the references to trees, streams and deer, when juxtaposed with the obvious lack of such properties, concentrate the mind on the possibility that the countryside is in imminent danger of complete engulfment. The film's unsettling implication is that this absence has become normative. Characters do not even appear to notice that there are few bucolic retreats remaining. Indeed, in one scene, Celia gathers flowers from among the wasteland's weeds. Here the camera directs a viewer to the poignant ignorance underlining Celia's action: she seems perfectly content, as if she were gathering wild flowers from a lush meadow. Part of the success of *As You Like It* is that it evokes a sense of contemporary crisis, a historical moment at which 'nature' has been distorted and compromised and hope in a better future has been eroded.

Viewed from a purist's perspective, Edzard's *As You Like It* seems perverse: in obstinately avoiding the pastoral, the film is diametrically opposed to Shakespeare's comedy. However, although a world apart in terms of verdancy, Edzard's urban scenario and Shakespeare's 'green world' do share a common point – like the pastoral scene of Shakespeare's play, the wasteland is a place of potential enlighten-ment. This barren site provides the only forum for reflection and reasoned debate in a world which has lost its ability to relate to the bucolic. Within it, homeless characters experience a vacuum of oppor-tunity and are forced to face their fears, not retreat from them: 'like the toad, ugly and venomous', the wasteland 'Wears yet a precious jewel in his head'.[11] If the wasteland makes an important thematic point, the corporate city is no less suggestive. Edzard's dichotomous metropolis ultimately shows two sides of the same coin, with the city as a whole becoming 'a metaphor – a dynamic configuration of the conflicting hopes and fears of the twentieth century'.[12] The two loca-tions signify a contradictory construction of the contemporary urban world, which displays a confident exterior but conceals a marginalized and abandoned material underside. Such a concern with the disjunc-tion between surface appearances and inner substance chimes with Jean Baudrillard's claim that the current age has no firmly established sense of 'reality'. Edzard's *As You Like It* may be seen as a moderate response to what Baudrillard calls 'the emancipation of the sign: released from any "archaic" obligation it might have to designate something, the sign is at last free for a structural or combinatory play that succeeds the previous role of determinate equivalence'.[13] In Edzard's film, the lack of a fixed relationship to Shakespeare's pastoral liberates the play from any 'archaic' indebtedness.

Despite entertaining scope for enlightenment, Edzard's wasteland still harbours incorrigible reprobates. As Edzard herself stated in inter-view, Arden comes across as 'bloody cold, harsh and dangerous':

> going out there isn't just a joke, which it tends to be when you show a pastoral theme or a woody glade. Today we are so yearning for pastoral bliss, many of us are particularly deprived of nature, and therefore nature seems much more attractive than I think in the text it's meant to be. I don't think that for a public of today a leafy glade would read as savage, or at least it would be very, very difficult.[14]

In order to underline a potential for savagery in the world that she constructs as Arden, Edzard dramatizes the lioness and snake episode of the play as a robbery. Thieves physically assault the sleeping Oliver (Andrew Tiernan), the latter's account of the event working as a voice-over. Through such scenic adaptation, Edzard provides an audience, unused to antique rhetoric, with a visual motif that might be readily appreciated. In this case, the visualization aids a traditional under-standing of the episode, and an audience is able to recognize that, in Richard Knowles' words, 'Oliver's conversion from sinfulness is brought about by Orlando's sacrifice.'[15] Such contemporary transla-tions assist Edzard's conception of the play and are certainly no more radical than those that theatre directors have been mobilizing for decades. Where Edzard is criticized for turning Arden into a 'concrete construction site', Peter Brook is eternally idolized for placing his Athenian wood in a white box.[16] More obscurely, the Canadian director Robert Lepage presented his *A Midsummer Night's Dream*, in the same year as Edzard, on a mud-strewn stage in a production which has been described as 'an extraordinary theatrical experience, often visually astonishing, sometimes hauntingly beautiful'.[17] Like Brook and Leparge, Edzard engages with a late twentieth-century unmooring of philosophical certainties to question stereotypical notions of her play's 'realities'; her filmic relocation, however, has yet to attract the praise that has been lavished on her theatrical counterparts.

Trouble in Utopia

In recent years, scholars have begun to turn their attention to the growing untenability of a utopian ideal at the end of the twentieth century. Escalating urbanization, periodic economic crises and global warfare have dealt a heavy blow to Utopian schemes, making their institutional possibility increasingly remote. As Robert Hughes states: 'we have got so used to accepting the failure of Utopia that we find it hard to understand our cultural grandparents, many of whom believed ... that its historical destiny was to succeed.'[18] Such a scepti-cal attitude towards the utopian construction might be exacerbated when another century is just around the corner, for, to cite Asa Briggs, 'in many quarters the arrival of a new millennium is awaited less with eager expectation than with a sense of resigned and even fatalistic inevitability ... Some observers ... have talked of eventual devasta-tion on an undreamed-of scale by such neo-Malthusian forces as AIDS, by global warming or by nuclear annihilation.'[19] These and similar *fin-de-siècle* anxieties, this section suggests, impact upon Edzard's *mise-en-scène* in *As You Like It*. Not only does Edzard purposefully omit a utopian investment in the pastoral; she also takes account of the fact that, for a late twentieth-century sensibility, there can be no reliance upon traditional notions of a rustic retreat.

By playing up the less palatable dimensions of *As You Like It*, Edzard follows in the footsteps of those critics who have identified in the play a harsher economic landscape that sits ill with its bucolic tendencies. Thus John Wilders notices that Arden is an essentially featureless locale described as 'a "desert": the banished Duke calls it "a desert city", and Orlando a "desert inaccessible". It is, simply, a deserted place'.[20] Similarly, Marilyn French reads *As You Like It* as concerned with 'the underside of society, made up of women, exiles, outcasts, the poor, the eccentric, and the low in status'.[21] The devotion given to the 'underside' in Edzard's film version of the play reveals that she, too, is engaging with a more general *fin-de-siècle* imperative to see Shakespeare's comedies as resonant and suggestive in modern terms.

In particular, Edzard stages her debate not so much in the country as its late twentieth-century equivalent, the city, preferring to use the Shakespearean text to investigate the dynamics of a modern, technologically dominated civilization. This more radical option avoids the incumbent problems of trying to create parallels with a now eclipsed agrarian environment. Furthermore, Edzard's refusal of stereotypical references (there are no shots of Big Ben, Westminster or Buckingham Palace) means that her setting takes on the qualities of a generic metropolis. The city is both nowhere and everywhere.

In this connection, Edzard's *As You Like It* may usefully be linked to other modern urban and dystopian films, such as Ridley Scott's *Blade Runner* (1982), Terry Gilliam's *Brazil* (1985) and, especially, Oliver Stone's *Wall Street* (1987). Both *As You Like It* and *Wall Street* unfold in a modern metropolis, utilizing the world of corporate finance to pass social comment. Edzard's corporate city, in fact, may be equated with Wall Street itself – 'a place where honour is traded for power and peace of mind for a piece of the action'.[22] The position of Duke Senior (Don Henderson) – he enjoys absolute rule, but must unexpectedly suffer the tribulations of exile – is represented as similar to that of a stockbroker, who deals in millions of dollars one day, but may be bankrupt and unemployed the next. Most illuminating, perhaps, is the implied connection between Gordon Gekko, *Wall Street*'s individualistic, amoral anti-hero, and Oliver. Both appear visually similar, with Edzard giving Oliver the clearly identifiable stockbroker 'uniform' of a bold striped shirt, double-breasted suit and slickbacked hair. In their obsession with increase, and lack of regard for emotion, both Stone's Gekko and Edzard's Oliver draw from, and feed into, the stereotype 'yuppie', a phrase coined in the 1980s to denote a particular breed of reprehensible capitalist, created and fostered by the politics of, respectively, Reagan and Thatcher. Gekko's philosophy states: 'You're a player or you're nothing. Everybody starts from the same place. It's not luck or circumstance – you screw the other guy before he screws you.' In *As You Like It*, Oliver's decision to impugn his brother's name (encouraging Charles, the wrestler, to break his neck) stems from his fear of the 'enchantingly beloved' (I.i.151) Orlando, whose naturally gentle humour causes the stockbroker to be 'altogether misprised' (I.i.155). With no compunction, Oliver and Gekko rid themselves of apparent enemies, and, although their methods differ, their irrational behaviour is in many ways comparable. By placing Oliver within the context of a business institution, Edzard underscores both the immense power invested in the hierarchical structures of large conglomerates and the multiplicity of methods for 'screwing the other guy'. Her filmic representation suggests that the brutal treatment meted out by Oliver towards Orlando may be seen as simultaneously literal and figurative.

Like Scott, Gilliam and Stone, Edzard exploits to the full the city's metaphorical valency. But Edzard also extends the metaphor, using binary opposition to depict not a one-dimensional city, but a dynamic urban contruct in which two separate universes compete for prominence. To be more precise, the director explores through her urban landscape 'the ideological border', as Johannes Birringer terms it, 'between the capitalist world and the socialist world'.[23] Adapting this distinction, the corporate city might be seen as the 'capitalist' hub (a plutocratic palace, presided over by a tyrannous managing director, connoting banks, the stock market and insurance) within which the inner city or wasteland is allowed to declare its 'socialist' credo. In the context of the early 1990s, such a mode of cinematic presentation carries with it an implicit 'post-Thatcherite commentary'.[24] Edzard's *As You Like It* is thus able to attack, if not negate, Thatcher's invidious comment that 'there is no such thing as society'.[25] For, in the wasteland, an audience experiences a move beyond individualism, encountering a place where a sense of communal feeling is generated – a new postmodern 'aesthetic paradigm' in which masses of people come together in temporary emotional groupings.[26]

What might be seen as a more communal manifesto emerges early in the film. When Orlando first disturbs the wasteland stockbrokers, they are gathered around a camp-fire made from a converted dustbin, and Jaques is reciting his 'seven ages of man' speech. As Helen Schaffer Snow states, the scene's sense of serene quiescence is established by the actor: 'James Fox's Jaques smiles through this speech, and his

measured, calm delivery is comforting and wise. This Jaques is an
ageing aristocrat, offering philosophical guidance through a topsy-
turvy world.'[27] Once Orlando disturbs the moment by running in
with his knife drawn, however, it becomes obvious that he has
misread the situation, and he immediately casts his weapon aside.
Orlando's initial perception of the *emigrés* as threatening is shown to
be based on appearance (they are dressed as 'down-and-outs'), and a
welcoming, generous air quickly reveals his judgement as erroneous.
Edzard's staging at this point capitalizes on Orlando's first response,
and in so doing invites spectators to questions their own preconceptions. For, in its construction of social distinctions, the film suggests
that, by eschewing material demands and artifice, the
stockbrokers/courtiers can concentrate on the value of human interactions. Although the virtues of such interaction are displayed most
eloquently in the representation of the Orlando/Rosalind relationship, they are no less in evidence in the film's evocation of the
experience of the Duke's court in exile.

In his recent study of Utopias, Robert Hughes has pointed out that,
in the twentieth century, 'the home of the Utopian impulse is architecture'.[28] Similarly, in Edzard's *As You Like It*, the deployment of
distinctive architectural landscapes is instrumental in making Utopian
(or, rather, dsytopian) points. In particular, Edzard seems to construct
her corporate city to mimic the over-confident univalence of
modernism, and the wasteland to connote the disillusioned multi-
valence characteristic of postmodernism, echoing Mike Featherstone's
observation that the 'modernist ... city's spatial form is dominated by
the grid-iron layout and high-rise ... architecture – [this] gives way to
the postmodern city within the confines of a "no-space place" in
which traditional senses of culture are decontextualized, reduplicated
and continually renewed and restyled.'[29] True to Featherstone's
dialectic, the corporate city in Edzard's film is strictly vertical and
claustrophobic, and we have views only of its interior. Close-up shots
are used to oppress individuals: the city is literally too small.
Characters are constantly being dwarfed and swamped by the architecture. Rosalind appears to be constricted by architectural weight,
and she is robbed of her customary dynamism. First seen standing
beside a huge door, she rests her head lightly against its frame: her
manner is morose, and she plays an insignificant role in the proceed-
ings. Likewise, when an audience first sees Orlando, he is waiting for
his brother, Oliver, and he leans awkwardly on a huge column. He
then crouches on the floor as he tells Adam of his miseries, the posture

of his body indicating a mood of heavy resignation. Also unshaven and dressed in an old, scruffy cardigan, Adam (Cyril Cusack) sits beside a revolving door which periodically turns of its own accord. The door suggests possibilities of escape to new opportunities. But at this stage both Orlando, cramped by his lack of educational vantage, and Adam, represented as a worthless outcast, seem trapped, caught in the foyer of Oliver's world and therefore restricted to its outskirts. The foyer might be regarded as an eternal waiting-room – one of the many ironic visual puns which the film exploits.

Conversely, the wasteland constitutes an open locale which assumes the pictorial value of a landscape painted on a huge canvas. Edzard provides us with a 'modern' city wasteland, 'stripped of all [its] signs, with walls bare like a guiltless conscience', which is redolent of Baudrillard's views on postmodernity.[30] With its huge vistas and distant industrial skyline, the wasteland, a horizontal space, has none of the court's claustrophobia. Filmed in the winter months, the sky has a pale hue and seems imbued with untested potentials. These constrictions and possibilities are captured in the film's camerawork: tracking and wide-angled shots indicate freedom and movement; conversely, static shots suggest confinement or stalemate. When Rosalind finds her tree poems, which have become graffiti sprayed in glorious technicolour on the wasteland walls, she is first shown in close-up. As she runs forward to read the words more easily, reciting as she moves, we see her in long shot. Touchstone (Griff Rhys Jones) proceeds to mock Orlando's verses, dancing around Rosalind as the camera tracks his progress. Rosalind, however, remains stationary, confused and unaware of who has penned the encomiums. At the end of the scene, she strikes Touchstone playfully, he begins to run away and she chases him: tracking camera shots now take over. In this scene, Edzard uses a mixture of close-up, medium and long shot, interspersed with tracking shots. The camerawork thus mimics the characters' fluctuating ascendancy (tracking camera shots) and descendancy (static camera shots), as, by turns, they subject each other to mockery.

Movement and space are not factors in the representation of the relationship between Phebe (Valerie Gogan) and Silvius (Ewen Bremner), so it is fitting that Edzard films the couple against a wall. Phebe is portrayed as a bored girlfriend who nonchalantly eats chips while Silvius pours his heart out to her. Significantly, Silvius perches uneasily beside blocks of discarded concrete. The camera is immobile, silently witnessing their futile courtship. In a comparable fashion, the scene between Corin (Roger Hammond), his one sheep and Touchstone is shot mainly with a static camera in front of the men as they sit.[31] Here, Touchstone and Corin deliver separate monologues on the corresponding advantages or disadvantages of 'city' over 'country'. They do not exchange views, and the camera highlights their deadlock.

Doubling Arrangements

The filmic decision to divide the city into two dystopian parts is complemented by the doubling of nearly all of the main characters. This directorial emphasis betrays that fascination with the arbitrariness of identity so evident in much of Edzard's other work.[32] Of course, directors and critics have long been sensitive to the comedies' doubling potential. For example, Alan Brissenden approves of the idea of doubling Oliver and Orlando, remarking that the two 'are in some respects reverse images of each other. Oliver is envious, murderous, deceitful ... devious and calculating, Orlando is hot-headed and passionate.'[33] However, Edzard's use of doubling in *As You Like It* is far more extensive, and sets her film apart from any other major film or stage production. As she stated in interview:

> Some parts are often doubled, and I thought it would give it more meat as well. It was absolutely a deliberate decision. But I don't think it would necessarily have worked with any actor, and it certainly was quite a challenge [for the actors concerned].[34]

Progressing beyond usual theatrical convention, Edzard also doubles the parts of Duke Senior, Duke Frederick (played by Don Henderson), Le Beau and Corin (played by Roger Hammond).[35] Multiple doubling grants the characters an added dimension, but, more intriguingly, it gives the impression that they lead parallel lives. Rather than simply deserting the corporate city to enter the wasteland, the courtiers/stockbrokers are fortunate in being able to experience both locations simultaneously: they are constructed as enjoying an unimpeded opportunity to populate two worlds. In this way, the film assumes a surreal tone, a fitting cinematic equivalent for a play in which familiar points of reference are continually dissolving.

Modern dress provides further opportunities to create visual links between the play's protagonists. This is particularly striking in the case of Rosalind and Orlando. The androgynous jeans-and-jacket outfit of Rosalind makes her a persuasive Ganymede, and, when she first meets Orlando, she finds her own situation echoed in his physical appearance. Usually, Rosalind as Ganymede is only able to represent a variation on the male and female mirror, but, in Edzard's film, it is Rosalind and Orlando who become mirror images of one another. Further illuminating the attention to doubling, Touchstone and Jaques are dressed alike in dark overcoats. The physical resemblance draws the two together and suggests that, following the view of Thomas McFarland, 'Touchstone is a mirror that not only reflects, but lightens, the malcontent of Jaques.'[36] Doubled courtiers work well, too: at the end of the film, in the corporate city, each meets his alter ego. Confused, the courtiers wave to one another. The felicity of this device is that the corporate world can now be seen to accommodate both Dukes, both brothers and both dimensions of a single individual. A corporate emporium is abandoned temporarily by the very same personalities who then return to find that it is not location that is important but perspectives on experience.

Not only does Edzard double characters; she also enlists mirrors and reflective surfaces to exploit the tension between surface and substance. The opulence of the corporate city's mirrored rooms, and the bleakness of the wasteland's watery appearance, are deployed metaphorically. As Ilona Halberstadt states:

> The opposition of court/City to forest/inner-city wasteland, of ruthlessness, ambition, greed, fear and dissatisfaction to flexibility, acceptance, generosity and sharing, is embedded in the very textures and gestures of the film. Glass chandeliers, glass doors and mirrors in the court interior fade into the pools of rain-water in the free space of Arden.[37]

Other material and physical properties are instrumental in drawing an audience's attention to questions of mimesis. During the conversation between Oliver and Charles (the wrestler), we see Oliver reflected in the highly polished surface of his office table. This not only echoes the motif of doubling but also underscores his environment's transparency and insubstantiality. There is no privacy here: characters are always reflected in a mirror or a table top, or they can be regarded through large panes of glass.

Through the translation of further shiny reflective surfaces into the 'Arden' wasteland, Edzard provides additional links to the corporate metropolis. Although Duke Senior instructs an attendant lord to 'kill

... venison' (II.i.21), he proceeds to open a vacuum sealed package of meat. The shiny cellophane in which the meat is wrapped provides a visual connection to the rest of the film, wittily recalling the city's glass perspectives. Nor is this visual logic neglected in the central scenes, for the mirrored rooms of the city give way to plastic tents in the Forest of Arden. At the end of the film, these elements are fused. In the final stages, the recollection of polythene tents fades into the image of court curtains and the transparencies of the brides' dresses, thus providing a concluding spectacle of the film's visual motifs.[38] The opening credits of the film appear on a static background of mirrored doors and painted wall hangings (significantly depicting stylized pastoral scenes). These dissolve into another, similar background, as Jaques, wandering through the corporate city, recites his 'seven ages of man' speech. It is only when Jaques begins to move that we realize we have been viewing him in a mirror, and we are reminded of the camera's ability to deceive. Edzard moves seamlessly from meta-theatre to meta-cinema, as Samuel Crowl observes: 'Edzard's camera captures [Jaques] through windows, in reflection, and standing in portals to emphasize his liminal relationship to the society he both shuns and seeks.'[39] Even in these preliminary sequences, therefore, the visual tricks, guiding perspectives and shaping angles that inform the film as a whole are apparent.

Conclusions

As You Like It represents an unsentimental rendering of Shakespeare's play, which rejects artifice and aestheticism. Edzard does not, to adopt Scott Wilson's words, 'search for poetic or aesthetic truth, an activity that would be at best useless if it were not ideological'.[40] Instead, she investigates, probes and redefines. In working to bridge the gap between what is pejoratively called 'high' and 'low' art, Edzard strives to establish a new genre. Her version of Shakespeare's play preserves Elizabethan language but refuses to figure England's national past through the haze of the doublet-and-hose heritage film.[41] Because of this, the film apparently appeals to no one group: it is not trendy or zany enough to be bracketed alongside Kaufman's *Tromeo and Juliet*. It does not have the star appeal of Luhrmann's *William Shakespeare's 'Romeo + Juliet'*. It does not attempt to appease or reaffirm the status quo, as does Kenneth Branagh's highly successful *Much Ado About Nothing*.

In short, Edzard has created a provocative work, but the director's resistance to lifting the film's mood and enticing the viewer makes it somewhat incompatible with a comedic core. Even in the final moments, the film settles into no tidy interpretative arrangement. The characters are gathered in the corporate city for the marriages of Rosalind and Orlando, Celia and Oliver. All is now bathed in a golden light. Yet the golden light may be an ironic vision of a 'golden' dusk or the breaking of a new dawn. Edzard seems acutely aware that Shakespearean marriages mark not only new beginnings but also finalities. The ending also allows us to consider the possibility that the film marks the dusk of a century fast concluding, which may just as easily create new horizons or a wasteland for society's less privileged members.

The film's commercial failure is perhaps due to its relentless desire to remind us that our civilizations are in danger of becoming 'soulless'. But its insistence on portraying *fin-de-siècle* societies as dystopian might also seem overly morose. Having said that, however, the film's refusal to provide something which even utopian schemes cannot supply may one day be seen as artistic integrity.

Notes

1. Interview with Christine Edzard, at Sands Films, Rotherhithe Studios, London, 31 July 1996. Most of the money came from Richard Goodwin's successes as a producer on such major British films as *Murder on the Orient Express* (1974) and David Lean's *A Passage to India* (1983). (Goodwin and Edzard are married and work together on smaller, avant-garde projects.) Some money for *As You Like It* was received from investors in Switzerland, Germany and the United States – namely, the Disney Corporation, who now hold the rights to the film but have 'deleted' it. The film has never been shown in the United States, but has been seen in Paris on at least two occasions, most recently in Spring 1998.
2. John Hill and Pamela Church Gibson, *The Oxford Guide to Film Studies* (Oxford: Oxford University Press, 1998), p. 395.
3. Interview with Christine Edzard, at Sands Films, Rotherhithe Studios, London, 31 July 1996.
4. Asa Briggs, 'The 1990s: The Final Chapter', in Asa Briggs and Daniel Snowman (eds), *Fins de Siècle: How Centuries End, 1400–2000* (New Haven and London: Yale University Press, 1996), p. 226.
5. Edzard cuts IV.ii and V.i, and passages from III.v and IV.iii. The epilogue is also cut because, as Edzard explained in interview, she was concerned 'about there being too many false endings'. Neither does Edzard show the wrestling match, preferring instead to focus on the reactions of the courtiers.
6. Raymond Mortimer, *The New Statesman and Nation*, 12 September 1936.
7. Jack Jorgens, 'The BBC-TV Shakespeare Series', *Shakespeare Quarterly*, 30 (1979), p. 412.
8. H. R. Coursen, *Shakespeare in Production: Whose History?* (Athens: Ohio University Press, 1996), pp. 98–9.

9. Russell Jackson, 'Shakespeare's Comedies on Film', in Anthony Davies and Stanley Wells (eds), *Shakespeare and the Moving Image: The Plays on Film and Television* (Cambridge: Cambridge University Press, 1994), p. 101.

10. Briggs, 'The 1990s', p. 226.

11. William Shakespeare, *The Complete Works*, ed. Stanley Wells and Gary Taylor, with John Jowett and William Montgomery (Oxford: Oxford University Press, 1987), II.i.13–14. All further references appear in the text.

12. Edward Timms, 'Theme and Variations', in Edward Timms and David Kelley (eds), *Unreal City: Urban Experience in Modern European Literature and Art* (Manchester: Manchester University Press, 1985), p. 4.

13. Jean Baudrillard, 'Symbolic Exchange and Death', in *Selected Writings*, ed. Mark Poster (Oxford: Polity, 1988), p. 125.

14. Interview with Christine Edzard, at Sands Films, Rotherhithe Studios, London, 31 July 1996.

15. Richard Knowles, 'Myth and Type in *As You Like It*', *English Literary History*, 33 (1966), p. 13.

16. Peter Brook, *A Midsummer Night's Dream*, The Royal Shakespeare Theatre, Stratford-upon-Avon (1970).

17. Robert Lepage, *A Midsummer Night's Dream*, Royal National Theatre, London (1992–3); Robert Smallwood, 'Directors' Shakespeare', in Jonathan Bate and Russell Jackson (eds), *Shakespeare: An Illustrated Stage History* (Oxford: Oxford University Press, 1996), p. 186.

18. Robert Hughes, *The Shock of the New* (London: Thames and Hudson, 1991), p. 164.

19. Briggs, 'Introduction', in Briggs and Snowman (eds), *Fins de Siècle*, p. 1.

20. John Wilders, *The BBC TV Shakespeare: 'As You Like It'* (London: British Broadcasting Corporation, 1978), p. 12.

21. Marilyn French, *Shakespeare's Division of Experience* (London: Cape, 1982), p. 111.

22. Video Sleeve to Oliver Stone's *Wall Street* (London: Twentieth-Century Fox, 1987).

23. Johannes Birringer, *Theatre, Theory, Postmodernism* (Bloomington and Indianapolis: Indiana University Press, 1991), p. 2.

24. Mike Davies, *Film Review*, November (1992), p. 24.

25. Margaret Thatcher, *Woman's Own*, 31 October 1987.

26. Mike Featherstone, *Consumer Culture and Postmodernism* (London: Sage, 1996), p. 101.

27. Helen Schaffer Snow, '*As You Like It*', in Keith Parsons and Pamela Mason (eds), *Shakespeare in Performance* (London: Salamander, 1995), p. 47.

28. Hughes, *The Shock of the New*, p. 163.

29. Featherstone, *Consumer Culture*, p. 99.

30. Baudrillard, 'Garap', in *Selected Writings*, p. 10.

31. Edzard's comments on the sheep are of general interest here: 'It didn't seem that there was any logic in using an urban wasteland and then having a flock of sheep. Roger [Hammond] said, though, that he was very keen to have at least a pet sheep. The sheep actually came from an urban farm next door, which was apt.' Interview with Christine Edzard, at Sands Films, Rotherhithe Studios, London, 31 July 1996.

32. Both *Little Dorrit* (1987) and *The Fool* (1990) trade in fragmented lives and doubled personalities.
33. Alan Brissenden (ed.), *As You Like It* (Oxford: Oxford University Press, 1993), p. 24.
34. Interview with Christine Edzard, at Sands Films, Rotherhithe Studios, London, 31 July 1996.
35. It is has become quite customary for the Dukes to be doubled. Of the many recent productions in Britain, Adrian Noble's 1985 production at the Royal Shakespeare Theatre, Stratford-upon-Avon, used doubling extensively. Edzard doubles the parts of Orlando and Oliver, obviously an impossibility on stage.
36. Thomas McFarland, *Shakespeare's Pastoral Comedy* (Chapel Hill: University of North Carolina Press, 1972), p. 107.
37. Ilona Halberstadt, 'As You Like It', *Sight and Sound*, 61, October (1992), p. 45.
38. For further discussion of these issues, see Halberstadt, '*As You Like It*', p. 45.
39. Samuel Crowl, '*As You Like It*', *Shakespeare Bulletin*, 11:3 (1993), p. 41.
40. Scott Wilson, *Cultural Materialism: Theory and Practice* (Oxford: Blackwell, 1995), p. 16.
41. For further discussion of these issues, see Andrew Higson, 'Re-presenting the National Past: Nostalgia and Pastiche in the Heritage Film', in Lester Friedman (ed.), *British Cinema and Thatcherism* (London: UCL Press, 1993), pp. 109–29.

6
Impressions of Fantasy: Adrian Noble's *A Midsummer Night's Dream*

Mark Thornton Burnett

When Adrian Noble's *A Midsummer Night's Dream* was performed by the Royal Shakespeare Company as part of its 1994–5 Stratford-upon-Avon and touring programme, the production attracted widespread acclaim. Eminent critics joined to sing the praises of a 'magnificent', 'notable', 'outstanding', 'stunning' and 'vibrant' reinterpretation of Shakespeare's play.[1] No doubt spurred on by this theatrical success, the RSC, in collaboration with Channel Four, quickly set about transferring the production to celluloid. The film version of *A Midsummer Night's Dream*, again directed by Noble, was commercially released to a limited number of cinemas in 1996 and, in 1997, made its way to a TV showing and the video market. But the passage from stage to screen proved an unhappy experience. As a film, *A Midsummer Night's Dream*, contrary to the expectations aroused by the reception of its previous incarnation, was roundly criticized. Directorial inadequacy had resulted in a 'botched' creation (stated *The Daily Telegraph*), an 'unmitigated disaster' (asserted *The Observer: Review*) and a 'highbrow pantomime' (agreed *The Sunday Times: Culture*).[2] Concluded *The Times*: 'Noble still thinks like a primitive', offers us a reading of the play that is 'charmless under the camera's close scrutiny' and 'puts the Bard's cause back a hundred years'.[3] Such a chorus of condemnation invites a considered response. In this essay, I aim to redress the filmic reputation of Noble's *A Midsummer Night's Dream* by concentrating on its stylistic felicities and postmodern aspirations. Rather than putting the Bard's cause back a hundred years, I will suggest, the film reinvents Shakespeare for the millennium, both recalling high Victorian decadence and looking ahead to the dawning of the new century. Before that argument can be developed, however, we need to return to the play itself.

In the opening scenes of *A Midsummer Night's Dream*, Egeus, outraged at his daughter Hermia's reluctance to accept his choice of marriage partner, accuses her lover, Lysander, of having 'stolen the impression of her fantasy'.[4] This printing metaphor is quickly taken up by Theseus, who reminds Hermia that her 'father should be as a god; / One that composed your beauties – yea, and one / To whom you are but as a form in wax / By him imprinted' (I.i.47–50). Thus does the play evoke women's positions in relation to patriarchal discipline and perceived malleability in the hands of fathers and governors alike. But the metaphors deployed here also suggest the role of the imagination in the artistic process: at one and the same time Hermia is a pawn in a struggle for an appropriate alliance and the raw material out of which will be fashioned a new entity. Indeed, the shaping 'imagination' (V.i.8) can be seen as essential to the action as a whole. It is not accidental that the 'mechanicals' are made up of carpenters and joiners (both types of artist). Nor is it irrelevant that Theseus should, towards the conclusion, play a variation upon his original argument, claiming that 'Lovers and madmen have such seething brains, / Such ... fantasies, that apprehend / More than cool reason ever comprehends' (V.i.4–6). In many ways, the power struggles of *A Midsummer Night's Dream* are conducted through representations of the myriad 'forms' (V.i.15) that the creative faculty is driven to produce.

In New Historicist criticism, in particular, these struggles have been read in terms of contemporary anxieties that obtained in the Elizabethan state. Louis Montrose, in a 1996 study, approaches *A Midsummer Night's Dream* by mapping the various contexts – the interplay among discourses of gender, social status and theatricality – that were a 'condition of the play's imaginative possibility'.[5] However, it also needs to be recognized that, as much as the play's prevailing concerns are in dialogue with the cultural complexion of the 1590s, they have an equally significant contextual location in later historical periods. Taking the various 'impressions' or 'forms' made by 'fantasy' or the 'imagination', Noble's filmic *A Midsummer Night's Dream* serves them up as a postmodern mixture of childhood reminiscences, self-conscious literary allusions, sexual awakenings and reminders of a turn-of-the-century environment.

Chiefly, it is through the interpolated character of the Boy (Osheen Jones) that the film manages to rewrite the play's imaginative topos. The film opens with the Boy asleep in his bedroom, which is crowded with books, puppets, a rocking-horse and a miniature theatre. It quickly modulates to the scene of the play itself – the Athenian court.

By placing the Boy first under and then at the table in this aristocratic world, the film grants him a key responsibility in the ensuing narrative: his is the guiding perspective, to the extent that he is capable, dramaturge-like, of giving birth to fairies from the bubbles created by his own toy pipe. At other points, the Boy assumes a more directive role still, as when he pushes Bottom's motorbike and propels forward a spherical moon, suggesting the centrality of the child's imperatives and projections to the play's unfolding events. Like Puck (Barry Lynch), the Boy has the power to activate and to generate. He 'bodies forth' (V.i.14) in the 'empty space' of his invention both the personalities and the properties that will people his dream.[6]

Crucial to the film are the ways in which the Boy's imaginative energies simultaneously empower and enslave. Even as he authors the 'forms' of his 'fantasies', appropriately envisioning the fairies as much younger versions of himself (their baggy trousers recall infants in diapers), the Boy is represented as the 'changeling' (II.i.120) over whom Titania (Lindsay Duncan) and Oberon (Alex Jennings) fight. During the realization of Titania's speech about the 'votaress' of her 'order' (II.i.123), the camera focuses in on a conventionally 'Indian' (II.i.124) image of the Boy in a turban – his distraught expression indicates his alarm at becoming the object of the King and Queen's dissension. In addition, when the toy theatre is magically transported to the forest, the Boy must struggle with Oberon for ownership of the puppets' strings. Oberon's seizure of a model figure from the theatre implies that he has no qualms in usurping the Boy's manipulative privileges. Power in Noble's conception of things is a matter of contest, and no one is permitted to exercise a secure and unchanging control. If, in the play, then, tensions cluster about the father's hopes for his daughter, in the film, they are extended to encompass wider generational conflicts and the predicament of a child in a divided familial landscape. In common with other recent 'Shakespearean' films, such as Lloyd Kaufman's *Tromeo and Juliet* (1996) and Jocelyn Moorhouse's *A Thousand Acres* (1998), Noble in *A Midsummer Night's Dream* deploys the Bard to hint at the increasing untenability of the late twentieth-century nuclear family as a practical ideal. For all his imaginative abilities, the Boy is still subject to the crises and estrangements of his adoptive parents.

To shore up the role of the Boy in the imaginative process, the film draws upon a variety of motifs from children's literature. Its opening frame of the Boy asleep is lent additional force by the copy of *A Midsummer Night's Dream*, illustrated by Arthur Rackham, which lies beside him on the bedclothes. When he falls through the night sky and a chimney pot to encounter the 'mechanicals', the descent of Alice down the rabbit hole in Lewis Carroll's *Alice's Adventures in Wonderland* (1865) and the depiction of the tornado in L. Frank Baum's *The Wonderful Wizard of Oz* (1900) are brought to mind. (Crying 'Mummy!' and screaming as he is pitched into darkness, the Boy seems on the point of entering not so much his dream at this point as his nightmare.) Each pivotal moment is accompanied by allusions to narratives that either evoke childhood richly or appeal to a collective children's memory. For instance, the flying umbrellas used by the fairies for their wonder-inducing entrances and exits recall P. L. Travers' *Mary Poppins* (1934); the departure of Bottom (Desmond Barrie) and Titania across the water in an upturned umbrella is reminiscent of Edward Lear's sea-loving and moon-seeking animals, the owl and the pussycat; and the scene of Bottom flying across the moon on his motorbike harks back to the escape of 'E. T.' in the film of the same name. The result is less an experience of Shakespeare as it is an intertextual rehearsal of familiar children's stories, past and present. In this way, Noble's *A Midsummer Night's Dream* pushes back the perimeters of what constitutes 'Shakespeare', combining elements from 'high' and 'low' cultural traditions and mixing 'old' and 'new' representational materials.

The film's investment in the trappings of childhood has a three-fold effect. First, the echoes of both literary and filmic forms point to the ways in which the imaginative impetus has assumed a wide range of manifestations across history. On the one hand, *A Midsummer Night's Dream* longs nostalgically for the heyday of children's literature in a late Victorian context; on the other, it revels in the possibilities afforded by a unprecedented wave of children's films, as references to 'E. T.' and *Home Alone* suggest.[7] (In this connection, the print culture outlined at the start is placed in a rivalrous relationship to the power of alternative media and new informational practices.) It is as if Noble seeks a mode of production that addresses the 'special effects' requirements of a younger, cinematically demanding spectator, while also answering to the more intellectual expectations of the twentieth-century Shakespearean filmgoer. The invocation of popular literary predecessors argues for the Bard's perennial appeal; the use of technological wizardry discovers the dramatist being appropriated to satisfy a modern sensibility.

Motifs from children's literature speak to the implied child in the audience in more specific ways, however. At a secondary level, the narratives alluded to in *A Midsummer Night's Dream*, like the film itself, work to equip the Boy (and thus the generation he represents) with important social skills and interpersonal capacities. Like Alice and Dorothy, to whom, in his parentless condition, he is allied, the Boy undergoes a series of extraordinary dislocations, as a result of which he is finally able to confront 'reality' in a more self-aware and constructive fashion than before.[8] This, of course, is the pattern elaborated in children's stories in their more traditional guise. As Paul Schilder states of the *Alice* stories, 'the child uses Carroll's ... anxiety situations in a way similar to the manner in which the child uses *Mother Goose Rhymes*. They take them as an understood reality which one can hope to handle better after one has played and worked with it.'[9] It is also the pattern characteristic of the fairy-tale, a form with a similar educative aspect. Bruno Bettelheim has said of fairy-tales that they explore the 'need ... to find meaning in our lives'. By suggesting 'solutions to perturbing problems', he argues, such tales reveal the 'struggle to achieve maturity' and 'caution against the destructive consequences if one fails to develop higher levels of responsible selfhood'.[10] Although *A Midsummer Night's Dream*, in its self-conscious elaboration of a child's experiences, follows neither of these trajectories exactly, the Boy's experiments with his creative abilities, involvement in his adoptive parents' conflicts and property disputes with a father figure reveal more than a passing resemblance to the generic processes whereby other fictional children are enabled to foster their personal development. They show the Boy testing and stretching the boundaries of childhood, striving towards a realizable autonomy.

A key element of the child's development is the confrontation with his or her own sexuality. In this regard, the third effect of Noble's investment in the cultural production of childhood comes into play. Through amalgamating a Shakespearean art form with the stuff of childhood 'fantasies', the director reactivates the sexual dimensions that underlie all mythic archetypes. In his classic *The Uses of Enchantment*, Bruno Bettelheim posits that fairy tales negotiate the uncertain sexual terrain between childhood, adolescence and adulthood, at times concerning themselves with specific crises such as 'Oedipal anguish'.[11] With reference to *Alice in Wonderland*, A. M. E. Goldschmidt makes more detailed claims for the sexual import of children's stories: the lock and the key, and the descent down the well, he contends, belong to 'the common symbolism of ... coitus'.[12] Nowhere in Noble's *A Midsummer Night's Dream* are obviously Oedipal crises hinted at; however, the film abounds in scenes of sexual revelation and voyeurism, which read in many ways as a working through of Goldschmidt's critical position. Sexuality in *A Midsummer Night's Dream* is initially brought to the Boy's attention via moments of heterosexual tension and displaced masculinity. Thus the Boy undergoes something of a primal scene when, at the start, he is privy to the chief protagonists' 'nuptial' (I.i.1) plans: Hippolyta's reference here to the 'silver bow / New-bent' (I.i.9–10) is, in Lindsay Duncan's delivery, made to bristle with all the erotic energy of unconsummated desire. More obscurely, perhaps, sexuality is paraded before the Boy during the rehearsals of the 'mechanicals', which take place in the war-time austerity of a corrugated hut. As Noble admitted in interview, a *Dad's Army* effect was aimed for in these scenes, and certainly the fire extinguishers, dartboards and old sporting trophies that adorn the hut walls appear as telling indicators of the 1940s.[13] But the temporal markers are also instrumental in constructing the 'mechanicals' as sexual outcasts, who can have no place in the war effort. The effeminacy of Francis Flute (Mark Letheren), it is implied, identifies him as an unfit soldier, while the braggadocio of Bottom, the film suggests, constitutes the sublimated sexuality of a man debarred from the battlefield. Because the Boy is simultaneously the voyeuristic auditor of the rehearsals, the film allows him to bear witness to a range of expressions of sexuality, from pre-marital badinage to compensatory theatricals. His is the blank page on which *A Midsummer Night's Dream* writes a vicarious experience of sexuality's frustrations and possibilities.

Nor do glimpses into the sexual world of adulthood end with the opening scenes. What might be termed a floating phallus is, via visual details and linguistic emphases, frequently tied to the Boy, suggesting a particularly forceful engagement with the archetypal paradigms that inform mythic narratives. The elongated handle of the sumptuous red parasol in which Titania drapes herself first suggests the male member, and the spectacle is lent an additional phallic flavour by the arch rendering of the accompanying song: 'You spotted snakes with double tongue, / Thorny hedgehogs, be not seen' (II.ii.9–10). That which the film suggests at the level of metaphor it soon takes up in physical action. Once Bottom, as an ass, has been granted a view of Titania's pudenda, he is spurred on to penetrate her violently from the rear. Given the graphic nature of Bottom's transformation, it therefore seems appropriate that the recollection of his 'vision' (IV.i.203) should be imbued with a sexual charge: with its bawdy 'methought I had' refrain, his account is presented as a reverie upon the delights of priapic tumescence. Dovetailing with, and suffused through, these moments are the Boy's responses. In them, an audience is prompted to discover the 'impression' of an awakening consciousness, one poised between the child's sense of sexual wonder and the adult's knowledge of sexual practice. Indeed, at one point the Boy actually assumes the phallic qualities that characterize his adult counterparts. Coming across Hermia (Monica Dolan) as she dreams of the 'crawling serpent [at her] breast' (II.ii.152), the Boy, magician-like, subjects her to levitation, thereby becoming, through a process of association, the phallus that is at the heart of the nightmare. Confirming the connection are the broader visual links forged between the Boy's stripy pyjamas, the strip flooring and the snaky implications of the parasol handle. Part of the business of achieving sexual responsibility, it might be argued, is knowing what to do with the phallus, and this is borne out in *A Midsummer Night's Dream* in which the Boy is chief participant in a number of organ-oriented scenarios. Dominated and dominant in his imagined universe, the Boy is forewarned of both the pleasures and the dangers of his future maturity.

Such is the nature of Noble's direction, moreover, that the Boy's experience is not restricted to examples of heterosexual behaviour alone. The film, in fact, is equally rife with interludes of homoerotic attraction. Perhaps inspired by recent queer appropriations of Shakespeare, Noble chooses to have Demetrius (Kevin Doyle) highlight the phrase, 'cheek by jowl' (III.ii.338), as part of a homerotic alliance with Lysander (Daniel Evans) against Helena (Emily Raymond). Similarly, just before he is turned into an ass, Bottom struggles to rid himself of Puck, who has climbed aboard his back. The implication is that the same-sex combination of fairy and mortal sets the seal on the weaver's subsequent bestial metamorphosis. While the Boy is not directly involved in these scenes, the underlying idea is still that sexuality is an uncertain property, that a child's gendered identity may be 'shape[d]' (V.i.16) by the external factors with which it comes into contact.

Cumulatively, and not surprisingly, the shifting sexual perspectives that characterize Noble's *A Midsummer Night's Dream*, as well as its ironic rewritings, invocations of modes of artistic production, confoundings of the states of 'fantastic' and 'real', conjurations of competing temporal markers and signifiers, and manipulations of forms of history mark the film out as a peculiarly postmodern phenomenon. As the late twentieth century draws to a close, Shakespeare and postmodernity, in fact, have become increasingly familiar bedfellows. In an age of post-capitalist 'mechanical reproduction', discussion invariably attends to the ways in which the dramatist operates less as a point of origin than as a prompt for all manner of cultural associations, a commodity that can be copied and imitated as well as applied and exploited.[14] Richard Burt's *Unspeakable ShaXXXspeares: Queer Theory and American Kiddie Culture* (1998), a study of the semantics of Shakespearean authority in modern American culture, is indicative of this shift in the critical mindset. If hybridity, pastiche, pluralism, cultural ransacking and the recourse to other texts and images are the defining marks of post-modernity, then the *mise-en-scène* of Noble's film makes a timely contribution to the postmodern debate.[15]

Through its self-conscious deployment of a number of representational 'forms', *A Midsummer Night's Dream* makes newly relevant the play's 'antique fables' and 'fairy toys' (V.i.3). In particular, by granting the parentless Boy some of the power of the dramaturge himself, it questions the extent to which Shakespeare still signifies an 'original', the 'parent' (II.i.117) to which the later development of the 'great literary tradition' can be traced. Even the set design functions as an important element in the film's interrogative confrontation with the Bard's mythic status. Numerous mirrors festoon the Athenian and forest interiors. At court, Helena contemplates her reflection in a glass; in the forest, Bottom glimpses pursuing fairies in the mirror of his motorbike. Privileging mirrors in this way serves a meta-cinematic purpose. It urges us to be sensitive to another reflective surface (the lens of the camera) and thus to recognize the constructed nature of the visions the film provides. Mirrors in *A Midsummer Night's Dream*, then, provoke an attempt to distinguish the authentic from the counterfeit, to adjudicate between the various accretions of Shakespearean doubling, reproduction and imitation in postmodern culture. Noble reminds his audience that he deals not so much in Shakespeare as in the meanings that a filmic engagement with the Bard might stimulate. 'Forgeries' (II.i.81), in short, *A Midsummer Night's Dream* implies, may eventually prove more resilient than the 'originals' to which they are parodically related.

Postmodernity, as critics have recently argued, cannot be linked to the twentieth century in its entirety. For it acquires much of its impact from an association with specifically *fin-de-siècle* anxieties. As Hillel Schwartz observes, 'what the postmodernist narrative celebrates is suspiciously millennial: a world of unending variety ... a world of transitive and playful identities, a world unencumbered by traditional demarcations of space or normative experiences of time'.[16] Ever alert to the implications of such connections, Noble's *A Midsummer Night's*

Dream elaborates its material in not one but several end-of-century modes. In itself, of course, as a play dating from 1594–5, *A Midsummer Night's Dream* is a millennial production, written in a decade of economic crisis. Ian Archer sums up the contemporary climate in the following terms: 'Harvest failures spelt impoverishment for the mass of the people, and crime soared ... Poor harvests in 1594 and 1595 were followed by two years of dearth in 1596 and 1597.'[17] The play is acutely responsive to this situation, and Titania's extended meditation on 'Contagious fogs' (II.i.90), the bank-breaking 'river' (II.i.91), rotting 'green corn' (II.i.94), 'distemperature' (II.i.106) and altered 'seasons' (II.i.107) can be profitably read as a nervous reaction to a desperate moment in England's economic fortunes. Noble's filmic *A Midsummer Night's Dream*, too, works to acknowledge the speech's point of origin in the fraught years of the 1590s. As Lindsay Duncan as Titania intones the celebrated words, the camera pans out to show mists gathering ominously over the sea and the music swells to climax on a foreboding note. True to the film's postmodern credentials, however, the montage here simultaneously invites spectators of the 1990s to assimilate messages pertinent to their historical location. For a late twentieth-century audience, the visual conjunction between water and fog points to chemically induced 'natural' disasters in the same moment as it precipitates memories of the Holocaust and fears of the imminent apocalypse.

Both the 1590s and the 1990s, however, are arguably overshadowed in the film by references to the nineteenth century's final decade. From the very start of *A Midsummer Night's Dream*, it is the symbolic appurtenances of the 1890s that predominate. The Boy's copy of the play, for instance, emblazoned with the name of Arthur Rackham, evokes that turn-of-the-century artist who enjoyed considerable success with his illustrated edition, published in 1900, of *Fairy Tales of the Brothers Grimm*.[18] The turn of the century is returned to again in the borrowing from L. Frank Baum's *The Wonderful Wizard of Oz*, also published in 1900, and finds cinematic confirmation in the scenes set at the Athenian court. Here, the cast-iron fireplaces, chandeliers, red and green corridors, sash windows, four-panelled doors and tessellated floors function as carefully chosen signifiers of a decadent late Victorian historical juncture: not surprisingly, Theseus comes into this *Homes and Gardens* setting dressed as a Wilde-attired aesthete. Commenting on the 1890s, Robert Newman observes: 'In ways that present striking parallels to the 1590s and the 1990s, the 1890s attempted to constrain threats to the social order in a context marked by shifting articulations of gender, sexuality, class and ethnicity.'[19] Newman does not elaborate, but it may be that he has in mind the traditional construction of the 1890s as a period in which the splendours of imperialism were beginning to be tarnished, in which fears of 'anarchism' circulated, in which established religion was on the decline, in which the so-called 'New Woman' was paving the way for the Suffragettes and in which belief was fading in the power of the middle classes.[20] As a transitional moment in history, then, the 1890s lend themselves well to the premeditated imperatives and overall effect of Noble's *A Midsummer Night's Dream*. Taking off from the 1590s, the film addresses the 1990s via a detour of the 1890s, borrowing from a spectrum of fantastic 'impressions' to reflect upon the future 'forms' that the 'Shakespearean' imagination will surely adopt or may never assume.

Nowhere are the connections between imagination and reproduction, overlapping sexualities and historical time-frames, and autonomy and domination more precisely illustrated than in the film's final moments. Earlier in the film, we have seen both the Boy and Puck as auditors at the rehearsals of the 'mechanicals', suggesting that each is an influence upon the ultimate shape of the play-within-a-play. This idea is elaborated upon in the closing stages of *A Midsummer Night's Dream*, where the imaginative impetus features not so much as an autonomous endeavour as an aspect of collaborative enterprise. Reciprocity is hinted at when Philostrate (Barry Lynch) takes the Boy's hand and leads him into the theatre where the amateur theatricals are about to take place. The theatre itself is an enlarged version of the toy theatre, earlier seen in the forest scenes and the Boy's bedroom. Such a shift in scale implies that the Boy's power will be diminished while that of the 'mechanicals' is about to be increased: no longer is a child able to aspire to absolute control over the imaginative experience. Nor is an audience frustrated in its meta-theatrical suspicions. As the performance begins, the Boy is seen in the wings raising the curtain and generally pulling at the ropes of the stage machinery. Even if he is able to conjure images and sequences from his favourite texts, the film suggests, the Boy requires the assistance of a host of underlings to bring his visions to life. Bruno Bettelheim has argued that fairy stories enable children to achieve 'meaningful and rewarding relations with the world around' them, since they concentrate on integrating isolated 'personalities' with the social and cultural collective.[21] A comparable operation can be detected in Noble's film, for it is only when he participates in a joint venture, rescinding theatrical authority to the 'mechanicals', that the Boy's dream can be fully realized.

Closely allied to his newly collaborative role is the Boy's developing grasp of the potential consequences of adult sexual conduct. The phallus, the film implies, cannot forever float irresponsibly, but must form part of an integrated whole. When the hymenal wall has been broken and the bloody 'mantle' (V.i.274) connoting deflowerment has been cast upon the stage, therefore, the mood of levity lifts, the Boy and the theatre audience becoming sober, calm and quiet. Along with his aristocratic auditors, the Boy hovers on the cusp of a liminal moment, an incipient awareness of the relationship between sexuality and mortality.

Illuminating still further the Boy's imaginative collaboration and evolving sexual identity is the film's concluding emphasis upon the restorative power of familial relations. Even before the closing cele-brations, the Boy has been prepared for the healing of fractured families, having overheard the prediction made by Oberon that the lovers will soon be 'Wedded with Theseus all in jollity' (IV.i.91). At the end, the focus of the film thus moves away from the isolation of the Boy in his private box and toward his incorporation within a series of new family scenarios. Once the 'mechanicals' have concluded their performance, the back of the theatre gives way to reveal a magical, moon-lit stretch of water. The liquid spectacle suggests rebirth, and this is clarified in the accompanying shot of the Boy being embraced by Oberon, Titania, Puck and the fairies. Picking up upon the refer-ences to 'nativity' (V.i.403) in Oberon's benediction, the film constructs the assembly as a welcoming family, as a parent, child and sibling group that only now can announce itself with certainty. Given its postmodern credentials, however, *A Midsummer Night's Dream* does not settle upon one family alone. The film's very last image is of the Boy in the lap of another family: returned to the theatre, he is cradled by the whole cast for the curtain call. It is, of course, to the cinema spectators that the cast appeals for applause, a move which neatly identifies us as the key collaborative element in the exercise of imagi-native judgement.

With these final moments, the film blurs purposefully once again the dividing-lines between its 'realities' and 'fantasies', court and forest locations, and characters and institutions. It hints, in fact, at the interchangeability of Shakespearean representations, reminding us, at a deeper level of its fabric, of the collaborative transferability of a production that, via a complex of funding agencies, managed to grav-itate from a stage performance to a screen presentation. The play, *A Midsummer Night's Dream*, the film wants to suggest, does not only exist on the printed page; rather, it consorts with, and is revitalized by, the new media and technologies that have revolutionized the twentieth century. As the clock chimes twelve in the closing sequence, harking back to the striking of midnight in the Boy's bedroom at the start, it seems as if one era has ended and another is about to commence.

Notes

1. Michael Coveney, 'Filth well worth revelling in', *The Observer*, 7 August 1994; Louise Doughty, 'Dream lovers', *The Mail on Sunday: Review*, 7 August 1994; John Gross, 'Heady stuff, this reality', *The Sunday Telegraph*, 21 August 1994; *The Sunday Times*, 7 August 1994.
2. *The Daily Telegraph*, 26 December 1997, p. 31; *The Observer: Review*, 1 December 1996, p. 12; *The Sunday Times: Culture*, 1 December 1996, p. 9.
3. *The Times*, 28 November 1996, p. 39.
4. *A Midsummer Night's Dream*, ed. Stanley Wells (Harmondsworth: Penguin, 1978), I.i.32. All further references appear in the text.
5. Louis Montrose, *The Purpose of Playing: Shakespeare and the Cultural Politics of the Elizabethan Theatre* (Chicago and London: University of Chicago Press, 1996), p. 160.
6. I am recalling here, of course, Peter Brook's famously unadorned production of *A Midsummer Night's Dream* in 1970–1 and the title of his book, *The Empty Space* (Harmondsworth: Penguin, 1980).
7. On the *Home Alone* parallel, see Richard Burt, *Unspeakable ShaXXXspeares: Queer Theory and American Kiddie Culture* (New York: St. Martin's Press, 1998), p. 3. *Peter Pan* (1953), *Pinocchio* (1940) and *Time Bandits* (1981) would be related films which transport a parentless child from 'reality' into an imaginative landscape.
8. For further Alice/Dorothy parallels, see Martin Gardner, 'A child's garden of bewilderment', in Sheila Egoff, G. T. Stubbs and L. F. Ashley (eds), *Only Connect: Readings of Children's Literature* (New York: Oxford University Press, 1969), p. 153.
9. Paul Schilder, 'Psychoanalytic Remarks on *Alice in Wonderland* and Lewis Carroll', in Robert Phillips (ed.), *Aspects of Alice: Lewis Carroll's Dreamchild as seen through the Critics' Looking-Glasses, 1865–1971* (Harmondsworth: Penguin, 1981), p. 343.
10. Bruno Bettelheim, *The Uses of Enchantment: The Meaning and Importance of Fairy Tales* (New York: Vintage, 1977), pp. 3, 5, 183.
11. Bettelheim, *Uses of Enchantment*, p. 115.
12. A. M. E. Goldschmidt, '*Alice in Wonderland* Psychoanalysed', in Phillips (ed.), *Aspects of Alice*, p. 330.
13. Matt Wolf, 'From Stratford', *The Times*, 19 December 1995.
14. I draw here, of course, on Walter Benjamin's essay, 'The Work of Art in the Age of Mechanical Reproduction'. See his *Illuminations*, ed. Hannah Arendt (London: Fontana/Collins, 1982), pp. 219–53.
15. See Zygmunt Bauman, *Intimations of Postmodernity* (London and New York:

Routledge, 1992), pp. 187–8; Hans Bertens, *The Idea of the Postmodern: A History* (London and New York: Routledge, 1995), pp. 54, 161; Angela McRobbie, 'Postmodernism and popular culture', in Lisa Appignanesi (ed.), *Postmodernism: ICA Documents 5* (London: ICA, 1986), pp. 54–7.

16. Hillel Schwartz, 'Economies of the Millennium', in Charles B. Strozier and Michael Flynn (eds), *The Year 2000: Essays on the End* (New York and London: New York University Press, 1997), p. 315.

17. Ian Archer, 'The 1590s: Apotheosis or Nemesis of the Elizabethan Régime?', in Asa Briggs and Daniel Snowman (eds), *Fins de Siècle: How Centuries End* (New Haven and London: Yale University Press, 1996), pp. 65, 71.

18. It might be suggested that Rackham is a particularly appropriate artist for the film to invoke. One of his reflections on his art – '[I believe] in the educative power of imaginative ... pictures ... for children in their most impressionable years' – is conducted in language redolent of Shakespeare's play. See Margaret Drabble (ed.), *The Oxford Companion to English Literature* (Oxford: Oxford University Press, 1985), pp. 806–7.

19. Robert Newman, 'Introduction', in Robert Newman (ed.), *Centuries' Ends, Narrative Means* (Stanford: Stanford University Press, 1996), p. 7.

20. See Asa Briggs, 'The 1890s: Past, Present and Future in Headlines', in Briggs and Snowman (eds), *Fins de Siècle*, pp. 157–95.

21. Bettelheim, *Uses of Enchantment*, pp. 11, 14.

7
'The Way the World is Now': Love in the Troma Zone

Margaret Jane Kidnie

In 'Brief Reflections on Popular Culture', Jean-François Lyotard comments that film and television should try to 'produce in the viewer or the client in general an effect of uncertainty and trouble ... You can't introduce concepts, you can't produce argumentation ... but you can produce a feeling of disturbance, in the hope that this disturbance will be followed by reflection.'[1] This essay considers Lyotard's vocabulary of disturbance and reflection through a close reading of the film *Tromeo and Juliet* (Lloyd Kaufman, 1996). *Tromeo and Juliet* is a parody of American culture in which the turn of the twenty-first century is heralded by macrobiotic diets and interactive computer sex, with the end of the lovers' night of love-making signalled, not by birdsong, but by the theme tune from the Regis and Kathie Lee show. Working within the horror/comedy/romance genres, and laying heavy narrative emphasis on cartoon violence, mutant monsters and soft porn, *Tromeo and Juliet* is a comic, and in places, shocking, reinterpretation of Shakespeare's *Romeo and Juliet*. Troma Films, founded in 1974 by Lloyd Kaufman and Michael Herz, is one of the few independent film companies still working out of the United States, and it has achieved cult status amongst its viewers through its determined resistance to the aesthetics of the mainstream Hollywood film industry. In turning his creative energy to Shakespeare's classic play, Kaufman, with co-writer James Gunn, upholds the Troma reputation for what he describes as 'extreme' scripts, delivering to his audience a film adaptation revealingly publicized with the tag line, 'Body Piercing. Kinky Sex. Dismemberment. The Things That Made Shakespeare Great!'[2]

While *Tromeo and Juliet* retains the broad Shakespearean story-line, even foregrounding the original five-act structure with choric voice-overs and breaks between the acts, the details of the plot have been thoroughly reconceived: new characters such as Juliet's cousin, Sammy, and his sister, Georgie, are introduced, and the action is relocated to modern-day Manhattan. The language, making use of an intrusive variety of registers, is a similarly hybrid creation. Realist dialogue, incorporating quotations from plays such as *Hamlet* and *As You Like It*, is spoken alongside adapted extracts from *Romeo and Juliet* and passages of modern iambic pentameter written to sound Shakespearean.[3] The fluid movement between each of these three registers makes it difficult always to be certain whether a character is speaking spontaneously or consciously quoting a literary text. When Juliet, for instance, says to Tromeo, 'Parting is such sweet sorrow', it is unclear whether she is delivering the line as Shakespeare's heroine, or simply using a well-known Shakespearean quotation that is especially appropriate to her present circumstances. This particular example is further complicated by the likelihood that the line was worked into the script simply to effect the comic juxtaposition of Shakespearean verse and modern speech afforded by Tromeo's response: 'Totally sucks.' Such linguistic confusion is typical of the film's broader, playful meta-theatricality; characters act out their parts in a Shakespearean drama, at the same time being aware of Shakespeare as an integral part of late twentieth-century culture.

Kaufman's decision to base a Troma film on *Romeo and Juliet* gives rise to other intertextual tensions. The visual wordplay at the end of the opening credits, for example, incongruously and disruptively fuses high culture with its subcultural revision, with the original title of the play, displayed across the screen in black capital letters on a yellowing parchment background, being suddenly transformed, to the crash of electronic music, into the Troma film title through the use of blood red graffiti. More subtly, *Romeo and Juliet* is one of the best known plays in the Shakespeare canon, with the names of the central protagonists entering modern vocabulary as synonymous with young love; in one of the film's many self-referential moments, their relationship is described as 'the greatest love the world has ever known'. Although a play such as *Titus Andronicus*, with its themes of mutilation, horror, violence and sex, is arguably more appropriate to the Troma ethos, the classic status of *Romeo and Juliet* allows Kaufman to exploit the gap between conventional ideological constructions of both romantic love and Shakespeare, and the reconstruction of those discursive categories in *Tromeo and Juliet*.

The compelling force of Shakespeare's tragedy of love and suicide derives from powerful cultural representations of romantic love as innate to human existence. Dympna Callaghan has argued, however, that *Romeo and Juliet* does not so much affirm as produce this essentialist understanding of romantic love. When historicized in the context of emergent social and religious theories of marriage in the early modern period, this play can be seen to have been instrumental in the creation and propagation of this particular ideology.[4] Only with the successful assertion of heterosexual, monogamous love as a dominant discourse has the social constructedness of the play's portrayal of desire become invisible.[5] The achievement of *Tromeo and Juliet* lies in its ability to make the invisible once again visible. By locating a theme as apparently universal and transhistorical as young love in unexpected or disturbing contexts, Kaufman renders the familiar strange, a process of cultural disruption which enables his audience to question and re-evaluate modern value systems in a reflective manner. The decision to update Shakespeare's story of romantic love provides Kaufman, moreover, with the opportunity to appropriate *Romeo and Juliet* as a vehicle for the articulation of distinctly end-of-the-century social anxieties.

Tromeo and Juliet, set against a backdrop of polluted foodstuffs, information technology and mutant children, offers a comically gruesome exploration of what the German theorist, Ulrich Beck, has labelled the 'risk society'. Beck's thesis is that we are now entering a period of late industrial capitalism in the western world in which priority is no longer placed on survival, but on attempting to control the latent hazards inherent in industrial production. Instead of interpreting western society as postmodern, Beck sees it as moving into an advanced state of modernization, in which those who most keenly perceive themselves at threat are precisely those who, released from subsistence concerns through wealth and education, have been able to make themselves aware of society's potential for mass destruction.[6] The effect on the individual of the need to cope on an everyday basis with hazards within the system is varied, fluctuating between fear or anxiety and indifference: 'Risks originate after all in knowledge and norms, and they can thus be enlarged or reduced in knowledge and norms, or simply displaced from the screen of consciousness. What food is for hunger, eliminating risks, or interpreting them away, is for the consciousness of risks. The importance of the latter increases to the extent that the former is (personally) impossible.'[7]

The flaws of industrial capitalism and the communal anxieties fostered by ever-increasing ecological contamination are not new territories for Troma Films. Two of the most successful Troma releases to date, *The Toxic Avenger* (1984) and *Class of Nuke 'Em High* (1986), explore in sensationalist manner the impact on society of toxic waste and nuclear energy, and the homicidal monsters featured in these films, whether operating for the public good or harm, are created from industrial accidents brought about by human error. *Tromeo and Juliet*, with similar insight into the public subconscious, treats the victimization of human and non-human life inherent in American society. The film develops this issue through its portrayal of the corporate world, exploring, in particular, the cultural significance of a contaminated meat industry. Juliet's father, Cappy Capulet, is the wealthy owner of Silky Films, a successful porn film company which was extorted years previously from Tromeo's father, Monty Que. Cappy now plots a billion-dollar merger of movies and meat through the marriage of his daughter to London Arbuckle, the sole heir of Meat World. Shakespeare's tale of young love provides the opportunity to examine the impact on individual lives of the peculiar circumstances of late twentieth-century western existence.

The latent risks of industrial society, emphasized by Beck as formative in the development of advanced modernity, are captured in the film's representation of London's meat packaging plant. The first, heavily ironic, image of Meat World is a shot of the company's logo on the wall of the factory, the logo consisting of two cutlets shaped in the form of a Yin-Yang, surrounded by the words, 'Meet You at Meat World'. Cutting inside the building, the camera presents us with the spectacle of plant workers mechanically ripping entrails out of a dead pig; this macabre shot is reinforced by the intrusive use of the song 'Gizzards, Snapple and Tripe' as soundtrack. London Arbuckle is presented as a manic, masochistic caricature of the young successful businessman, his actions and words comically editorialized through a range of background sound effects. The standard of quality control operating within the meat industry is viciously satirized as London first reprimands a worker for cutting off too much fat, and then considers how best to make use of a slime-covered, partly decomposed corpse found lying in a corner, an animal that looks like it 'crawled through the cellar window and died'. Thrusting a slice of 'raisin loaf' in Juliet's face, he exults in the fact that he's 'finally figured out something to do with those pigs' ears'. The effect of this early scene is to demonstrate the manner in which London's single-minded determination to increase production and profits renders him indifferent to the quality of food intended for human consumption. Moreover, it suggests the extent to which London devalues non-human life by reducing animals to an edible mass of snouts, tails and hooves. Kaufman thus constructs Meat World as a food processing catastrophe waiting to happen.

The centrality of this critique of the meat industry to the broader concerns of the film is suggested through ubiquitous verbal and visual references to meat and animals. Juliet, for example, is a macrobiotic vegetarian who cradles a cow doll in her sleep, while Tromeo arrives at the Capulet ball in an elaborate cow costume. Much later in the film, after learning that his daughter has broken her engagement to London, Cappy orchestrates a humiliating dinner scene in which Juliet is forced to beg her former *fiancé* to take her back, as the family cook, Ness, standing behind Juliet's chair, slaps meat onto her plate. Most spectacularly, in a bid to escape her unwanted marriage to London, the heroine ingests a drink which temporarily transforms her into a grotesque cow-like figure. Recent ecofeminist theory addressing the parallels between the relations of production within patriarchy which have led to the oppression of women by men, and the relations of production within capitalism which have led to the oppression of the ecology by humans, provides a useful theoretical reference point in understanding the thematic significance of these and other similar images. Ecofeminist stances, like feminism itself, are widely varied, but have in common the conviction that the gender hierarchy is only challenged meaningfully through corresponding resistance to other economic and social hierarchies which value life primarily, or exclusively, in terms of productivity.[8] Karen J. Warren has described the relations between humans and the ecology as characterized by the 'logic of domination': humans, unlike non-human life, have the capacity to change the community in which they live; this power makes humans morally superior to non-human life; and human moral superiority justifies the subordination of non-human life.[9] Warren argues that this oppressive conceptual framework, located within patriarchy, is used within western culture to sanction the subordination of women to men on the grounds that women are identified with nature and the realm of the physical.[10] Women and non-human life are rendered subservient to the dominant capitalist imperative to maximize profits; striving constantly for more, rather than enough, the relationships between men and women, and between humans and the ecology, become ever more violent and polluted. *Tromeo and Juliet* offers a perceptive critique of such relationships, emphatically portraying both markets – meat and marriage – as exploitative and profit-oriented.

Juliet's horror at the fate of cattle screaming on their way to slaughter is, in an important sense, horror in the face of her own destiny, as she is forced to enter into a loveless, but profitable, marriage. This thematic connection is strikingly conveyed in the scene in which the heroine's defence of animal rights prompts an intimate discussion of her sense of resigned defeat in face of the forthcoming marriage to London: like London's animals, Juliet feels powerless to do anything but submit to her father's desire to get his hands on the Arbuckle fortune. In a revealing figure of speech, Capulet subsequently compares his daughter to Arbuckle's cattle, confidently reassuring his future son-in-law that after their marriage, Juliet will become 'a docile little bovine'. Both women and animals are presented as tamed, brought into the service of a masculinist, capitalist ethic. Sharp parallels are thus drawn early on between the abuse and exploitation of women by men, and of the ecology by humans, each relationship shaped by the same destructive impetus. Juliet's subconscious fears that she is valued by a capitalist system only in so far as it can control her reproductive potential is shockingly conveyed through a dream sequence in which she gives birth to rat-infested popcorn which is eagerly consumed by her lover, Tromeo. Juliet's body – more specifically, her womb – in this nightmare sequence is represented as contaminated, and entirely at the service of male hunger. This dream is further significant in that the pollution of Juliet's reproductive system can be read as the direct result of Tromeo's visionary ambitions to set his mark upon the world. Grasping his lover to him after slipping through her bedroom window, Tromeo imperiously declaims what they will accomplish through their love: 'Together you and I will replenish the world; kill hunger, and thirst, and hate, and bear the new era of grace!' (There is a roll of thunder as Juliet collapses on the bed.) Juliet's dream betrays the young woman's repressed fears of living in a society in which outdated goals of conquering subsistence needs threaten the very continuance and propagation of existing life. This anxiety, according to Beck's construction of the risk society, derives from an awareness of the need to balance further progress with the recognition that such progress, if not fully modernized according to new principles, will result in the destruction of all forms of life.

The difference between Juliet's prospective marriage partners is highlighted at the Capulet ball, where London arrives dressed as a milkman, and Tromeo as a Friesian cow, a commercially farmed breed of dairy cattle. This costuming, while comic, is also thematically significant. The milkman outfit metaphorically likens London's relationship with Juliet to the dominant hierarchical power the young entrepreneur commands over non-human life at Meat World, and emphasizes the problematic dynamics already implicit in the surname 'Arbuckle', an oblique reference to Roscoe 'Fatty' Arbuckle, the comedy film actor tried in 1921 for the rape and murder of Virginia Rappe.[11] Tromeo, by contrast, visually aligned with subordinated non-human life, is presented as occupying a position of vulnerability within this capitalist and patriarchal economy.[12] Juliet's instant and unreasoned attraction to the cow on the dance floor, and subsequently, to the unknown man inside the costume, only confirms the sense of identification with non-human life she has already been portrayed as feeling. The ensuing love between Juliet and Tromeo thus comes to embody a form of resistance, or even escape, from distinct, but linked, systems of oppression institutionalized within American society. The climax of the movie, in which Juliet is monstrously transformed into a cow on the morning of her wedding day, makes literal the ideological connection between animals and women as so much meat. The magic potion given to Juliet by the apothecary, Fu Chang, is a mixture of herbs deliberately concocted 'to scare the shit right out of any meat freak who admires too much your surface, not enough the person beneath'. It is Juliet's beauty that makes her a marketable commodity in a marriage exchange, and, by corrupting that beauty, the potion renders her worthless. Unsurprisingly, London's love sensationally fails to extend 'beneath the hide'. Horrified and disgusted by his *fiancée*'s appearance, and reduced to violent and copious vomiting, London breaks their contract of marriage by throwing himself out of Juliet's third-floor bedroom window.

The character most insistent on this arranged marriage, however, is not London, but Juliet's father. The extent to which Capulet dominates his daughter in order to maximize the wealth he can make from transferring her, still a virgin, to a husband in marriage is highlighted throughout the movie: Juliet complains, for example, that she is never allowed out of the house, and Capulet beats her violently after learning that she has broken her engagement with London. Cappy Capulet, outwardly suave and sophisticated, is a corrupt, power-hungry film mogul who controls his wife and daughter through fear and domestic violence. Capulet's feelings towards his daughter are further problematized by the two episodes in which Juliet wakes in terror from a nightmare, only to find her father lying beside her in bed. Drunkenly running his hand over Juliet's scantily clad body, and luridly accusing her of waking him with screaming orgasms – 'probably dreaming of getting fucked in the ass' – Capulet's patriarchal need to control her sexuality becomes overlaid with incestuous desire. In the second of these encounters, a scene provoked by Juliet's popcorn-birthing nightmare, he drags her by her hair into the Time Out Room, a blacked-out, sound-proofed room in the upper storey of the house. Capulet's abusive treatment of Juliet throughout this scene is punctuated by allusions to texts which pointedly assert the patriarchal authority of the father, both human and divine. First illuminating a raised plexiglass cube with the Biblical command, 'Let there be light', Capulet proceeds to chain his daughter to the floor of the cube, ominously paraphrasing another Shakespearean father, King Lear, with the words, 'How much sharper than a serpent's tooth it is to have a thankless child.'[13] His parting comment to a subdued Juliet, caged in the box, emphasizes the extent to which he believes such abusive domination is validated by their distinct and innate roles within a set of current social hierarchies: 'Children should behave themselves, my sweet, all women should. That's what they're here to do.'

The subtextual current of erotic desire underpinning Capulet's financial interest in his daughter finally erupts in the scene immediately following London's suicide, when Capulet bursts into his daughter's bedroom. Angrily surveying Juliet's face, he slaps her onto the bed, saying, 'You might as well have slipped your hand into my pocket and taken out a billion dollars, girl.' When provoked further by Juliet's attempts to escape his grasp, Capulet, with chilling menace, resolves, 'Oh, God. I'm going to kill you. I'm going to kill you and fuck you at the same time.' It is only with Tromeo's sudden entrance that this threatened rape is prevented. The sense of horror and disturbance prompted by Capulet's brutal treatment of his daughter mutually reinforces the comic disruption generated by Arbuckle's gleeful disregard for animal life at Meat World: in each instance, the film unsettles its viewer through a reading of commonplace social hierarchies as the abusive exploitation of either human or non-human life. Kaufman's insistent portrayal of these contaminated relationships as the consequence not of individual, but societal, corruption offers very little scope for the consoling belief that these are just sick perversions of an otherwise viable system. Manhattan society, founded on power structures premised on oppression and degradation, is breaking down at all levels through the sheer pressure of ever-increasing emotional, economic and social violation.

Capulet's subsequent overthrow at the hands of Juliet and Tromeo thus represents the revolt of both non-human life and women. Magically transformed by her lover's kiss from a cow back into a beautiful young woman, Juliet initiates an assault on her father which can only be seen as a peculiarly female form of revenge on a figure who has come to embody, and indeed epitomize, the evils of society. Juliet first beats Capulet away from the body of her unconscious lover by branding him in the face with a hot curling-iron, and then converts into weapons other cosmetic appliances and products scattered around her bedroom. She drives bobby pins into his ears, stabs him repeatedly in the back with a nail file, thrusts a blowdryer into his mouth and turns it on, and then Tromeo, recovering consciousness, grabs two tampons from Juliet's dresser and shoves them up Capulet's nose. Tromeo strikes Capulet with Juliet's copy of *The Yale Shakespeare*, and Juliet steps up behind her kneeling father to drop her computer monitor onto him with such force that his head is encased in the screen. This confrontation, however, is only concluded after Capulet, recovering from this assault, forces the lovers up the stairs into the Time Out Room, a room which by now resonates with the horrors of patriarchal authority and female disempowerment. As the camera fixes on the plexiglass cube towards which the three of them, now off-screen, are steadily moving, the apparent victor quietly intones the words, 'Behold how Capulet brings civilization to animals.' Related, but hitherto distinct, hierarchical systems are thus conflated in the closing moments in one revealing, life-denying assertion of power. But the literary context of Capulet's last, proudly referenced, quotation exposes the vulnerability of even dominant cultural forces. With poignant dramatic irony, Capulet imposingly recites from Shelley's 'Ozymandias' the legend just visible amongst the ruined remnants of the statue of the once indomitable, but now forgotten, conqueror: 'Look upon my work, ye Mighty, and despair!'[14] It is left to Juliet to deliver the final blow to secure her freedom. As Capulet absorbedly moves into the plexiglass cage to prepare it for his victims, she grips the plug of the computer monitor still on his head. Defiantly and powerfully rejecting the demeaning identity imposed on her from childhood – 'I'm not Daddy's little Charentais melon any longer' – Juliet thrusts the plug into the electrical socket beside her.

By dramatizing abusive relations of power and drawing attention to compelling parallels between the meat industry and marriage as different forms of systematized oppression, *Tromeo and Juliet* offers a disturbing commentary on western society. As Lyotard has suggested, such disruption of expectations and preconceptions is an important effect, as it may subsequently provoke the viewer to considered reflection. Troma Films, however, could have achieved this effect without self-conscious recourse to *Romeo and Juliet* as a source text. The emphasis placed on Shakespeare, consequently, seems designed as a means by which to interrogate, not only interdependent issues of love, marriage and the ecology, but also constructions of Shakespeare himself as a cultural icon. The by now familiar appropriation of this author to a conservative, or even reactionary, political agenda is apparent through the manner in which Capulet's aspirations to conquer and dominate other forms of life are inflected through frequent, and ostentatious, quotation of the canon. Capulet attempts to identify himself with the prestige of Shakespeare, and of high culture more generally, as an ideological means by which simultaneously to justify and exploit the diseased social system from which he profits.[15] His hegemonic assertion of power is frustrated, however, by the presence of a non conformist youth culture premised on dance music, promiscuity, crystal meth and body adornment. Capulet's perception of youth culture as transgressive and potentially subversive of the public order on which his authority depends is most clearly articulated as he beats his daughter after learning that she has broken her engagement with London: 'Aren't there any boundaries at all anymore? Are there any lines that can't be crossed by your generation of freaks?' A power-base founded on canonical literature, capitalist markets and the brutal assertion of patriarchal authority is thus explicitly set in opposition to a supposedly degenerate youth culture.

Significantly, however, the cultural weight of Shakespeare is not entirely surrendered to dominant values; although Capulet may appropriate to himself as a powerful legitimizing strategy Shakespeare's status as an artistic genius, the currency of this author amongst a younger generation remains evident. Juliet's edition of *The Yale Shakespeare* is always prominent in the scenes shot in her bedroom, resting on her dresser or lying open on her bed, and Tromeo owns a CD-ROM porn collection entitled 'Shakespeare Sex Interactive'. As Tromeo flicks through the CD-ROM cases, eventually settling on 'As You Lick It', the camera lingers over the other SSI titles: 'Et Tu Blow Job', 'Merchant of Penis' and 'Much Ado About Humping'. In addition, the lovers' speeches are peppered with verbal allusions to the plays: Juliet, for example, delivering a line resonant with connotations of abused familial trust, lashes out at her father as she attacks him with the hairdryer, saying, 'you sick bastard – vicious mole of nature'.[16] By positioning Shakespeare on both sides of the generation divide, *Tromeo and Juliet* resists any simple opposition between high culture and youth culture, dominant ideology and subversive resistance. Instead, the film problematizes a whole range of assumptions attendant on complacent assertions of moral and social deviancy, and raises the question as to which characters, if any, can lay claim to the politically and ideologically powerful category of 'normal'. The Shakespearean canon emerges within this debate as an important site of struggle.

This issue of what can be read as 'normal' is central to *Tromeo and Juliet*, with words such as 'pervert', 'sick' and 'freak' resounding throughout the film; crucially, images of deviancy are neither unique to the streets and bars nor restricted to one or other side of the Capulet/Que class divide. Benny (Benvolio), disgusted by the mutilation of a pigeon and a squirrel carried out by members of each of the two families, highlights the gap between their everyday behaviour and more conventional notions of family life. Concentrating on the real-time nipple-piercing with which he is engaged, he briefly pauses to tell Murray (Mercutio) and Tromeo, 'You're supposed to be normal people, leading normal lives. Working 9 to 5. Going to church on Sunday. Normal. Maiming, murdering, crippling park animals, it's a little abnormal, you know what I mean?' But the apparent disorder inherent in Manhattan society, far from representing a localized aberration, is put forward elsewhere in the film as ordinary. As Sammy puts it, while trying to cajole his sister into having sex with him, 'you know the way the world is now. We've got pantyliners, we've got perverts, we've got anorexia, everything's in style – if we just throw a little incest into the mix, pretty soon the world will be like one great big hug!' The abnormal, in other words, has become normal. Reflecting in the Time Out Room on their abusive and violent upbringings, Tromeo comments to Juliet that maybe they are both 'warped', but goes on to suggest that it has become impossible any longer for either them to distinguish between normal and its opposite: 'if you've been told a curved line is straight your whole life, you start to believe it.'

Tromeo and Juliet disrupts our ideas of normal in all sorts of ways, without providing any comforting or easy answers. Traditional social boundaries, such as those espoused by Capulet, are not only transgressed, but exposed as morally untenable, and the film, denying any fixed points from which deviancy may be measured, makes it difficult to determine where exactly those lines between normal and abnormal

should be redrawn. It is the manner in which *Tromeo and Juliet* nego-
tiates the theme of romantic love at the heart of Shakespeare's play,
however, which provides the key to the film's success as subversive
theatre. Tromeo's aspiration, as described early on in the action to
Murray and Benny, is one day to achieve through marriage a middle-
class, suburban existence, complete with family picnics and barbecues
in the backyard; alternative sexualities and lifestyles, set against this
Utopian ideal, are subsequently marginalized as poor substitutes. Friar
Lawrence's memory of pederastic love is portrayed only fleetingly in
flashback, and Juliet abandons her lesbian lover, Ness, immediately
after meeting Tromeo; Tromeo, by contrast, is not even aware of
Murray's feelings for him until the moment of his best friend's death.
The ideological distance between Tromeo's celebrated heterosexual
love for Juliet, and Murray's repressed homosexual love for Tromeo, is
summed up by Benny's bemused reaction to Murray's deathbed
request for a farewell kiss: 'Fuck – Murray was a fag.' The primacy of
the lovers' relationship is not seriously challenged even when the
angry, mutilated ghosts of Sammy, Murray and Tyrone (Tybalt)
demand a hallucinating Juliet to justify the hitherto unspoken
premise that her love for Tromeo is all important: 'You find the greatest love the world has ever known. And on the way we have to pay for
it with our lives?' But with the startling and unexpected discovery in
the closing moments of act five that Juliet and Tromeo are sister and
brother, the last remaining social boundary – that separating true love
from taboo sexuality – is erased.

The spectre of incest haunts the margins of this film: Capulet's
desire for his daughter serves throughout as an index to his moral
depravity, and, as early as the opening scene, Sammy's insistent
advances on his sister are repulsed as perverted, Georgie dismissing
her brother's ecstatic vision of their sexual union as part of a new
world order with the matter-of-fact retort, 'Yeah, I'm sure, Sammy –
me, you and our mutant in-bred children.' By forcing the viewer to
reconcile essentialist notions of young love to incest, the film exposes
the romance on which the story-line is premised as simply another,
alternative form of sexual desire, constructed within (or against) social
convention. Supposedly firm boundaries between valid and transgressive
sexualities crumble, as Shakespeare once again provides the territory
over which the lovers' happiness is negotiated. In a scene that echoes
the recovery of lost family at the end of such plays as *Twelfth Night*
and *The Comedy of Errors*, the astonished lovers regard each other for
a long moment in wonder. Finally, and with a fitting sense of context,

they resolve on a course of action through an exchange of quotations from *As You Like It* and *Much Ado About Nothing*. Juliet tentatively offers her lover the lines, 'Sweet are the uses of adversity / Which, like the toad, ugly and venomous, / Wears yet a precious jewel in his head', to which a comprehending Tromeo confidently responds, 'Let every eye negotiate for itself, / And trust no agent.'[17]

The impetus provided by children who challenge and ultimately prevail over their parents' attempts to stand in their way of marriage is a plot device typical of Shakespearean comedy, and Kaufman's revisionist reading of the play, with the young lovers escaping both money-grabbing parents and the violence of Manhattan to marry and raise a family in Tromaville, New Jersey, conclusively reorients the film away from tragedy, towards comedy. *Tromeo and Juliet* can be read in all sorts of ways as the product of the late twentieth century, and like many *fin-de-siècle* narratives, it regards its age as simultaneously the source of despair and hope, pessimism and optimism.[18] Human and non-human Manhattan society may be breaking down through violence and exploitation, but there is an impulse towards an as yet unseen future order, a belief, as Sammy puts it, that this world 'herald[s] the dawning of the age of Aquarius – just like in *Hair*'. This indistinct promise is realised in the epilogue to the film, set six years later in Tromaville, New Jersey: 'The New World'. The happy lovers, hosting a backyard barbecue, are surrounded by Tromeo's father, Monty Que, close friends and two playful, in-bred daughters sporting mutant faces on the sides of their heads. Hearing the baby, little Murray, start to cry in the play pen, Tromeo leaves the hot dogs on the barbecue to walk over and pick up his son. As his wife, family and friends gather round, Tromeo turns little Murray in his arms to present to the camera an apparently undeformed baby boy. The final chorus, spoken by Lemmy from the 'House of Motorhead' as a voice-over to this sustained image of domestic fulfilment, reworks the final lines of Shakespeare's play to situate this scene and the preceding action within the confusion and disorder generated by the approach of the millennium: 'So this is the dawn of the twenty-first age, / Where love ever rules and all is insane. / And all of our hearts free to let all base things go / As taught by Juliet and her Tromeo.' *Tromeo and Juliet* enthusiastically affirms the idealized and proverbial love shared by Shakespeare's protagonists, but the troubling form that love takes is not easily reconciled to conventional belief systems. In this way, even the essentialist category of true love is finally exposed as historically and culturally determined, shaped by the social pressures brought to bear on successive generations. By constantly, and deliberately, wrong-footing its audience, and drawing into question at every turn complacent and restrictive assertions of 'normal', *Tromeo and Juliet* jolts its viewers out of mute complacency, challenging them to reflect upon, and interrogate further, the belief systems on which structures of power are premised.

This is not to suggest, however, that *Tromeo and Juliet* offers viable solutions to the problems facing western society, since the various forms of systematized exploitation brought into sharp relief over the course of the film remain in place at the close of the action. Tromaville, New Jersey, far from representing a distinct, alternative utopian order, is really just an extension of Manhattan, and the hot dogs grilling on the barbecue suggest the degree to which the comfort of the New World is predicated on systems of exploitation the lovers have supposedly left behind. Instead of escaping an oppressive society, the lovers simply relocate to a different geographical position within it, their identities as residents of the suburbs remaining caught up in the ideological constructs of the urban centre. The family's cheerful consumption of processed meat products, however, is only one indication in this closing scene of the absence of any coherent oppositional politics. Another is the viewer's first glimpse of Juliet, in which can be read society's on-going exploitation of women. Unlike Tromeo and Benny, who chat with each other by the barbecue, Juliet is portrayed in silent solitude, reclining in a garden lounge chair, staring sidelong into the distance. This sequence of images locates activity and subjectivity in the male characters, while projecting an understanding of the heroine as the beautiful, passive object of the viewer's meditative gaze.

This closing scene is thus of a piece with the filmic treatment elsewhere in *Tromeo and Juliet* of Jane Jensen, the actor playing Juliet. During the adapted balcony scene, for example, Tromeo enters the Time Out Room to find a semi-naked Juliet chained in the plexiglass box. As Tromeo, standing hidden and unseen in the shadows of the room, praises her beauty, the camera shifts between the two characters, cutting at the line, 'See how she leans her cheek upon her hand' (II.i.65), to a shot of Juliet's hand resting on her buttock. The focus of the camera alternates between the woman, still and silent in the cube, and the male protagonist, who in turn gazes at the woman. Postponing the moment at which Juliet reciprocates her lover's gaze by opening her eyes, Kaufman presents her as a static thing of beauty, fit both for her lover's, and the viewer's, admiration.[19] This objectification of the female body is carried over into the ensuing sex scene, in which the camera concentrates exclusively on the woman's, rather than the lovers', facial expressions, Juliet's head and face foregrounded within the frame of the picture. The female body becomes the site of another's activity, the activity being located simultaneously in the male character who makes love to the woman, and in the viewer who watches the woman being made love to. The pleasure provided by the encounter staged in the raised glass box thus depends on constructing the heroine, in Laura Mulvey's words, as 'an object of sexual stimulation through sight'.[20] The exploitative manner in which Kaufman handles the lovers' sexual initiation reproduces the impact of the earlier lesbian encounter between Juliet and Ness, both scenes transforming women into objects to be looked at and desired. Kaufman's revisionist narrative may allow the character of Juliet to escape the pressures of market commodification inherent in an arranged marriage to London, but this potentially liberating feminist treatment is undercut by the exploitative manner in which the camera continues to film the actor's body after Capulet's death. To this extent, neither Juliet nor Jane Jensen avoids limiting and misogynist constructions of female identity and sexuality.

But the recognition of an inability or unwillingness ultimately to provide coherent resistance to dominant ideologies which oppress women and non-human life is not necessarily to read the film through a thesis of containment, or to suggest that the film is an aesthetic or political failure. Instead, it seems most useful to interpret *Tromeo and Juliet* as a thoroughly modern narrative, in the sense of Beck's (arguably postmodern) construction of risk society. The film's ambivalent ending comes into particularly sharp focus when approached through this theoretical framework. Individuals in a self-reflexive risk society are forced to make choices not about whether or not there will be risks, but the manner and extent to which they will let those risks impact on their lives. The lovers' method of coping with the hazards attendant on modern life is to manage risk by ignoring it, a strategy emphatically set in place with Juliet's exhilarating response to her mother's revelation of their incestuous love: 'Fuck it – we've come this far.' The lovers neither escape nor resolve the horrors of late twentieth-century existence; on the contrary, they negotiate what seems to them a tolerable position within the system by moving far enough away from the urban nightmare to allow them to pretend it is not there. However, the unpredictable and uncontrollable conditions of end-of-the-century western society are manifest on the bodies of their three children, little Murray's apparent physical health only emphasizing the arbitrary nature of risk.

Tromeo and Juliet asks unsettling questions without offering tidy answers. As Lyotard observes, however, it is perhaps not necessary, or even possible, to offer argumentation; the power of a film such as this lies precisely in its ability to disturb the belief systems and apparently stable categories of truth held by mainstream culture. The film's closing image is a shot of an actor, cleverly made up and costumed to look like Shakespeare, laughing into the camera. This clip is presumably intended to legitimize, and even authorize, Troma Film's playful adaptation, visually reinforcing the appeal to authorial intentions printed on the cover of the video to the effect that 'TROMEO & JULIET containes [*sic*] all the car crashes, alternative rock music, eroticism and special effects that Shakespeare wanted but never had'. But as the laughter continues with a disconcerting insistence, the image drains of meaning; rather than sharing the joke, viewers begin to feel as though the joke might be on them. Staring back at the decontextualized figure, and continuing to listen, after the picture fades to black, to the now disembodied laughter, the comic delight afforded by the sight of Shakespeare brought to life is replaced, once again, by unease.

Notes

1. Jean-François Lyotard, 'Brief Reflections on Popular Culture', in Lisa Appignanesi (ed.), *Postmodernism: ICA Documents* (London: Free Association Books, 1989), pp. 181–2.
2. This publicity soundbite, written by production assistant, Michael Shapiro, derives from one of Kaufman's many comments on the film, which were intended, as he puts it in his memoirs, to 'provoke a reaction' (Lloyd Kaufman and James Gunn, with introduction by Roger Corman, *All I Need to Know about Filmmaking I Learned from 'The Toxic Avenger'* [Berkeley: Putnam Berkeley Group, 1998], p. 285). The screenplay, drafted by Kaufman in 1992, was thoroughly reworked by Gunn three years later, and the shooting of the film, which began in June 1995, was completed before Baz Luhrmann went into production with his *William Shakespeare's 'Romeo + Juliet'*; both movies were released in 1996 (Kaufman, *All I Need*, p. 298). I should like to thank Lloyd Kaufman and Troma Films for their helpfulness throughout the writing of this essay. They provided me with publicity material, reviews, the third draft of the screenplay (21 February 1995) and a pre-print copy of the final chapter of Kaufman's memoirs, '*Tromeo & Juliet* and the Future of Troma'.
3. There are three sustained passages of Shakespearean verse found in *Tromeo and Juliet*. The balcony scene, as in the source text, is spoken at the lovers' first private encounter, but the lines have been ironically adapted to a

revised setting, Tromeo entering the Time Out Room to ask in wonder, 'What light from yonder plexiglass breaks? / It is a right-angled cosmos, and Juliet is its sun' (II.i.44–89). The other two passages occur during the Capulet ball: Tromeo, setting eyes on Juliet, delivers a version of the 'teach the torches to burn bright' speech (I.v.43–52), and the lovers subsequently speak most of Shakespeare's shared sonnet (I.v.92–106). The switch from realist dialogue to iambic pentameter, a device frequently employed in the movie, is readily apparent in the two scenes in which the history of the Capulets' adulterous relationship and the takeover of Silky Films is told through flashback and voice-over. As the final version of the screenplay is unpublished and unavailable, all quotations from *Tromeo and Juliet* have been transcribed from the film. All quotations from the plays of Shakespeare have been taken from Stanley Wells and Gary Taylor, with John Jowett and William Montgomery (eds), *The Complete Works: Compact Edition* (Oxford: Clarendon Press, 1988).

4. Dympna Callaghan, 'The Ideology of Romantic Love: The Case of *Romeo and Juliet*', in Dympna Callaghan, Lorraine Helms and Jyotsna Singh, *The Weyward Sisters: Shakespeare and Feminist Politics* (Oxford: Blackwell, 1994), p. 88.

5. Callaghan, 'The Ideology of Romantic Love', pp. 60–2.

6. Ulrich Beck, *Risk Society: Towards a New Modernity*, trans. Mark Ritter (London: Sage, 1992), pp. 19–27, 51–84. Beck explicitly rejects the description of western society as 'postmodern', and emphasizes instead the continuity which prevails between classic industrialism and self-reflexive modernization, arguing that 'we are witnessing not the end but the beginning of modernity' (*Risk Society*, p. 10). Beck's reading of current social changes as a break within modernity, rather than as a departure from it, none the less shares a number of common features with theories of postmodernism. This problem of terminology, as Krishan Kumar argues, confirms that any clear demarcation between historical periods is difficult, if not impossible, the 'postmodern' always embodying within itself its modernist heritage (*From Post-Industrial to Post-Modern Society: New Theories of the Contemporary World* [Oxford: Blackwell, 1995], pp. 143–4).

7. Beck, *Risk Society*, p. 75.

8. See, for example, Victoria Davion, 'Is Ecofeminism Feminist?', in Karen J. Warren, with Barbara Wells-Howe (eds), *Ecological Feminism* (London: Routledge, 1994), pp. 8–28; Ynestra King, 'Healing the Wounds: Feminism, Ecology, and the Nature/Culture Dualism', in Nancy Tuana and Rosemarie Tong (eds), *Feminism and Philosophy: Essential Readings in Theory, Reinterpretation, and Application* (Boulder: Westview Press, 1995), pp. 353–73; Carolyn Merchant, *Earthcare: Women and the Environment* (New York: Routledge, 1996); and Karen J. Warren, 'The Power and the Promise of Ecological Feminism', *Environmental Ethics*, 12 (1990), pp. 125–46. The political and intellectual distinctions between a range of ecofeminist perspectives are discussed by Carolyn Merchant in *Earthcare*, pp. 8–18.

9. Warren, 'The Power and the Promise of Ecological Feminism', p. 129.

10. Warren, 'The Power and the Promise of Ecological Feminism', p. 130.

11. The circumstances of the Arbuckle trial are discussed by Richard Dyer in *Stars*, with supplementary chapter and bibliography by Paul McDonald

(London: BFI Publishing, 1998), p. 178.

12. The affinity between Tromeo and animals was earlier established through the transition from the scene in which the viewer sees Tromeo at home in his cow outfit, to the first scene set at Meat World, where the sound of Tromeo's 'mooed' response to his friend, Murray (Mercutio), blends seamlessly into the sound of real cattle as the camera cuts to show Juliet walking along the sidewalk up to the factory door.

13. Genesis 1:3; *The Tragedy of King Lear*, I.iv.268–9.

14. Shelley's poem reads 'works' in place of Cappy's 'work' (Percy Bysshe Shelley, 'Ozymandias', in *Poetical Works*, ed. Thomas Hutchinson, corrected by G. M. Matthews [Oxford: Oxford University Press, n.d.], p. 550, line 11).

15. While the plays of Shakespeare feature most prominently in Cappy's dialogue, he also, as noted, quotes Shelley, while his confident familiarity with the great names of modern art is comically pointed when he fires his crossbow at Murray and Benny (Benvolio), asking how they would like him to 'use your guts to Jackson Pollock the streets'.

16. Juliet's description of Capulet alludes to the speech in which Hamlet criticizes his uncle's reinstatement of Danish drinking rituals after the murder of Hamlet Senior (*Hamlet*, Additional Passage B, line 8 [I.iv.26]).

17. *As You Like It*, II.i.12–14; *Much Ado About Nothing*, II.i.168–9.

18. Krishan Kumar, in his analysis of late twentieth-century western society, notes parallels between the current postmodern condition and forms of thought historically inspired by the ends of centuries, arguing that, although postmodernism is distinct in many ways from the sort of prophetic thinking typical of turns of the century, it has none the less become caught up in a sense of the apocalypse: 'the onset of the end, not just of another century but of another millennium, is bound to have an effect on the theories under consideration ... [E]ven though many of the theories were elaborated before a strong sense of *fin de siècle* came upon us, they have come to be identified with its mood and to shape themselves, in part at least, according to its expectations' (*From Post-Industrial to Post-Modern Society*, p. 151).

19. A similar moment occurs during the Capulet ball, when Tromeo catches sight of Juliet across the room seated in a chair; Ness, positioned slightly behind and to one side, frames the heroine's body for the camera. Unaware that she is being watched, Juliet looks in front of her in silence as Tromeo describes her beauty. Laura Mulvey argues that this split between active/male and passive/female is a typical effect in movies, resulting from broader sexual imbalances within society: 'The determining male gaze projects its fantasy onto the female figure, which is styled accordingly. In their traditional exhibitionist role women are simultaneously looked at and displayed, with their appearance coded for strong visual and erotic impact so that they can be said to connote to-be-looked-at-ness' ('Visual Pleasure and Narrative Cinema', in *Visual and Other Pleasures* [London: Macmillan, 1989], p. 19).

20. Mulvey, 'Visual Pleasure and Narrative Cinema', p. 18. Although Ness enters the room unnoticed by the lovers to watch them have sex, the potential voyeuristic pleasure of the scene is located in the viewer. The two

gazes represented at this point in the scene, that of Ness and the viewer, are distinct in so far as the former serves to enhance the erotic spectacle for the latter, the camera turning only briefly from the action in the box to register the impact on Ness of watching her former lover with a man.

8
'These Violent Delights Have Violent Ends': Baz Luhrmann's Millennial Shakespeare

James N. Loehlin

Baz Luhrmann's 1996 film, *William Shakespeare's 'Romeo + Juliet'*, is necessarily a central text for any consideration of Shakespearean film-making at the millennium.[1] Of all the Shakespeare film releases of the 1990s, it is the one most obviously oriented toward the twenty-first century. Along with its effective plundering of youth culture and its aggressive marketing toward a teenage audience, it employs post-modern aesthetic strategies that set it off from the substantial body of teen-star-crossed-lovers films from which it derives. Luhrmann's flashy, eclectic visual style and ultra-hip ironies earmark *William Shakespeare's 'Romeo + Juliet'* as *fin-de-siècle* spectacle; yet the gesture to bardic authority in the film's title, and the watery cocoon in which Luhrmann shelters his young lovers, evince a romantic nostalgia that is a surprising and poignant response to the frenetic excess of late twentieth-century culture.

Luhrmann's resetting of the play is explicitly millennial: 'Verona Beach' is a near-future urban dystopia of guns, drugs, conspicuous consumption and civic breakdown. Filmed in Mexico City, *William Shakespeare's 'Romeo + Juliet'* depicts a multiracial society where lavish wealth exists alongside grinding poverty, and the sensation-crazed, trigger-happy populace are kept in check only by police helicopters and riot squads. Social organization is a strange amalgam of late-model capitalism, Catholicism and feudalism: the smoggy skyline is dominated by a monumental statue of Christ flanked by the skyscrapers of the Capulet and Montague empires. The rival families are powerful factions whose members drive flashy cars with vanity licence plates (CAP 002, MON 005) and carry high-tech sidearms marked with the family crests. Despite this post-millennial setting, Luhrmann's basic approach to the story is not new: teenage lovers resist the corrupt values of their parents and so fall victim to a violent and uncaring society. The generation-gap emphasis of *William Shakespeare's 'Romeo + Juliet'* links it to a whole series of teen films from the 1950s forward.

The teen film was part of the emergence of a distinctive youth culture in the decades following the second world war. Unsupervised teenagers with time on their hands formed both a national social concern and a fertile commercial market. Hollywood responded to this phenomenon with some films that portrayed teens as menacing delinquents (such as *The Blackboard Jungle* and, to some extent, *The Wild One*), but just as often with films that showed them as sensitive idealists misunderstood by their shallow, vain and greedy parents.[2] Films like *Are These Our Parents?*, *Where Are Your Children?* and *Youth Runs Wild* placed much of the blame for teenage tragedies on the older generation, but the most influential of all was Nicholas Ray's 1955 *Rebel Without a Cause*. *Rebel* introduced the archetypes of James Dean as the troubled, brooding youth, Natalie Wood as the neglected daughter who falls for him, and Sal Mineo as his wealthy, emotionally wounded, presumably homosexual friend: a variation on the Romeo/Juliet/Mercutio triangle. Natalie Wood went on to play love-struck tragic teens in *Splendour on the Grass* and the Bernstein/Wise/Robbins musical, *West Side Story*, both in 1961. When Franco Zeffirelli released his immensely popular film of *Romeo and Juliet* in 1968, it joined a flourishing cultural tradition of young love crossed by parental opposition.[3] Historically, Romeo and Juliet had mostly been played by mature actors, as in the 1936 George Cukor film version, with Norma Shearer and Leslie Howard; Zeffirelli's stage and film versions of the play, along with *West Side Story*, redefined them as rebellious adolescents.[4] This tradition of star-crossed love extended beyond the movies to all aspects of youth culture, including rock-and-roll, which produced such tragic hits as 'Teen Angel' and 'Leader of the Pack' ('My folks were always putting him down / They said he came from the wrong side of town').[5]

William Shakespeare's 'Romeo + Juliet' repeatedly associates itself with this tradition. The sweet-faced young leads, Claire Danes and Leonardo DiCaprio, came to the film with established credentials as misunderstood adolescents (*My So-Called Life*, *This Boy's Life*, *The Basketball Diaries*). The Montague and Capulet parents are played as wealthy, status-conscious and stereotypically out of touch with their children. Gloria Capulet (Diane Venora) is a chain-smoking, pill-popping trophy wife with no time for her daughter's problems; Ted

Montague (Brian Dennehy) watches Romeo gloomily out of the tinted window of his limousine, unable to speak to his son. Luhrmann conceived Romeo in terms of the teen film archetype: 'In a way, he was the original rebel without a cause, the first James Dean. He is someone who is a young rebel in love with the idea of love itself.'[6] The first shots of DiCaprio in the film, wandering the beach to avoid his parents, replicate the tilted head, hanging forelock and introspective squint of Dean's Jim Stark. DiCaprio's anguished cry – 'Then I defy you, stars!' – perhaps unconsciously, exactly matches the tone and cadences of Dean's trademark outburst, 'You're tearing me apart!'[7] Luhrmann follows *West Side Story* in recasting Shakespeare's feuding families as rival gangs; his Montague and Capulet boys duplicate not only the ethnic affiliations (Anglo and Latino) but also the colour schemes (gold and blue *versus* black and red) of the Jets and Sharks.[8] Romeo and Tybalt's duel even includes an automotive 'chicken run', recalling that in *Rebel Without a Cause*. Yet Luhrmann's film distances itself from the teen film tradition by virtue of the qualities that mark it as a postmodern production: an aggressively fragmented aesthetic, a highly self-conscious, ironic intertextuality and a cynical fatalism tinged with nostalgia.[9]

The film's frenzied camera movement, staccato editing and pop music score led many critics to compare it to the quintessential postmodern product, MTV.[10] Luhrmann, together with his cinematographer, Donald McAlpine, and editor, Jill Bilcock, uses a whole range of self-conscious cinematic tricks and rock-video flourishes. The film reels with dizzying hand-held shots, slam zooms and swish pans, as well as the changing film speeds, jump cuts and lush, unnatural saturation of colour that made Luhrmann's one previous picture, *Strictly Ballroom*, so visually distinctive. *William Shakespeare's 'Romeo + Juliet'* foregrounds its own status as a mediated representation; it wears its visual bravura on its sleeve, begins and ends as a television broadcast, and sets several scenes in an abandoned cinema, the Sycamore Grove.[11] The film features an elaborate sound design with sophisticated layering and sampling, amplified sound effects and a wide range of musical styles, including many alternative pop songs commissioned especially for the film and incorporating lines from the play, such as the pounding hardcore rap of 'Pretty Piece of Flesh' by One Inch Punch. This sonic and visual flair is needed to balance out weaknesses in the film, notably the vocal shortcomings of the cast. For the most part, the actors speak with toneless naturalism, their reedy voices flattening out the elaborate poetic conceits of one of

Shakespeare's most self-consciously verbal plays. In the tradition of innovative Shakespearean filmmakers like Welles and Kurosawa, Luhrmann finds visual and aural replacements for the lost poetry. Claire Danes doesn't do much with Juliet's wish to take Romeo 'and cut him out in little stars' (III.ii.22), but she is backed up by Stina Nordenstam's haunting song, 'Little Star', and the lines recall the film's image of Juliet, in white party dress and angel's wings, standing dreaming on her balcony, with slow-motion fireworks drifting like stars around her head. Leonardo DiCaprio mumbles through Romeo's premonition that 'Some consequence yet hanging in the stars / Shall bitterly begin his fearful date / With this night's revels' (I.iv.107–9), but Luhrmann supports him with a brief, eerie flash-forward to Romeo walking among the shimmering candles and dying flowers of Juliet's tomb. Luhrmann replaces the linguistic complexity of the play with cinematic wit of equivalent virtuosity: his delight in his own medium matches the young Shakespeare's, even while the poetry dies in his teen actors' mouths.

One of the chief aesthetic devices of *William Shakespeare's 'Romeo + Juliet'*, and one of the hallmarks of postmodern cinema, is intertextuality – the reference to other works, genres and styles, whether as homage, parody, simple imitation or even unconscious duplication.[12] Luhrmann's film is a compendium of references to twentieth-century popular culture. His avowed intention in creating this bricolage was simply clarity:

> The idea behind the created world was that it's a made-up world comprised of twentieth-century icons, and these images are there to clarify what's being said ... The idea was to find icons that everybody comprehends, that are crystally, overtly clear. The hope was that by associating the characters and places with those images, then what is being said is freed from its cage of obscurity.[13]

However, the overlapping and intersecting meanings of Luhrmann's allusions actually do much to complicate and enrich the film. *William Shakespeare's 'Romeo + Juliet'* continually and playfully juxtaposes contemporary kitsch with the high-culture world of Shakespeare, classical music and Renaissance art and architecture. In Catherine Martin's Fellini-inspired production design, the phantasmagorical mixes with the social real in a wealth of telling details.[14] The Capulet mansion is a Florentine palazzo, decked out for the masked ball with Christmas lights and metal detectors at the gates. Capulet and his wife host the party costumed as Antony and Cleopatra: grotesque parodies of great Shakespearean lovers, complete with garish makeup, sweaty toga and glittering gold dress. Luhrmann delights in forcing Shakespearean language and ideas into his squalid late capitalist world: the gangs wield flashy handguns with brand names like 'Rapier' and 'Sword 9 mm'; Romeo and his friends hang out at the Globe Theatre pool hall; a billboard advertises Prospero Scotch Whiskey ('Such Stuff as Dreams Are Made On'). Friar Laurence's message fails to reach Romeo in Mantua through the incompetence of an overnight delivery service called 'Post Haste Dispatch'.[15] In spite of these satirical touches, the film is far from being the kind of all-out cynical parody of Lloyd Kaufmann's *Tromeo and Juliet*, discussed elsewhere in this volume by Margaret Jane Kidnie. Luhrmann's attitude towards its Shakespearean source is often quite reverential. He retains much of the text that Zeffirelli left out, including the Friar's meditation on plants in II.iii, the complex bantering exchanges between Romeo and his friends in I.i and II.iv, and much of Juliet's 'Gallop apace' and potion speeches (III.ii and IV.iii). As Luhrmann's title suggests, the film depends on the cultural authority of Shakespeare even as it playfully undermines it.[16]

*

The opening sequence of *William Shakespeare's 'Romeo + Juliet'* provides a good instance of the film's intertextual allusiveness: its combination of parody and bardolatry nicely encapsulates Luhrmann's ambivalent attitude towards his sources. Shakespeare's prologue is read by a news anchorwoman on a low-tech, 1970s era television which hangs suspended in darkness, then gradually moves forward until it fills the screen. The anchorwoman (played by a real TV newsreader, Edwina Moore) uses the sympathetic but upbeat, half-smiling style characteristic of local broadcasts, and reads the lines with sincere banality. Over her shoulder is a projected headline icon reading 'Star-Cross'd Lovers' and showing Romeo and Juliet's broken wedding ring. At the line, 'the two hours' traffic of our stage' (Prologue, 12), the film cuts to a montage of urban violence, backed by a bombastic choral piece, a pastiche of Orff's 'O Fortuna' entitled 'O Verona'. Over this, a deep, grave, Shakespearean-sounding male voice repeats the words of the prologue, which now appear on the screen in the film's trademark baroque font (the uncredited voice sounds like that of Pete Postlethwaite, who plays Friar Laurence, an RSC veteran and the most 'authentic' Shakespearean in the cast). As the montage reaches a frenzied climax, the words are again flashed at unreadable speed, followed by the film's title, *William Shakespeare's 'Romeo + Juliet'*. This doubled presentation of the prologue, once in a cheeky pop-culture parody, once with grave seriousness and an earnest bow to textual authority, sums up the film's divided approach to the chaotic world of Verona Beach and the timeless tragedy of the lovers.

The brawl scene that follows continues the postmodern tendency toward pastiche, parody and pop culture. The Capulet/Montague feud is rendered in the style of action-film *auteurs*, Sergio Leone and John Woo. Guitar chords and eerie whistlings evoke Ennio Morricone's trademark western scores, while close-up slow-motion and freeze-frame shots of Tybalt lighting a cheroot, then crushing out the match with the silver heel of his cowboy boot, quote shots of Clint Eastwood in *A Fistful of Dollars* and Charles Bronson in *Once Upon a Time in the West*. The freeze-frame introduction of the characters with onscreen titles ('Tybalt Capulet, Prince of Cats, Juliet's Cousin') recalls the opening of *The Good, the Bad and the Ugly*. Once the showdown starts, the fast editing, changing camera speeds, and especially the slow-motion shots of the leaping Tybalt firing two guns at once, are clearly a parody of, or homage to, the Hong Kong director, John Woo. Luhrmann's use of flashy action-film devices both engages and distances the audience – we vicariously experience the intoxicating fun of violence, while being perfectly aware that this is a spectacle staged for our pleasure. The later fight between Mercutio and Tybalt is staged very differently, in *cinéma vérité* style, with a hand-held camera thrust among the awkwardly scuffling combatants – a device Zeffirelli also used in his version of the fatal duel.

The pervasive keynote of hip irony returns again and again throughout the film. Romeo laboriously writes out his Petrarchan conceits in a journal ('O brawling love, O loving hate, / O anything of nothing first create!' [I.i.174–5]), then impresses Benvolio with his poetic romanticism by seeming to invent them *extempore*. Gloria Capulet's metaphorical praise of Paris as a book of love – 'Read o'er the volume of young Paris' face' (I.iii.81) – is mocked by a magazine cover showing a smiling Dave Paris as 'Bachelor of the Year'. Romeo and his friends learn of the Capulet ball, not from a servant, but by watching an *Entertainment Tonight*-type TV show, whose garish hostess winks the camera an invitation: 'if you be not of the house of Montagues … come and crush a cup of wine' (I.ii.81–2).

Not all of the film has this degree of wit and invention. Sometimes Luhrmann's allusions seem to be merely failures of imagination, simple replications rather than pointed reworkings. His frequent borrowings from Zeffirelli's *Romeo and Juliet* tend to fall in this category. Harold Perrineau's Queen Mab speech, for instance, is a clumsy copy of John McEnery's from the earlier film, though making 'Queen Mab' a hallucinogenic pill on Mercutio's forefinger is an inspired touch. Perrineau builds to misogynistic fury on the account of Mab's nocturnal assaults on maids, then repeats his final 'This is she' (I.iv.95) in rage and confusion, whereupon Romeo's hand on his shoulder causes him to start and wheel towards the camera in startled recollection of his senses. The sequence matches the exchange between John McEnery and Leonard Whiting almost shot for shot, down to the blue light haloing the two young men as Romeo embraces Mercutio to calm him down. The real revelation of Perrineau's Mercutio comes immediately after, in the party scene, where he vogues through a glitzy camp performance of 'Young Hearts Run Free' that combines Busby Berkeley with *Paris is Burning*. This memorable performance, atop a brightly lit staircase, in high heels, spangled bra and Jean Harlow wig, serves the structural function of the Mab speech, encapsulating the brilliancy, imaginative energy and homosocial bonding of Mercutio's world, just before Romeo meets the woman who will draw him away from it. The whole sequence exemplifies Luhrmann's characteristic technique of replacing or supplementing the verbal text with a cinematic equivalent.

The balcony scene begins as a witty parody of Zeffirelli, playing on the audience's conventional expectations for the scene. In mid-long shot, Romeo emerges from the foliage into a dreamy, moonlit Renaissance courtyard; the camera angle, lighting and mood match Zeffirelli's treatment of the scene exactly. Suddenly the courtyard is bathed in searchlights: Romeo has set off the security system's motion detector, and he trips over the poolside furniture in a clumsy panic. Collecting himself, Romeo climbs a trellis toward Juliet's balcony, where a shadowy form appears on the illuminated curtains. No sooner has Romeo intoned, 'It is the east and Juliet is the sun!' (II.ii.3), than the windows are flung open to reveal the portly middle-aged Nurse; meanwhile, Juliet walks out of an elevator next to the swimming pool. Romeo's approach to the startled Juliet ends up tumbling both of them into the pool, where Romeo must hide underwater while Juliet smiles winningly at a bemused security guard who comes to investigate.

The parodic comedy of the first part of the scene frees the young actors from expectations of grand and lyrical passion. Having invoked and discarded the traditional trappings of the famous love duet, Luhrmann can film an appealing scene about two wide-eyed kids in a swimming pool. Whispering and kissing in a tight close-up, Danes and DiCaprio are convincingly love-struck, and the awkwardness and danger of their situation excuse the low-key approach to the poetry. They communicate their desire not with their words but with their eyes, which appear huge and shining in the surreal light from the pool.

This scene forms a crucial part of an ongoing visual metaphor associating the lovers with water. The first image of Juliet in the film, as described here in the screenplay, shows her face underwater: 'INT. JULIET'S BATHROOM. DAY. The still, serene, submerged features of a beautiful young girl. Dark floating hair gently frames the face. Heavy liquid eyes stare up through the water.'[17] A similar shot of Romeo's face submerged in a bathroom sink precedes his initial meeting with Juliet. They first see each other through a huge salt-water aquarium which forms the wall separating the men's and women's guest bathrooms at the Capulet mansion. The blue calm of the water, with its glowing tropical fish, replaces the deafening revelry of the party as the lovers stare at each other, entranced, through the glass. Luhrmann's use of water helps remove the lovers from the noisy and frenetic world of Verona Beach, sheltering their story in a silent element that seems outside of time.

Luhrmann's aquatic insulation of the lovers leans toward sentimentality, but it is actually part of the film's fatalism. Romeo and Juliet's love literally has no place in this world. Luhrmann reminds us of this repeatedly through brutal editing that shatters his lovers' idylls. During the 'Gallop apace' speech (III.ii.1–31), Juliet's enraptured face fills the screen as she calls on the night to bring her Romeo; the image is suddenly replaced by a shocking match cut of Romeo's face, bloody and contorted with hate as he races his car after Tybalt in the 'chicken run' duel. When Romeo shoots Tybalt, Luhrmann intercuts a half-second image of Juliet in her bedroom, as if hearing the shots. This effect is reversed in the morning scene (III.v). The camera glides slowly down on the twined, discreetly nude bodies of the lovers, again recalling Zeffirelli's film; a sudden cut to Tybalt's bullet-riddled body jerks Romeo awake in terror. The lovers' private world is always vulnerable to the sudden intrusion of violent death.

William Shakespeare's 'Romeo + Juliet' is a love story for a generation that can't imagine a future, and this is what sets it off so completely from the teen-star-crossed-lovers films it otherwise resembles. *Rebel Without a Cause* ends with a rehabilitation of the older generation, and a hope for better communication. *West Side Story* ends with Maria's passionate denunciation of the cycle of violence the gangs have been perpetuating. Zeffirelli's film focuses on the final reconciliation of the two households, who walk together in a moving and orderly funeral procession. In all of these films, the Romeo and Juliet characters are ahead of their time; their love points the way to a better future, a new unity beyond the greed, anger and factionalism of their parents' world. But Luhrmann's Romeo and Juliet live after their time. The film repeatedly associates them, not with the future, but with the past. At the Capulets' masked ball, the future is represented by the smiling, smug Dave Paris, the young business school type, who is costumed as an astronaut. Romeo and Juliet, by contrast, are dressed as a knight in shining armour and a Botticelli angel; costumes that look nostalgically back to a cultural past that could embrace their love. Throughout the film they wear simple clothes in blue, silver and white, making them appear watery and spectral amid their gaudy surroundings. It is only in their timeless underwater world that they can shut out the frenetic present of Verona Beach and sustain their love.

Accordingly, the tomb scene is completely isolated and self-contained, intruded upon by neither Paris nor the Friar. Romeo, dodging police helicopters and machine guns, breaks into the church where Juliet's body is laid, and suddenly he is in another world. Hundreds of candles and blue neon crosses give the tomb a shimmering aquatic glow, as if Romeo and Juliet were indeed underwater. This beautiful refuge is the scene of the film's final, cruelly cynical trick on the self-immersed young lovers. Juliet stirs and wakes, smiling to see Romeo with her; too wrapped up in his grief to notice, he drinks the poison just as her hand reaches up to stroke his cheek. The device of having Juliet awake before Romeo dies was common in the eighteenth century, and was apparently used in a 1916 film with Theda Bara.[18] None the less, its effect here is profoundly shocking and painful. For a few tortured seconds the lovers try to cling together in life, staring at each other in horrified realization. Kenneth Rothwell aptly describes these cruel moments as breaking through the romantic isolation Luhrmann has previously afforded his lovers: 'In an ironic way the last scene critiques the narcissism the movie might elsewhere be seeming to uphold.'[19]

Alone with Romeo's corpse, Juliet sobs for a moment, then pulls out his pistol. She fumbles slightly with the hammer, which makes a frighteningly loud click in the silent tomb, then puts the gun to her head and shoots herself. After the double suicide, the watery romantic isolation of the lovers returns for a poignant moment. The last phrases of Wagner's 'Liebestod' from *Tristan und Isolde* play during an overhead shot of the bodies surrounded by a sea of candles. Once again Romeo and Juliet are associated with a mythic medieval past of chivalry and courtly love, rather than the raucous present of the rest of the film. Juliet's violent suicide is washed over by the ecstatic love-death of Isolde, swooning in bliss on the body of her lover: 'ertrinken, versinken – unbewußt – höchste Lust!' ('To drown, to sink – unconscious – highest pleasure!').[20] As the camera floats over the entwined lovers, the film cuts to a brief montage of their happy moments together, concluding with a slow-motion shot of them kissing under water. As the Wagner fades from the soundtrack, the screen whites out, then resolves to a bleak image of two shrouded corpses on hospital gurneys being loaded into an ambulance.

The film ends with this harsh and reductive scene. The Capulet and Montague parents, emerging from their limos in front of the church, look stunned and bleary in the pre-dawn light, but make no move towards each other. Luhrmann's film offers neither the orderly reconciliation of Zeffirelli's ending, nor the distancing irony of Michael Bogdanov's stage version, where the families continued their rivalry in the competing public relations gestures of erecting golden statues of their dead children. The deaths of Luhrmann's Romeo and Juliet bring no resolution; they become merely another lurid image for a media-besotted culture, body-bagged victims in a grainy news video, as the film returns to the newscast framework of the opening. The bland anchorwoman recites the closing words of the epilogue, then moves on to the next story as the TV screen dissolves in static snow.

*

The grim conclusion of *William Shakespeare's 'Romeo + Juliet'* signals a fatalistic acceptance of the triumph of the postmodern world of Verona Beach. There is no refuge for the lovers, even in romantic death; their idyll is interrupted, reduced, commodified, turned into televised spectacle. Yet Luhrmann's final pessimism seems to smack slightly of bad faith, given the film's involvement in a whole range of mediated commercial practices. Unlike previous Shakespeare films,

William Shakespeare's 'Romeo + Juliet' relates not only back to an authorizing text but forward and outward to a whole network of cultural and commercial enterprises: merchandising tie-ins, two soundtrack albums, a screenplay/text edition and an interactive CD-ROM. The official Twentieth-Century Fox website features a 'Verona Beach Visitor's Guide' instructing users on 'what to wear, what to buy, and what to drive', as well as pop-psychology character biographies condemning the older generation: 'Lady Capulet really blew it and got into a co-dependency thing, while her husband abused her daughter, much to his later regret.'[21] At the UK *Romeo + Juliet* website, 'You can choose an alternate future for the star-cross'd lovers or go to Verona Beach school to learn more about the film and the play.'[22] Another website includes 230 'Signs that you are obsessed with *Romeo + Juliet*', among them:

7. You spend hours thinking up R+J merchandise – 'Montague and Capulet guns', 'Romeo and Juliet clothing line', 'The "Fair Verona" play-set (dolls included)' ...
10. You used to check the Internet everyday to find out when the second soundtrack was coming out.
11. You suddenly have an obsession with angels, Catholic imagery and bright Hawaiian shirts.[23]

The distinctly commercial and materialist aspect of many responses to the film suggests that its young viewers were attracted largely by fashion, as well as by its heart-throb stars. The film was immensely successful with the teen audiences it carefully courted (test-marketers nervously asked young viewers 'whether the Shakespeare language in the film bothered you or not').[24] *William Shakespeare's 'Romeo + Juliet'* did well at the 1997 MTV Movie Awards, with Danes winning for Best Female Performance, along with nominations for Best Male Performance, Best On-Screen Duo, Best Song and Best Kiss. Peter Newman quoted a number of teenage responses in *Shakespeare Bulletin*, and some show a degree of sophistication: 'the scenes flip-flop from extravagance and grace to poverty and despair. Luhrmann uses every opportunity to display the tumult and passion of teenagers' lives'. But many teenagers seemed to approach the film at a lowest common denominator level: 'Orlando DiCaprio [*sic*] is hot!'; 'It was almost like watching an MTV video'; 'I thought it was going to be a girly film, but there was a lot of killing – that was cool'.[25] Needless to say, this response delighted Fox executives. 'From the very first screening, we knew it would attract younger audiences,' said Tom Sherak, head of distribution, after the film grossed a chart-topping $11.6 million in its opening weekend. 'If you don't believe this remains the greatest love story ever told, look at these numbers.'[26]

These somewhat depressing responses to the film do not necessarily invalidate Luhrmann's achievement. *William Shakespeare's 'Romeo + Juliet'* is a flagship Shakespeare film for the new millennium in part because it is able to assimilate and exploit the materials of contemporary culture, while keeping them in a relationship of provocative tension with the Shakespearean source. The lurid contemporary setting and the ageless love story criticize and comment on each other in ways that bring both into sharper relief. Like several of the films discussed in this volume, *William Shakespeare's 'Romeo + Juliet'* reinvents the conventions of Shakespearean filmmaking in a self-consciously postmodern way. Like Adrian Noble's *A Midsummer Night's Dream*, discussed by Mark Thornton Burnett, it interrogates the mythic status of the text by reframing it within a complex network of cultural associations. Like Christine Edzard's *As You Like It*, discussed by Amelia Marriette, it uses a contemporary urban setting to reverse audience expectations of Shakespearean 'prettiness' and to engage, in a limited way, with modern social concerns. Like Richard Loncraine's *Richard III*, discussed by Stephen Buhler, it quotes a range of cinematic styles and genres to create unsettling juxtapositions between different cultural modes.[27] And, as is the case with *Richard III*, I believe that the juxtapositions in *William Shakespeare's 'Romeo + Juliet'* – of teen films, MTV culture, various Hollywood genres and courtly romance – go beyond mere playful pastiche or ahistorical nostalgia.

Frederic Jameson, in his critiques of postmodernism, attacks what he calls 'the nostalgia film' for presenting a pastiche of past representational modes that is essentially detached from history.[28] According to Jameson, films like *American Graffiti*, *Chinatown* and *Body Heat* are not about a real historical past, but instead merely recreate the look and feel of existing representations of the past. By depending on an intertextual pastiche of other cultural productions, postmodernism has become divorced from history and from the real, 'as though we have become incapable of achieving aesthetic representations of our own current experience'.[29] *William Shakespeare's 'Romeo + Juliet'* seems in many ways to be susceptible to this critique. Not only does it exploit a whole range of cultural styles and *clichés*, but its use of teen film archetypes suggests a strong connection to the era Jameson most condemns as an artificial past, the Eisenhower 1950s of *Rebel Without a Cause*. Yet the intertextuality of *William Shakespeare's 'Romeo + Juliet'* goes beyond being a mere self-referential hodgepodge; Luhrmann confronts the social realities as well as the media modes of the new millennium. As Barbara Hodgdon has pointed out in a compelling paper, *William Shakespeare's 'Romeo + Juliet'* points to how 'there seem to be no answers, fictional or real, religious or legal, to gender, ethnic and class differences and conflicts, to generational strife, or boys with guns'.[30] The film's unresolved ending, with the lovers' timeless idyll reduced to a grim TV news item, is an honest response to the culture of the new millennium. The nostalgia with which Luhrmann enshrouds his Romeo and Juliet inevitably gives way to the violent and media-crazed culture of which they are, necessarily, already a part.

Notes

1. *William Shakespeare's 'Romeo + Juliet'*, directed by Baz Luhrmann, Twentieth-Century Fox, 1996. The film's title is noteworthy, not only for its claims to literary legitimacy in invoking the author's name, but for the use of the cross in place of 'and': both the standard formula for youthful love inscriptions ('Romeo + Juliet = Love 4 Ever') and an allusion to the Catholic iconography that dominates the production design. The cross thus functions as a small emblem of the film's juxtaposition of contemporary and historical sign-systems.
2. John Lewis, *The Road to Romance and Ruin: Teen Films and Youth Culture* (New York: Routledge, 1992), p. 3.
3. The story of doomed young lovers battling parental or societal opposition has been repeatedly reinvented by Hollywood in fascinating ways, from melodramas like *Splendour in the Grass* or Zeffirelli's *Endless Love* to crime odysseys like Terence Malick's classic *Badlands* or the Tarantino-scripted *True Romance*. (The archetype is also frequently recast in the comic mode, as in *Pretty in Pink*, *Say Anything* and their ilk, or the much darker *Heathers*.) The staggering success of Jim Cameron's *Titanic* must be blamed, in part, on the popularity of the *Romeo and Juliet* archetype, as well as on Leonardo DiCaprio's appeal as a teen tragic hero.
4. The treatment of the play as a contemporary socio-economic parable, in which the young lovers reject the materialist values of their parents' generation, became fairly common on the stage, most notably in Michael Bogdanov's 1986 modern-dress production for the Royal Shakespeare Company, which in many ways anticipated Luhrmann's film.
5. Michael Barson and Steven Heller, *Teenage Confidential: An Illustrated History of the American Teen* (San Francisco: Chronicle Books, 1998), pp. 88–9.
6. Baz Luhrmann, quoted in Twentieth-Century Fox promotional material, http//www.clairedanes.com/rjintro.html.
7. *Romeo and Juliet*, ed. Brian Gibbons (London and New York: Methuen, 1980), V.i.24. All further references appear in the text.

8. Race functions in the film in a somewhat ambiguous way. The Montagues and Capulets are plainly represented as Anglo and Latino, but Gloria Capulet (Diane Venora) and Juliet (Claire Danes) have fair hair and skin and do not use the Hispanic accents adopted by the other Capulet actors, including the Italian-American Paul Sorvino (Fulgencio Capulet) and the English Miriam Margolyes (Nurse). The character of Escalus, who mediates between the two households, is represented as an African-American police chief, Captain Prince; his kinsman, Mercutio (Harold Perrineau), is also African-American, but his other kinsman, the Governor's son, Dave Paris, is white (Paul Rudd). The other African-Americans in the film are not involved in the feud, and may be viewed as sympathetic to the lovers: they include the newscaster who frames the story (Edwina Moore), the diva who sings Romeo and Juliet's love ballad (Des'ree) and the boy chorister who sings at their wedding (Quindon Tarver). I am indebted here to the comments of Margo Hendricks and Barbara Hodgdon (in Hodgdon's 'Totally DiCaptivated: Shakespeare's Boys Meet the Chick Flick', a paper first presented at the International Shakespeare Conference, Stratford-upon-Avon, August 1998).

9. See Steven Conner, *Postmodernist Culture: An Introduction to Theories of the Contemporary* (Oxford: Basil Blackwell, 1989), pp. 73–81.

10. See Jay Carr, *Boston Globe*; Roger Ebert, *Chicago Sun-Times*; and Janet Maslin, *New York Times*: all 1 November 1996.

11. Luhrmann is explicit about his use of cinematic conventions: 'In fact, what we've done was set the film in the world of the movies. You will notice that the film changes in style very dramatically, echoing very recognizable film genres, from Busby Berkeley to 70s' naturalism to even European expressionism. These severe changes of style refer to cinematic worlds or looks or ideas that audiences are familiar with on some level; using them to construct this "created world" will hopefully produce an environment that can accommodate a stylized language and make it easier for the audience to receive this heightened language'. Baz Luhrmann, quoted in Twentieth-Century Fox promotional material, http://www.clairedanes.com/rjintro.html.

12. See Susan Hayward, 'Postmodernism', in *Key Concepts in Cinema Studies* (London: Routledge, 1996), pp. 259–72.

13. Baz Luhrmann, quoted in Twentieth-Century Fox promotional material, http://www.clairedanes.com/rjintro.html.

14. Martin sought to imitate 'the heightened reality of a Fellini film; the way that Fellini can have this incredible dream sequence in a particular situation that has an exceptional reality about it. They are always extraordinarily well observed'. Quoted in Twentieth-Century Fox promotional material, http://www.clairedanes.com/rjintro.html. The numerous helicopter shots of the monumental Christ statue overlooking the city may be a homage to the opening of Fellini's *La Dolce Vita*.

15. One such allusion – a building-site hoarding reading 'retail'd to posterity by Montague construction' – deserves special mention. It derives from a scene in *Richard III* (ed. Antony Hammond [London and New York: Routledge, 1990]) where young Prince Edward, about to be sent to the Tower and his death, innocently discusses the history of the building with his treacherous uncles, Richard and Buckingham. Assured by Buckingham

that the Tower's foundation by Julius Caesar is 'upon record', Edward goes on to moralize upon the importance of truth having an existence independent of historical evidence:

> *Prince.* But say, my gracious lord, it were not register'd,
> Methinks the truth should live from age to age,
> As 'twere retail'd to all posterity,
> Even to the general all-ending day.
> *Rich.* [*Aside*] So wise so young, they say, do never live long.
> *Prince.* What say you, uncle?
> *Rich.* I say, without characters fame lives long.
>
> (III.i.75–81)

By using 'retail'd' in its modern capitalist sense, and applying the doomed prince's words to one of Montague's hastily erected skyscrapers rather than the Tower of London, Luhrmann's film neatly pinpoints a postmodern world of transience and consumption, where truth lives not from age to age, nor even from minute to minute, but only in a Jamesonian perpetual present.

16. In the introduction to the published screenplay, Luhrmann performs the common directorial strategy of enlisting Shakespeare to justify his approach: 'Shakespeare's plays touched everyone, from the street sweeper to the Queen of England. He was a rambunctious, sexy, violent, entertaining storyteller. We're trying to make this movie rambunctious, sexy, violent, and entertaining the way Shakespeare might have if he had been a filmmaker.' Baz Luhrmann, 'A Note from Baz Luhrmann', in *William Shakespeare's 'Romeo & Juliet': The Contemporary Film, the Classic Play* (New York: Bantam Doubleday, 1996), p. i.

17. Luhrmann, *William Shakespeare's 'Romeo & Juliet': The Contemporary Film, the Classic Play*, p. 32.

18. Kenneth Rothwell, 'The Luhrmann *Romeo and Juliet*: Yesterday and Today, from Nickelodeon to Megaplex', p. 8, a paper prepared for the Shakespeare and Film Seminar, annual meeting of the Shakespeare Association of America, Washington D.C., March 1997.

19. Rothwell, 'The Luhrmann *Romeo and Juliet*', p. 8.

20. Richard Wagner, *Tristan und Isolde*, 1865. The film uses a recording by Leontyne Price.

21. http://www.romeoandjuliet.com.

22. http://www.geocities.com/Hollywood/Lot/1767/links.html.

23. http://www.geocities.com/Hollywood/9251/signs.html.

24. Quoted in Lynda E. Boose and Richard Burt, 'Totally Clueless?: Shakespeare Goes Hollywood in the 1990s', in Lynda E. Boose and Richard Burt (eds), *Shakespeare, the Movie: Popularizing the Plays on Film, TV, and Video* (London and New York: Routledge, 1997), p. 18.

25. Peter Newman, 'Luhrmann's Young Lovers as Seen by Their Peers', *Shakespeare Bulletin*, 15:3 (1997), pp. 36–7. The four comments quoted came respectively from L. A. and C. L., both aged 15, and M.S., aged 14.

26. Quoted in Judy Brennan, 'Where Art Thou? In First Place', *Los Angeles Times*, 4 November 1996.

27. See also James N. Loehlin, '"Top of the World, Ma": *Richard III* and Cinematic Convention', in Boose and Burt (eds), *Shakespeare, the Movie*,

pp. 67–79.

28. Frederic Jameson, 'Postmodernism and Consumer Society', in E. Ann Kaplan (ed.), *Postmodernism and Its Discontents* (London: Verso, 1988), pp. 18–20 and *Postmodernism: The Cultural Logic of Late Capitalism* (Durham, NC: Duke University Press, 1991), pp. 19–20.
29. Jameson, 'Postmodernism and Consumer Society', p. 20.
30. Hodgdon, 'Totally DiCaptivated'.

9

'Either for tragedy, comedy': Attitudes to *Hamlet* in Kenneth Branagh's *In the Bleak Midwinter* and *Hamlet*

Emma Smith

During the mid-1990s, the British actor-director Kenneth Branagh, in association with Castle Rock Entertainment, made two films based on *Hamlet*. *In the Bleak Midwinter* (1995) is a low-budget, feel-good comedy set among a troupe of actors rehearsing and performing *Hamlet* in a disused church. *Hamlet* (1997) is the fullest version of the play ever committed to celluloid, running at over four hours and stuffed with special effects and star cameos. While on the surface the two films could hardly be more different, they are, in fact, intimately connected. Both films have a particular *fin-de-siècle* self-consciousness about their Shakespearean material: explicitly in the case of *In the Bleak Midwinter*, implicitly in the case of *Hamlet*. A close analysis of *In the Bleak Midwinter* reveals some of the ways in which it anticipates and allegorizes the contemporaneous pre-production travails of Branagh's ambitious *Hamlet*, at the same time as it mediates the broader relationship which has vexed a century of Shakespeare on film, that between theatre and cinema. Most crucially, it is also an attempt at a scapegoat, diverting what is potentially ridiculous and laughable about the play itself, siphoning off *Hamlet*'s dangerous proximity to comedy, and leaving the film of *Hamlet* as generically pure and serious high art. Together, the two films recapitulate a century's filmic encounter with the *Hamlet* play, an engagement perpetually pulled between deferential homage and irreverent parody. As Branagh admitted in an interview, 'When people ask, "Why do *Hamlet*?", I say all the answers are contained in *Bleak Midwinter*.'[1]

Serious, 'straight' *Hamlet*s on film often, it seems, need to have their comic supplements. The pretensions of the play teeter on the brink of burlesque – long, histrionic speeches, acts of rash, almost casual violence – and, in order to retain its serious character, this potential laughter needs to be diverted. The tradition of Shakespearean burlesque from the eighteenth- and nineteenth-century theatre has been adopted and extended by its successor, the cinema. In the earliest days of British Shakespearean film, for example, Cecil Hepworth's aspiring *Hamlet* of 1913, featuring the recently knighted stage actor, Sir Johnston Forbes-Robertson, was followed by his parody animations, *Oh'phelia* and *'Amlet* (1919). The silent era, with its appetite for burlesque comedy, actually saw more *Hamlet* parodies than straight versions, including *When Hungry Hamlet Fled* (US, 1915), *Pimple as Hamlet* (GB, 1916), *Colonel Heeza Liar Plays Hamlet* (US, 1916) and *Hamlet Made Over* (US, 1916). More recently, Laurence Olivier's *Hamlet* (1948) and, more obliquely, Mel Gibson's action *Hamlet* (1990) were parodied by Arnold Schwarzenegger in *Last Action Hero* (1993). The familiarity of the play's central premise, the resonances of its high declamatory acting style and the recognizability of its most famous lines make it ripe for parody. Even its length, which was a special feature of Branagh's film of *Hamlet*, has been a source of much humour in, for example, Tom Stoppard's *A Fifteen-Minute Hamlet* and the Reduced Shakespeare Company's bravura five-minute stage *Hamlet*, speeded up to 45 seconds, and then, in a fine spoof of the reversing trick encore of the early cinema projectionists, replayed backwards.[2] Just as Hamlet has been a prime role for the greatest actors of the century, so *Hamlet* burlesques have exercised the greatest comedians. Alongside Henry Irving, Laurence Olivier, John Gielgud, Ralph Richardson and Derek Jacobi must therefore be allowed Buster Keaton, Eric Morecambe, Tommy Cooper, Les Dawson and Benny Hill: every serious actor is flanked by his comedic counterpart. What is potentially comic about the serious role is drawn off by the parody, and the parody is funny because it identifies and magnifies those elements of the ridiculous which productions of the play must attempt to suppress. Much of the laughter at *Hamlet* spoofs arises from audience recognition and relief, but, in presenting the play as a source of comedy, parodies betray an uncertainty about how to approach canonical high art in an age of ironic aesthetic detachment.

Branagh's approaches to *Hamlet* in the 1990s combine the two strains of classical theatrical acting and pantomimic burlesque, bringing previously bifurcated traditions into postmodern collision. *In the Bleak Midwinter* serves as the comic forerunner, purging the play of its ridiculous elements in order to preserve *Hamlet* as epic, sober and permanent. Whereas *In the Bleak Midwinter* as a film is as transient as the ragged *Hamlet* it describes, the film of *Hamlet* has altogether more weighty aspirations: the home-made posters outside the church where the actors are scratching together their version of the play contrast sharply with the incised lettering of *Hamlet* in the film, as the ephemera of theatrical performance is set against the monumental permanence of film. Branagh made *Hamlet*, it seems, with an eye to posterity, to the new century, but subsequence and posteriority are the predominant modes of *In the Bleak Midwinter*'s bitter-sweet homage to repertory theatre and black-and-white cinematography.

No parody can ever be an integral, distinct aesthetic experience, as by definition it is forever in dialogue with the parodied, only gaining meaning through tacit comparison. *In the Bleak Midwinter*'s primary host text is, of course, Shakespeare's play, but in retrospect it can be seen to achieve its full signification in relation to Branagh's *Hamlet* film. Many of the jokes in *In the Bleak Midwinter* resonate archly in the context of the subsequent *Hamlet*. First among these is the relation to the text. Branagh's *Hamlet* was sold as the fullest text of the play ever filmed – the video was marketed, in a tongue-in-cheek allusion to a context both cinematic and textual, as 'the writer's cut' – and its length was one of the main topics of interest in its reviews and reception. 'Other actors', one journalist observed in the flurry of newspaper interest around the film's British *première* early in 1997, 'have had a stab at *Hamlet* on film. But only Branagh's includes every line written by Shakespeare, without excision of sub-plots or minor characters'. This was echoed in most of the notices, which were divided between praising the film's claims to be a definitive version and criticizing its duration as an unwieldy imposition on cinema scheduling.[3] *In the Bleak Midwinter* explicitly addresses the issue of the play's length. Joe, the director-Prince, begins to tell his actors about his vision of the play: 'I see it as a very dark play.' The irrepressibly camp Terry (John Sessions), playing Gertrude, interrupts: 'I see it as a very long play. Sally Scissors is going to appear, we hope'.[4] Joe concedes that he has 'a lot of cuts' but that the first stage of their rehearsal process will be 'to read the whole thing'. 'Oh great', interjects the gloomily acerbic Henry (Richard Briers), cast as Claudius: 'We've only got ten days' rehearsal but let's spend fifteen hours reading the whole bloody thing on day one'. Tom (Nicholas Farrell) plays Laertes and badgers the director about the 'four key lines' which have been cut from his part – and ironically, in Branagh's film, the uncut role is played by the director, Michael Maloney.

The fear that *Hamlet* is actually rather tedious pervades the difficult period of rehearsal. Joe's sister, Molly, a local teacher, has arranged for him to put on a play, but she does not know what he has chosen. Her hope for 'something Christmassy – a comedy' is frustrated, and she is horrified at his choice because she does not see that it will attract a young audience: 'Great. Oh hello, kids. Do stop watching Mighty Morphin Power Rangers and come and watch a four hundred-year-old play about a depressed aristocrat. I mean, something you can really relate to.' A populist appeal to an audience is a prime consideration of the stage *Hamlet* in *In the Bleak Midwinter*, but fears that Branagh's film version was compromising on Shakespeare in order to appease a young cinema-going audience were prevalent in press reports about the film. These were fuelled by the publication of the screenplay in advance of the film's British *première*, in which Branagh's interpolations in Shakespeare's play, particularly the comment about Claudius going 'into Norman Schwartzkopf mode', were criticized as 'crass'.[5] Branagh's attempts to draw parallels with contemporary culture in his mediation of Shakespeare's play in print are an implicit rebuttal of Joe, who says the unmentionable, but seemingly unavoidable, truth: 'Finally it's Shakespeare, and nobody's interested.' So, while the final climactic performance of *Hamlet* in *In the Bleak Midwinter* is apparently a personal and theatrical success, the film itself seems nervous of overloading its audience with the play. *Hamlet* emerges from this film as some set-pieces, some famous speeches, a swiftly edited and fast-moving 'greatest hits' of fighting and ranting in front of a rapt audience. By contrast, in order to get support for his own film of *Hamlet*, however, Branagh's confidence in his, and the play's, ability to sustain an audience's interest must be unwavering. By allowing doubts about the accessibility and relevance of *Hamlet* to surface in, and to be allayed by, *In the Bleak Midwinter*, Branagh attempts to evacuate a cultural and a personal space for his self-confident and summative presentation of the play on film.

While all its cast experience doubts about the project, *In the Bleak Midwinter* ultimately affirms the relevance of Shakespeare's play in two ways. First, it uses the script of the play as a way of reflecting and resolving conflicts in the cast's offstage lives. Often these correspondences and echoes are unexpected and painful. Rehearsing the 'closet scene', Terry finds his son Hamlet's recriminations too aching to bear, and he later confesses to his unlikely friend, Henry, that he himself has an estranged son who is ashamed of his father's lifestyle and profession. Nina (Julia Sawalha) is urged, as Ophelia, to express her character's sense of sadness and loss at the death of Polonius, and she draws on her own experience of bereavement to do so, until her tears are all too real. Through the trials and frictions of rehearsal, the cast establishes new and poignant relationships, all of which are resolved through the final show. Here Nina's distant father, the mother Carnforth (Gerard Horan) always felt to be disappointed in him, and Tom's son all appear in the audience and claim their respective families in a moment of *rapprochement* achieved through performance. *Hamlet* is revealed as a play with cathartic powers. As Nina tells Joe: 'we needed this play'. The cosy consequence of the experience has been to heal and to reunite, co-opting Shakespeare to the library of 1990s' self-help and self-fulfilment. Strikingly, it is precisely these same popular psychological valences that Branagh wants to invoke for his own *Hamlet* film: 'I find [Hamlet's] struggle, his journey through the play, feels very contemporary. When I go to book shops, I see shelves full of "How to love yourself". "How to help yourself", "Seventeen ways to discover the baby in you" – we're forever looking for the secret, some way of accepting that life is a rocky road, a bit of a tricky business.'[6]

Second, *In the Bleak Midwinter* validates the unlikely choice of *Hamlet* through its ultimate performance of the play, asserting that some kind of community in a fractured and depressed area can be achieved through theatre. The earnest Molly has high hopes for the troupe's play in a village symbolically named Hope, where 'there is nowhere for people to go': 'we need this place to give people a focus. Prove to the council that there is a community worth maintaining – that there is a community.' As the doors open for the performance, a carefully representative audience files into the church and settles itself among the cardboard people manufactured by Fadge (Celia Imrie), the dizzy designer, to pad out the crowd. As the camera cuts to reaction shots at key moments in the play, their excitement at the spectacle is clear. *Hamlet* is exciting. The power of the play and of live theatre to re-establish community bonds is affirmed. It is, however, only a momentary victory in the middle of winter: the lights and warmth of Christmas as a fleeting reprieve from the dark and cold. The sense of communal purpose and convergence experienced both by the cast and its audience is only temporary. The days of the repertory theatre are gone, and the film's profound nostalgia serves only to emphasize their passing. In an outburst of misery after a particularly trying day's rehearsal, Joe rails against the futility of the whole enterprise: 'Churches close and theatres close every week because, finally, people don't want them'. When Terry and Henry talk about Henry Irving and the great days of British theatre, it is with a regretful awareness that they have been left behind. The ironically jaunty background music asks 'Why must the show go on?': the first performance of the Hope *Hamlet* is a terminus. Its ultimate irony is that this paean to live theatre is, of course, not live theatre but film. One of *In the Bleak Midwinter*'s naggingly implicit questions – and one in which it is absolutely enmeshed – is the role of cinema in the decline of theatre. It is significant that a self-conscious reference to photography sparks real fury from Tom. Vernon (Mark Hadfield) is recording the process of rehearsal on his video camera, in a short sequence which prompts questions about the film itself: 'Why does everybody have to see behind the scenes these days? What happened to all the bloody mystery?' For Branagh, it seems that demystification of the theatrical illusion of *Hamlet* is the province of *In the Bleak Midwinter*, with its comic scenes of warm-up exercises and the slapstick of actors tumbling about the makeshift stage. It is the film of *Hamlet* which maintains the mystery, with its use of special effects and trick photography, and with its period of rehearsal carefully tucked away behind the scenes. Even this, though, is revealed and commodified through the film diary appended to the published screenplay. It is a curious feature of the late twentieth-century cultural fascination with costume drama, including Shakespeare, that such effort should be put into creating period illusion, at the same time as documentaries and books on 'the making of' show the cast wearing trainers under their farmers' smocks or tons of mud being layered onto tarmac roads.

In the Bleak Midwinter's relationship with its voluminous companion piece, *Hamlet*, is a troubled one, as Shakespearean film's uncertain relationship with its theatrical past is imperfectly worked out by *In the Bleak Midwinter*. The film romanticizes the theatrical experience, both for a cast and an audience, while itself eschewing it. It also romanticizes *Hamlet*, while at the same time suggesting that what is most interesting and affecting is not *Hamlet* itself but the interactions of the ordinary, flawed people trying to rehearse it. *Hamlet* is presented in a kind of shorthand, in contrast to the longhand approach of Branagh's film of the play. *In the Bleak Midwinter* cannot rely on the entertainment value of the play itself, and it is only a belief in this that can sustain a four-hour filmic *Hamlet*. *In the Bleak Midwinter* pits Hollywood as the enemy of small-scale and sincere theatre: it tempts as the moral and artistic opposite of the worthy ensemble-playing in the church, even while Branagh himself is working within Hollywood to secure funding for his film of *Hamlet*. Joe is beguiled by his agent (Joan Collins), who has scooped for him a deal in a new science fiction film trilogy, on the condition that he fly to America immediately, leaving his fellow-actors in *Hamlet* in the lurch on their opening night. *In the Bleak Midwinter* is uneasily caught between parody and hagiography, or, rather, its version of parody is ultimately a vehicle for reification. On the one hand, the film treats the play of *Hamlet* as an 'absurdly solemn prism through which to view the world'.[7] Tom voices this extreme position in his audition: 'Hamlet isn't just Hamlet. Oh no. Hamlet is me. Hamlet is Bosnia. Hamlet is my grandmother. Hamlet is this desk. Hamlet is everything you've ever thought about.' The film makes it clear that these claims are laughable, yet, in his publicity interviews for the release of his *Hamlet* film, Branagh himself expressed a similar sense of the play's fullness: 'It's marvellous. It's ridiculous. Its meaningful. It's meaningless.'[8] Claims audiences were allowed to laugh at as preposterous in *In the Bleak Midwinter* are here packaged as insight and justification.

The success of the production of *Hamlet* in *In the Bleak Midwinter* thus presents a fantasy, a wish-fulfilment scenario for the relevance, the success and the appreciation of the big-budget film of *Hamlet* which, in retrospect, is always in the background. But it also rehearses the anxieties attendant on such a challenging project. Perhaps nobody will want to come and see it. Perhaps the money will run out. Perhaps Shakespeare isn't relevant or accessible or interesting. Although Branagh is credited as director and screenwriter of *In the Bleak Midwinter*, his physical absence from the film allows Joe to function as a kind of substitute or projection. Joe's intermittent doubts that his dream will ever be realized serve as a displacement of the unspeakable taint of failure attaching itself to Branagh's next production. Writing in the introduction to the screenplay of *In the Bleak Midwinter*, Branagh admitted, 'there is much of me in Joe', adding a quick, defensive parenthesis, '(although not the terrible experience of a year's unemployment)'.[9]

There are many indicators that *In the Bleak Midwinter* is intended to be read as a version of autobiography – of both Branagh himself and of his filmed *Hamlet*. Like Branagh, when he played a full-text Hamlet for the Royal Shakespeare Company, the actor-director Joe is thirty-three years old – and this correspondence identifies Joe's production of *Hamlet* with Branagh's stage experience rather than with his contemporaneous work on the play for the big screen. Like Joe, who demands that his actors develop their characters from their own experiences, Branagh described his 'full emotional commitment to the characters, springing from the belief that they can be understood in direct, accessible relation to modern life'.[10] Joe tells his sister how he saw the play when he was fifteen, and it changed his life. This information is also relayed by Branagh in his introduction to his screenplay of *Hamlet*: 'It set my heart and my head racing … I was fifteen … I believe that much of what has followed in my life was affected by that experience.'[11] For Branagh and Joe, the production of *Hamlet* is a long-held ambition: in both cases, it is their commitment to the play that drives the action. Joe admits that much is riding on the success of the project: 'I did [fail] once before. Different show, same bull at a gate mentality, complete cock-up. All money lost, all confidence lost with it. The day it went bust, my *fiancée* left me for another man.' It is hard not to see a parallel with Branagh, whose previous film, *Mary Shelley's 'Frankenstein'* (1994), had been panned by the critics and coincided with his public break-up with his actor-wife, Emma Thompson. *In the Bleak Midwinter* is preoccupied by cashflow, from the small loan Joe squeezes from his agent, to Fadge's sale of her beloved van to pay the actors' rent. Joe admits that his budgeting has been based on a wholly unrealistic prediction of box office takings: Branagh's own financial planning relied on an expectation of returns at the box office. 'Can Hamlet be a commercial success?' mused one newspaper report, and, in his introduction to the screenplay, Branagh admitted that persuading the Hollywood film companies to finance his dream was a slow process: 'My attempts to finance a film version [of *Hamlet*] had been in motion since the opening of *Henry V*.'[12] Even the look of the two versions of the play is similar: both Hamlets fight in shirt and braces, and the same actors recur, although not in the same roles. Michael Maloney is Hamlet and Laertes, Richard Briers plays Claudius and Polonius. Both films are nostalgic: for the heyday of repertory theatre and village community in the melancholic *In the Bleak Midwinter*; for the pomp and nobility of a bygone age symbolized by the late imperial costuming of *Hamlet*. Both films are set in winter: the snowy winterscapes are borrowed from an earlier, more innocent age and have a distinctly *fin-de-siècle* air of wistfulness and regret. This mood is peculiarly appropriate to the theme of retrospection in the play (itself, of course, a *fin-de-siècle* cultural production) and to the broader cultural context of its late twentieth-century reworkings.

If *In the Bleak Midwinter* serves to divert and displace some of the obstacles – for audiences as well as for the director – to a successful film of *Hamlet*, this function is also provided by a television documentary which was transmitted on commercial British television to coincide with the release of Branagh's *Hamlet*. Again, the uncertainty of tone which dogs theatrical Hamlets is much in evidence, here given a postmodern twist. *In Search of Hamlet with Jonathan Ross* alludes to a different kind of contemporary Shakespearean cinematic appropriation, the documentary *Looking for Richard* (1996), starring Al Pacino. Ross uses his characteristic chat show format to publicize Branagh's film and the play, with comic appearances by 'Shakespeare' as an unwilling interviewee, revealing, in answer to a question about language from Jack Lemmon, who played Marcellus in the film, 'It all had to sound like bollocks, but actually mean a great deal.' An interview with Richard Briers, ostensibly talking about his role as Polonius, reverted to questions about his long-running role in television's comedy series, *The Good Life*. Viewers were given two telephone numbers to register their preference for 'to be' or 'not to be', and, in an extended parodic masterclass, Kenneth Branagh himself is directed to make a mockery of the soliloquy 'To be or not to be' in a ridiculous accent. Like one of the unlucky hopefuls auditioning in *In the Bleak Midwinter*, Branagh utters the speech through a ventriloquist's dummy. A version of *Hamlet* in the style of American soap opera called 'Dane-Nasty' adds to the catalogue of parodic abbreviations, as does a carefully spliced montage of moments from the Olivier film and from Branagh's film presenting the key iconic scenes and lines in a matter of seconds. Throughout the programme, short clips from the film, showing Hamlet and Ophelia (Kate Winslett) making love, or Gerard Depardieu as Reynaldo, are interspersed with this parodic commentary. *In Search of Hamlet with Jonathan Ross* is a distinctly postmodern televisual product: short montage sequences, heavy on irony and pastiche, and overlayered with a kind of detached knowingness.

The existence of this programme, apparently made with the full backing of Branagh and Castle Rock Entertainment, attests to the same uncertainty about the seriousness of *Hamlet* as was writ large in *In the Bleak Midwinter*. It suggests that the only way to approach what is potentially farcical or grandiose about the four-hour film is bathetically to pre-empt and occupy the parodic territory. As the programme's 'Shakespeare' tells the audience, in a version of Puck's epilogue to *A Midsummer Night's Dream*, 'Twas but meant as harmless frolics, / Not as arty-farty bollocks'. The fear that to take Shakespeare seriously is to be 'arty-farty' pervades the programme, and this unease sits uncomfortably with its ostensible purpose of promoting the longest, and arguably the most earnest, Shakespeare film of the century. Shakespeare's cinematic predominance at the *fin de siècle* has not, it seems, banished doubts about the play's relevance to film audiences, nor has it alleviated the need for apologies and justifications.

For all its grandiose glamour and its aspirations to be definitive, *Hamlet*'s generic instability is enforced, rather than dispersed, by the existence of cinematic parodies and spoofs. Far from cauterizing the play's tendency towards self-parody, *In the Bleak Midwinter* and *In Search of Hamlet* serve to reinforce it, and in doing so, they threaten to bring down the epic filmic edifice of Branagh's *Hamlet*. Branagh's vision of the play, and its role in his own career, are ultimately self-consuming: in place of Polonius' generic division 'either for tragedy, comedy' is the instability of farce, parody and burlesque. Like the ill-fated and bathetic Millennium Dome of London's Greenwich, Branagh's large vision does not have the courage of its own convictions: the heroic *Hamlet* is insistently eroded by the forces of bathos which it has, in part, generated.

Notes

1. David Gritten, 'The Film's the Thing', *The Daily Telegraph*, 11 January 1997.
2. Tom Stoppard, *A Fifteen-Minute Hamlet* (London: French, 1976); Jess Borgeson, Adam Long and Daniel Singer, *The Reduced Shakespeare Co. Presents 'The Compleat Works of Willm Shkspr' (Abridged)* (New York: Applause Books, 1994).
3. Gritten, 'The Film's the Thing'.
4. All quotations are from *In the Bleak Midwinter*, directed by Kenneth Branagh, 1995. The screenplay was published as *A Midwinter's Tale* (New York: Newmarket Press, 1995).
5. Kenneth Branagh, *'Hamlet' by William Shakespeare* (London: Chatto and Windus, 1996), p. 12; Nigel Reynolds, 'Branagh edition of *Hamlet* features Stormin' Norman', *The Daily Telegraph*, 23 November 1996.
6. Hugo Davenport, 'Don't get mad, play Hamlet', *The Daily Telegraph*, 15 February 1997.
7. David Jays, *'In the Bleak Midwinter'*, *Sight and Sound*, 5:12, December 1995, p. 47.
8. Gritten, 'The Film's the Thing'.
9. Branagh, *'A Midwinter's Tale'*, p. vi.
10. Branagh, *'Hamlet'*, pp. vii–viii.
11. Branagh, *'Hamlet'*, p. v.
12. Gritten, 'The Film's the Thing'; Branagh, *'Hamlet'*, p. vii.

10
The End of History and the Last Man:
Kenneth Branagh's *Hamlet*

Julie Sanders

No literary critic reflecting on the events and images of the first week of September 1997 in Great Britain can have failed to make some very Shakespearean connections. On 31 August, Diana, Princess of Wales had died, along with her companion, Dodi Fayed, and their driver, Henri Paul, in a horrific car crash in a Paris road tunnel. A remarkable week of national mourning followed – one which witnessed genuine challenges to the power of the monarchy in Britain, and, in particular, to the public conduct of the House of Windsor. Undoubtedly, the British media were instrumental in orchestrating these challenges, depicting the Royal Family as cold-hearted in their response to the death of a woman they had in previous years, and in full public view, removed from their ranks, stripping her of her royal title and casting aspersions on her psychological stability. In the immediate aftermath of the Princess' death, Queen Elizabeth was forced into several symbolic positions initially resisted by the monarchy, such as making a live address to 'the grieving nation', lowering the Union flag over Buckingham Palace and, perhaps most significantly, allowing a state funeral.

That funeral itself contained one of the most trenchant challenges to the House of Windsor, in the guise of the pulpit oration of Diana's brother, Charles, Earl Spencer, and his assertion of the rights of the Spencer family in overseeing the upbringing of the young princes, William and Harry: 'I pledge that we, your blood family, will do all we can to continue the imaginative and loving way in which you were steering these two exceptional young men, so that their souls are not simply immersed by duty and tradition, but can sing openly.'[1] Subsequently engulfed by much publicized personal scandal, Spencer's motivations for making such a speech have been questioned, but, in the context of the moment (surely crucial in understanding the iconic power of the event), the tribute was one which won the spontaneous applause of those listening. The power of this rival aristocratic family, the Spencers, was felt to be so strong at that moment in history that, on the day of the funeral itself, Elaine Showalter had claimed in *The Guardian*: 'Make no mistake; this is the defining moment of the *fin de siècle* monarchy ... As in Shakespeare's plays, a new dawn is signalled when a new dynasty moves in. Symbolically now, Prince William represents the House of Spencer; a new beginning for a new millennium.'[2] In retrospect, such claims may appear far-fetched, but Earl Spencer's dramatization of his relationship with his sister in that funeral oration certainly brought to mind two specific characters from one Shakespearean play, *Hamlet*. In his depiction of Diana and himself as devoted siblings, united in their youth, but now torn prematurely asunder by the sister's untimely death (that sister the spurned lover of an heir to the throne, and the brother forced to deal very publicly with his grief and anger), Spencer recalled for many the story of Ophelia and Laertes, not least the latter's own melodramatic funeral declaration: 'I tell thee, churlish priest, / A minist'ring angel shall my sister be / When thou liest howling.'[3]

The newspapers of that September week and the days following Diana's funeral had evoked several parallels with Ophelia, not least when remarking upon the 'maimed rites' (V.i.212), at least as originally planned, of the event.[4] Both women were presented as victims of patriarchal culture, forced by the unnatural pressures of their lives into psychological instability and self-harm. Of course, it is important to register the connections between Spencer's mythologizing of his sister as 'Diana the hunted' (playing on the associations of her name with the forest-dwelling goddess-hunter), his claims to her memory (and indeed her children) and Laertes' own claims to emotional and familial rights over his sister – physically contested with Hamlet over her corpse in the play. But this is not an essay about direct connections between *Hamlet* and Diana's funeral. Instead, I am employing a narrative of that event, in a self-consciously anecdotal fashion, in order to indicate the way in which Shakespeare seems inextricably tied up with the presentation and understanding of monarchy in the last decade of this millennium. In the process, I want to argue that, in an oddly prescient way (since it was on release in British cinemas in the months preceding Diana's death), some striking intertextual links between Kenneth Branagh's 1997 film of *Hamlet* and this seminal cultural moment might be found.

I

John Taverner's 'Song for Athene', which accompanied Diana's coffin as it departed Westminster Abbey, was a lyrical amalgam of Shakespeare and the Bible.[5] Combining elements of the Orthodox funeral service with the eulogy delivered by Horatio over Hamlet's corpse – 'flights of angels sing thee to thy rest' (V.ii.365) – Taverner's composition captured that oddly British dependence on Shakespeare at times of ceremony and crisis.[6] As the BBC cameras panned away from the coffin, the television audience's dominant visual image was of ranks of gathered spectators standing on the abbey's stone floor. The person the camera then chose to focus upon, and who was later invited to offer a personal commentary on the service for BBC viewers, was the film director and life-peer, Lord (Richard) Attenborough, a friend and confidant of the late princess. For a literary critic trained to contextualize, this particular image provided an immediate analogue to Branagh's directorial sense of an ending when filming his monumental four-hour plus version of *Hamlet*. In the film, on the black-and-white marbled floor of the Palace of Elsinore, Hamlet and Laertes duel to the death on a red carpet. The bloody scene of royal family anguish is then spectated and commented upon following the belated arrival of the English ambassador, come to Denmark with news that 'Rosencrantz and Guildenstern are dead' (V.ii.376). In Branagh's film, the role of the English ambassador was taken by one Richard Attenborough. No one would want to suggest that Branagh had psychic powers in foreseeing Diana's death and its cultural impact during the making of his film. What I do want to suggest is that Branagh's *Hamlet* film is dependent, in often problematic ways, upon the iconography of monarchy and absolutism which is deeply inscribed on the British psyche, and indeed upon the sense of an increasing crisis within the British Royal Family in the 1990s. This was already a hugely topical issue when Branagh commenced filming.

Branagh's particular interpretation of *Hamlet* is a self-consciously millennial one in that it exploits the *fin-de-siècle* anxieties of the original play. *Hamlet* was first performed in 1600–1, the declining years of the illustrious reign of the Virgin Queen, Elizabeth I, and, accordingly, years of worry about the succession. This was the era of the Earl of Essex's ill-fated rebellion and of widely expressed concerns about the reign to come. *Hamlet* is concerned with a transition of reigns, with a political system in a state of flux, and with multiple 'senses of an ending'.[7] The play and its eponymous protagonist are both imbued with a *fin-de-siècle* mentality and so, too, is Branagh's film. This essay will identify common patterns between the late 1990s and the themes of the play as developed in Branagh's big-screen version. Specific parallels between the film's themes and contemporary society's concerns will be identified and discussed, such as a widespread anxiety about political tyranny and the oppression of human rights, the breakdown of the family as a social unit (under threat internally, not least from the spectre of sexual abuse) and the extreme pressure on individuals, which manifests itself in physical and psychological disorders, including anorexia, bulimia and nervous breakdowns.

Branagh finds in the aforementioned crisis of the British monarchy in the 1990s, and in the figure of Princess Diana in particular, a facilitating idea for exploring these themes, as he finds them, in *Hamlet*. The film's millennial anxieties are played out through various linked ideas and images of a monarchy under threat or in decline. The murder of Old Hamlet becomes, accordingly, a site both of nostalgia and confused critique. Nowhere is this more evident in the film's narrative than in the multivalent (and potentially self-cancelling) significance of the opening and closing shots of Old Hamlet's stone statue, which I will explore in detail. Indeed, I want to go so far as to suggest that confusion, ethical incoherence even, is at the core of Branagh's project and that this is in itself a very real reflection of the millennial state of mind.

Branagh's *mise-en-scène* will prove central to an exploration of the contradictory treatment of monarchy in the film. The palatial setting and its snowbound landscape, with Blenheim Palace operating as Elsinore, evoke a series of complex associations with monarchy and absolutist power, both nineteenth- and twentieth-century in derivation. The Russian connotations of this are particularly potent – from the evocation of Napoleon's winter-time retreat from Moscow after the Battle of Borodino in 1812 through to the execution of Tsar Nicholas II at Ekaterinburg a century later, both of which are dealt with in a highly romanticized and idealized fashion.[8]

Integral to Branagh's exploration of the fate of modern monarchy in his interpretation of *Hamlet* is an examination of a world in which the lines and demarcations between public and private life prove dangerously blurred. This, it will be seen, is most evident in his treatment of the character of Ophelia, whose trajectory in the film – from secret lover of Hamlet to betrayed partner and daughter to very public psychological breakdown – undoubtedly conjures the popular press images of Princess Diana. The royal family, in this respect (in the play, the film and contemporary life), becomes a metonym for the fate of the family unit in society at large, depicted, as it is, as under duress and dysfunctioning to the point of disappearance. Quintessential aspects of *fin-de-siècle* society are explored in Branagh's film, from incest and family tragedy, through to secularization and the loss of faith, and the 'Woman Question'. By emphasizing these elements, the director insists his film speaks to the present age, although occasionally this has unexpected results.

Finally, this essay will argue that Branagh's millennial anxieties and doubts, pervasive in his treatment of themes of royalty and family in the film, also manifest themselves in the aesthetic and material aspects of his *Hamlet*. To this end, his casting decisions and his choice of format will be discussed. In conclusion, I will suggest why it is *Hamlet* specifically, as a play, that Branagh looks to in order to make his millennial screen gesture – why that play's themes are seen to speak so clearly to the confusions and concerns of the late 1990s. Branagh's *other Hamlet* film, his 1995 black-and-white comedy, *In the Bleak Midwinter* (retitled in the US as *A Midwinter's Tale*), will be discussed in this respect, not only as a comic counterpart to the full-blown tragic version of the play, but as revelatory of the special significance Branagh accords this playtext in terms of its power to shape our politics, personal and otherwise.

The treatment of questions of monarchy and power will, then, be used to expose both Branagh's seemingly contradictory drive towards making a definitive *Hamlet* for the twentieth century and the production of a film riven with doubt and uncertainty about its subject matter. Ultimately, this will be seen less as a personal flaw in Branagh's *oeuvre* than an inevitable reflection of British self-doubt, cultural and political, on the verge of the new millennium.[9]

II

In its preoccupation with public image and with the surveillance and monitoring of individuals within the palace of Elsinore, the House of Denmark in Branagh's *Hamlet* has very real links with that of the House of Windsor at the end of the twentieth century. Admittedly, Branagh does not set his film in the late twentieth century, opting instead for the analogous period of the nineteenth century, but in seeking parallels, such as the Diana–Ophelia one, he refracts 1990s' concerns into the past. In the published screenplay, Branagh describes selecting 'a period setting that attempts to set the story in a historical context that is resonant for a modern audience but allows a heightened language to sit comfortably'.[10] Yet the question remains as to why Branagh felt the nineteenth century would have particular resonance for a late twentieth-century audience. The simple answer would be that this century represents recent history and is therefore more likely to be known. Certainly, Branagh's Denmark has a distinctly English imperialist air. The exterior scenes of the film were shot at Blenheim Palace, the reso-nances of whose epic architecture were not lost on Branagh or his reviewers.[11] Mark Thornton Burnett has commented on the associa-tions (aesthetic and political) of that spatial setting:

> Following the defeat of the French at Blenheim in 1704, the palace was constructed for the Duke of Marlborough as thanks for the landmark victory. Sir Winston Churchill was born at Blenheim in 1874, and members of the family still live at the palace. With these contexts in mind, it can be argued that Branagh's *Hamlet* operates as a metaphor for historical conflicts between England and France, between England and Germany, and even between the English Royal family and a more powerful political entity.[12]

Whilst the national and international inflections Burnett identifies raise intriguing questions about the politics of this production, my concern here is ostensibly with the latter observations on the role that Blenheim plays in constructing, and to a certain extent deconstruct-ing, a sense of a Royal Family, both that of the play and that of Britain in the 1990s.

Undoubtedly, by reinserting the political scenes excised by both Laurence Olivier's and Franco Zeffirelli's film versions (1948 and 1990 respectively), Branagh invites his audiences to make associations of this kind. The new political world of might and expediency that Fortinbras represents at the end of the play could be identified with the secular power of a Churchill in the twentieth century, and the Churchillian referents are expanded on by Branagh in the screen-play.[13] But in Branagh's film, Fortinbras (played by Rufus Sewell as a sulky victor), though he may slouch in the throne of Denmark, does put on the crown, thereby associating himself with sovereignty, however ill-fitting or uncomfortable that stance might appear. So what is the political point being made here? That royal families, once overthrown, are only replaced by new tyrants? The problematic and potentially contradictory images of the final few minutes of the film do leave us uncertain as to the future that lies ahead for Elsinore.

Blenheim/Elsinore and their statues, very visibly pulled down in the closing sequence of the film, seem to represent a past world of absolutist rule, but it is unclear whether Branagh intends this to be applauded or lamented.

The crisis of the monarchy in the 1990s is inextricably connected to the perils of increased media exposure and has led to extended and ongoing debates about press intrusion in the UK. This was a decade in which the private lives of the royals were made public in ways scarcely imagined by deferential preceding generations. The stories of various royal romances and divorces and of scandals engulfing the Royal Family, the secret taping of private telephone calls and the decision of a number of members of the Royal Household to talk 'off-the-record' to journalists have reduced the previously aloof entity of the monarchy to little more than a soap opera. The British tabloids have been at the heart of this enterprise, although the 1990s have also seen the proliferation on newsstands of so-called 'celebrity spotting' magazines, such as *Hello!* and *OK*, publications which depended on photo-stories of Diana in particular to maintain their hold on the market.

In devising his set, Branagh intended to exploit or reproduce this fascination of the 1990s with the private lives of public individuals. Commenting on his version of the royal court in *Hamlet*, he stated: 'I wanted it to be a very glamorous court, a very glamorous-looking place, somewhere where you could understand the fascination of the nation. Which I think is in tune with some part of Shakespeare's interest in it which was to look at the very private lives of very public individuals. If you like, these people could be stepping out the pages of a nineteenth-century *Hello!* magazine.'[14] That Branagh might have found salient the very contemporary haunting of the private life of Diana, Princess of Wales by the world's media seems a reasonable extrapolation, not least because *Hello!* magazine was a major exponent of that journalistic voyeurism. As the 'most photographed woman in the world' and as the subject of many *exposés* (self-generated or otherwise), Diana symbolized for the 1990s the public/private debate in a very unique way. Branagh finds a parallel figure for this in his film in the character of Ophelia, subjecting her to a series of voyeuristic intrusions: for example, the reading aloud to the court of Hamlet's love letter to her (an action she is initially forced to undertake, her father stepping in only when her own voice falters) and the selfconscious spectating of her mental disintegration in a padded cell.

Ophelia is not, however, the only victim of this 'culture of intimacy'.[15] The claustrophobia of the duel scene, which sees the court crowded into the central hall and the doors locked against the outside world, is telling. This is the culminating image of a series of court 'shows' which commences with Claudius' post-marriage address (staged as a 'performance' applauded by courtiers) and continues with the vertiginous seating of the audience for *The Mousetrap* (a spatial decision, which ensures that every word exchanged between members of the Royal Family can be heard). A recurring element of Branagh's *Hamlet* is the sense that royal families have no private life, and the director has explained the mirror motif of the film in the following terms: these are 'people forever being watched or forever watching themselves'.[16]

In that final court scene in the film, everyone's focus is on the ultimate emblem of royal rule, a red carpet. As if to emphasize the inward-turned and restricted vision of the Elsinore community, whilst the court's attention is consumed by the events unfolding themselves on that carpet, the scene for the cinema audience is punctuated by images of Fortinbras' army, advancing through the snows, breaking down the barriers between them and the seat of power (doors and thresholds, which have played a considerable role in the construction of the court throughout the film) and finally crashing through the windows into the central hall. Something is indeed rotten in this state of Denmark: this is an unsustainable world, which has eaten itself apart with corruption and betrayal, yet it is also one that Branagh's film seems inexplicably nostalgic for and sentimental towards. This is the fundamental incoherence of the film's ruminations on power and royalty, and one which I identify less as a criticism of Branagh's inconsistent politics than as a revealing mirror of blurred millennial thinking on such matters. The 1990s, as I suggested earlier, have witnessed a comparable crisis of their own in thinking about political and royal authority, and it is not one from which we have yet emerged.

Blenheim Palace enables in the film one further analogy, hinted at in a throwaway comment in Russell Jackson's production diary. He calls Blenheim, in an entry reflecting on artificial snow put down for filming, a 'formidable Winter Palace'.[17] This evocation of a building seminal to late nineteenth- and early twentieth-century Russian history is more telling than the light-hearted context of Jackson's comment suggests. One of this century's most poignant, and indeed romanticized, images of the fall of monarchy is the murder of Tsar Nicholas II and his family and aides in 1918 by the advancing Russian revolutionaries. That brutal act came, however, in the wake of the Romanov family's own tyrannies against the Russian people (not least the 1905 St Petersburg [then Petrograd] massacre of protestors in the snow outside the Winter Palace).[18] The recent ceremony held over their corpses, identified through DNA testing, and the controversies it provoked, indicate the political confusions these events still generate, echoing, in its problematic and sometimes diffuse mobilization of popular and political sentiment in the former Soviet Union, the complex impact of Diana's funeral. The British Royal Family is closely related to the Romanovs, and this lends poignancy to these embedded allusions in Branagh's film.

The events of the Russian Revolution embody the paradoxes of politics in the twentieth century, not least due to that popular revolution's rapid descent into tyranny and dictatorship. In his controversial book, *The End of History and the Last Man*, Francis Fukuyama posited the notion of '*post-histoire*', arguing that liberal democracy could be seen as the 'end point of mankind's ideological evolution', the 'final form of human government' and, as such, the 'end of history'.[19] He sees in this the culmination of a lengthy historical and political process, declaring that 'The most remarkable development of the last quarter of the twentieth century has been the revelation of enormous weaknesses at the core of the world's seemingly strong dictatorships'.[20] Branagh's *Hamlet* undoubtedly engages with this fundamental weakness at the heart of tyrannies. The film is characterized by a determination to interrogate particular forms of government. But what is produced ultimately by Branagh's nostalgic script of the demise of a royal household, one which is in many respects produced by current debates in the 1990s about royalty and society, is less Fukuyama's 'endism' than a sense of irresolution and repeating political and social cycles.

At the tail-end of the twentieth century, we have tangible images of the collapse of Russia's second cycle of political tyranny, with the fall of communism in the late 1980s and the early 1990s. Many will feel that the most abiding image of that political outcome remains the dismantling of the Berlin Wall by the people of the former East and West Germany in 1989, but another must be that of the pulling down of huge statues of communist leaders across the former Soviet Union. Branagh's *Hamlet* chooses to open and close with a monumental statue of its own, that of Old Hamlet, which is placed on the threshold of Elsinore. The film commences with a striking emphasis on text – the stone lettering of the name 'Hamlet' on the statue's plinth. This enables a clever trick whereby we move from text into 'reality' as the camera pans sideways and we realize we are at the gates of the palace. The image also suggests something of the stature of Old Hamlet, preparing us for the significance of his ghostly apparition. It is important that Old Hamlet's ghost appears as the statue comes to life in full military armour: this is no flesh-and-blood patriarch but a ruler of a warring nation, an emblem and a myth. This all seems to tally unproblematically with a film in which the director seeks to win sympathy for his protagonist's, and his nation's, plight.

The closing invocation of the statue is more ambiguous. Branagh elects to end his film not with the heartstring-pulling image of Hamlet's corpse borne aloft (Christ-like though the image is) but with Fortinbras' foot soldiers hammering away at the edifice of Old Hamlet's statue. As the chipping away at this image of power provides a poignant close-up, what questions are we meant to pose? Is the action meant to suggest the desecration of something great, or is it, as I am suggesting, almost unavoidably, meant to remind audiences of those fallen statues of Stalin and others? If the latter is true, then the conclusion must be that Old Hamlet was a tyrant, one whose representational apparatus needs to be dismantled for history truly to find an 'end'. Such an interpretation can be supported by another Romantic evocation: the fragments of the statue of the fallen dictator, Ozymandias, in Shelley's eponymous poem:

> Two vast and trunkless legs of stone
> Stand in the desert ... Near them, on the sand,
> Half sunk, a shattered visage lies, whose frown,
> And wrinkled lip, and sneer of cold command,
> Tell that its sculptor well those passions read ... [21]

Yet, once again, Branagh's choice of a sentimental musical overlay at this point in the film confuses the effect upon watching audiences. The politics of this *fin-de-siècle* rumination are incoherent at their heart and at their close. Branagh seems at turns appalled and enticed by the power invested in a figure such as Old Hamlet. As a result, his film effects as its only certainty an implicit association between the *fin-de-siècle* moment and a crisis of political authority.

The end of the nineteenth century has long been recognized as sharing concerns and a sense of crisis with our own millennial moment. Elaine Showalter observes: 'From urban homelessness to imperial decline, from sexual revolution to sexual epidemics, the last decades of the twentieth century seem to be repeating the problems, themes, and metaphors of the *fin de siècle*'.[22] She goes on to identify these problems as the breakdown of the family unit, the decline of religion and the question of sexual rights. All these themes feature in Branagh's cinematic recreation of the nineteenth century and all find parallels in our own age. The issue of the breakdown of the family is writ large in Branagh's *Hamlet*. This might seem unavoidable in any production of a play at whose centre lies fratricide ('Thus was I, sleeping, by a brother's hand / Of life, of crown, of queen at once dispatch'd' [I.v.74–5]) and an incestuous coupling ('the rank sweat of an enseamed bed' [III.iv.92]), but it is given special prominence in Branagh's production, partly due to his decision to work with the 'fuller text' *Hamlet*, a complex combination of Folio and Second Quarto texts. Running at over four hours, this fuller text allows the play's 'second family' to emerge with greater power than in previous film versions.

The Polonius–Laertes–Ophelia family, as portrayed in this film, offers a multifaceted point of comparison for the Claudius–Hamlet–Gertrude triad. Branagh has identified this as a major advantage of playing the fuller text, commenting on the way it highlights a 'double family tragedy'.[23] As if to further the comparison with Hamlet's situation, Branagh's interpretation of this second family tragedy, where another son loses a father and embarks on revenge, and where another woman is manipulated by powerful patriarchs, makes explicit the incestuous potential that has been identified by critics in the Polonius group.[24] More usually this subtext is located in the father–daughter relationship: Ophelia, it is argued, loses a second lover when her first stabs her father behind the arras. In a mirror action, she is driven mad by her inability to alter this situation, and her singing, in madness, of sexually bawdy lyrics may refer to relations with her dead father as much as her estranged lover. An act of sexual control is therefore ascribed to Polonius' interference in his motherless daughter's relationship with the Prince.

Certainly, this film's Polonius (Richard Briers) is linked at particular moments to a brutalized form of sexuality. In the Reynaldo scene (another crucial reclamation for this *Hamlet* that Branagh's full-text decision enables), where Polonius employs a secret agent to spy on his own son and catch him 'drabbing' (II.i.26), Polonius himself is seen in his private chambers with a hired woman. The hypocrisy would seem clear, but one of the inconsistencies of the film is that this glimpse of a machinatory Polonius is shied away from elsewhere, as if a sentimental reading of the part creeps back in by one of the film's endless side-doors and secret passages (and this is perhaps true of the film as a whole: sentimentality seems to overtake any political concerns

staked out by the opening sections).[25] After the nunnery scene's trau-
matic subjection of Ophelia to Hamlet's rage, this Polonius rushes to
comfort his daughter: only Claudius (Derek Jacobi) remains self-
possessed. Yet the Polonius who comforts his daughter, and who
regrets his misunderstanding of the depth of Hamlet's affection for
Ophelia, does not tally with the Polonius portrayed elsewhere in the
film – a man depicted as Claudius' prime ministerial cohort, and one
who exposes Ophelia to several painful, public humiliations.

Branagh and Briers appear undecided as to Polonius' role in affairs
and, as a result, what incestuous subtexts there are to this family are
focused not on the paternal but the fraternal male: Laertes. Early on,
in one of Branagh's favoured long tracking shots, we see Laertes
(Michael Maloney) advising his sister (Kate Winslet) how to deport
herself in his absence (I.iii). The earlier juxtaposed requests of Laertes
and Hamlet to return to their places of study, Paris and Wittenberg
respectively, have prepared audiences for parallels between them. The
two men are further paralleled with another son avenging wrongs
done to his father, forming a triad with Fortinbras of Norway. There
are also significant ways in which the text constructs Hamlet and
Laertes as duelling lovers as well as grieving sons, and Branagh's film
makes that point explicit. This reading is clearly one Branagh himself
intended, since, in the screenplay, he notes of the Laertes–Ophelia
advice scene: 'As they walk with their arms around each other, they
are very, some might say unnaturally, close.'[26] Laertes is in competition with Hamlet for Ophelia's favour: this is not obvious fraternal
behaviour and provides a context for the graveside battle over who
loved Ophelia more.

The film's shift of focus away from father–daughter incest, and on
to the sexual relations of the younger members of the play's two families, is telling in terms of Branagh's priorities. The paternal abuse
theme might have seemed more relevant to the 1990s, but Branagh's
own ongoing competition with other film Shakespeares militated
against it. Franco Zeffirelli's 1990 screen version starring Mel Gibson
as Hamlet and Glenn Close as Gertrude offered a particular focus of
that rivalry.[27] That the prince and his mother were the stars of that
production tells us much about Zeffirelli's directorial emphases. Like
Olivier before him, Zeffirelli cast a Hamlet and Gertrude who were
extremely close in age, heightening the potential for Oedipal
constructions.[28] As if mere suggestion were not enough, Zeffirelli also
opted for several onscreen kisses between his protagonists and,
indeed, Gibson and Close in the closet scene engaged in physical

simulation of the sexual act. Branagh seems to move away from this interpretative possibility in his film, by choosing instead a stately and oddly unsexual Gertrude (despite much smoothing down of the marital bed) in Julie Christie, and also by rather heavy-handedly using flashbacks to emphasize the contrasting physicality of Ophelia and Hamlet's relationship. Flashback images of the couple making love occur not only when Polonius instructs his daughter about men's intentions towards women, but also during Ophelia's mad scenes. This serves to suppress the ambiguity of reference in her songs, which I identified earlier as crucial to the tracing of any incestuous subtext to the Ophelia–Polonius relationship. Family breakdowns and incest are still themes in Branagh's *Hamlet*, but we find them, like the flashbacks, avoided at more canonical (or obvious) moments. The one 'true' family unit of the film proves, ironically, to be that of the travelling players.

The breakdown of a religious framework in this Elsinore is signified by the abuse of the space of the confession box at several moments in the film. It is in and around this ecclesiastical site that Polonius interrogates his daughter about her relationship with Hamlet: poignantly, it is also against the screen of this space that Ophelia will hurl herself when she learns of her father's death. This marks her movement into madness, and is the first of many scenes when we will see her body pushed up against physical constraints: from walls and doors, to cells and straitjackets. Here, too, Claudius delivers his 'O my offence is rank' soliloquy (III.iii.35) and Hamlet imagines killing him (the film makes that image explicit in a brief but dramatic dream sequence). The privacy of personal faith and space is denied in this secular, corrupt community.

By setting his film in such a vividly realized context, Branagh is able to suggest the patriarchal constraint of women in the nineteenth century. His Ophelia is constructed and portrayed in terms of that period's understandings of female insanity.[29] Her madness is directly associated (via those flashbacks) with her sexual experiences and interpreted as a kind of erotomania. Her treatment – straitjackets, padded cells and enforced cold showers – is witnessed by the audience, often mediated through a sympathetic observer (sometimes Laertes, most often Horatio). Once again, modern approaches to care in the community and to specifically female disorders (at least in terms of their media portrayal), such as bulimia and self-harming, and their relevance to the 'Diana myth', add their own contemporary poignancy to these scenes.

There are many ways in which Branagh relates the nineteenth-century *mise-en-scène* of his film to twentieth-century issues, not least to questions of monarchy and power. The 'millennial consciousness' of this film is not, however, confined to these subjects. The aesthetics of the film are informed by the same. It was much observed at the time of the film's release that it was shot in 70 mm wide-screen format and that it offered a 'complete' text. It serves to ask why these were viewed as defining aspects of this production. 70 mm film has four times the normal definition of ordinary film, and this does give the production a particularly vivid visual style, particularly in terms of colour and costume. Traditionally it is the gauge used for epic films, for 'spectacle-centred projects'.[30] This tells us much about Branagh's motives when making this film, but also about the contradictions it embodies. However critical a stance the film might wish to take on the glamorous Elsinore court and the power-politics it represents, the camera is enamoured by the epic grandeur of that court's self-representations. Again, this may be more revealing of the paradoxes inherent in the treatment of the British Royal Family in the 1990s than Branagh had intended.

One reason for the 70 mm gauge and the 'full' text is Branagh's sense of the momentous occasion of the film and its time of production. This is a *Hamlet* intended to supersede other film *Hamlet*s of the century: in interview, Branagh was quick to stress all the extra dimensions his full-text version could offer, not least the 'second family tragedy' and the restoration of the political element. This desire to provide something definitive for the millennial moment is obvious in other more materialist ways, such as casting. Branagh's *Hamlet* contains many Hamlets other than his own. He himself has written at length about the influence the BBC Television production of the play starring Derek Jacobi had on his acting career and his lifelong engagement with Shakespeare.[31] Branagh self-consciously casts Jacobi as Claudius and both bleach their hair so that Hamlet resembles his uncle more than his late father. Pre-release articles about the production made much of Jacobi's presentation of a copy of the play to Branagh, which is traditionally handed to the 'Hamlet of his generation'.[32] This suited Branagh's aim with regard to the production, that of providing a *Hamlet* for this millennial generation, but, more than that, the *Hamlet* for the twentieth century, a self-conscious summation of what preceded it. And for that reason Jacobi is not the only former Hamlet to appear: Michael Maloney, a much-heralded stage Prince but also Hamlet in Branagh's own comic film about an amateur production of the play, *In the Bleak Midwinter*, appears as Laertes, and John Gielgud plays a silent role as King Priam (visualized during the Player King's speech), thus allowing the film to evoke (and transcend?) screen and stage Hamlets from the start of the century to the end.

In the Bleak Midwinter also exposes Branagh's grandiose intentions with regard to *Hamlet*. As Emma Smith's essay in this volume explores in greater detail, the film sits in an odd relationship to Branagh's epic production. It tells the story of a group of unemployed actors staging a Christmas-time production of the play in a threatened church. The Christmas setting is sentimental, but once again the play is employed at a time of need, a liminal moment, and contributes to the resolution of the various life crises of its cast. We might expect Branagh to want to distance his serious film version of the play from one that is (deliberately) full of parodic and *cliché*-ridden approaches to the text, and the black-and-white format of *In the Bleak Midwinter* may be explained by this.[33] Yet in many ways Branagh invites connection between the two. Many of *In the Bleak Midwinter*'s actors reappear in *Hamlet*, although always in a displaced role – the aforementioned Maloney, but also Nicholas Farrell (Laertes in *In the Bleak Midwinter*; Horatio in *Hamlet*) and Richard Briers (Claudius; Polonius). It is as if these actors are integral to Branagh's filmed Shakespeares (Briers has also appeared in his *Henry V* and *Much Ado About Nothing*) or to filmed Shakespeare more generally (Maloney is in Zeffirelli's *Hamlet* and Oliver Parker's *Othello* [1995], which also stars Branagh as Iago; Farrell is in the same *Othello* and also Trevor Nunn's *Twelfth Night* [1996]). There is, then, something authenticating about their presence. Of course, there is the flip-side argument that filmed Shakespeare has been reduced to something of a clique, and one controlled by Branagh at that, but it remains for the next century of filmed Shakespeare to offer its own challenges to that speculation.

What does become overridingly clear from Branagh's two film explorations of *Hamlet* in the 1990s is his belief that the play has the power to change us, even at our most millennial and cynical. Moments of importance in *In the Bleak Midwinter* prefigure crucial points in his *Hamlet* film, even its very making. Michael Maloney's character, Joe, says: 'I saw this play when I was fifteen. It changed my life. You don't forget that.' The story is, in fact, Branagh's, and he retells it in his introduction to the printed screenplay of his *Hamlet*. Throughout his acting career, Branagh has seen and drawn parallels between himself and the role. In his published autobiography, he ends with a glance towards the future with the statement that 'The readiness is all'; he closes his introductory essay to the screenplay with the same line, and in a televised interview drew attention to this speech as the most important of the play.[34] In *In the Bleak Midwinter*, the speech is, touchingly, handed over to a spear-carrier; it is delivered off-stage and with reference not to the play's context of political and family breakdown but to the individual situations of the actors. In the end, this is perhaps why Kenneth Branagh felt so driven to make a *Hamlet* for the 1990s, even a *Hamlet* for the millennium, because he believes it matters, and believes it can make a difference to individual spectators and audiences.

III

But there is no 'end of history' here, nor does Branagh prove to have the last word where *Hamlet* is concerned. Ironically, in his drive towards making something definitive and life-enhancing, Branagh's film, despite numerous strengths and local insights, results in being politically and ethically fissured and, at times, simply confusing. His screenplay seems irretrievably torn between lamenting a lost ideal of imperial power and conducting a critique of political dictatorship. It indicts the cruelties of a governmental system that destroys the fragile individualism of a Hamlet or an Ophelia, whilst appearing seduced by the same. Once again, the state funeral of Diana, Princess of Wales, and the ambivalent responses (towards the institutions of the monarchy and the press) that it evoked, may prove an instructive analogy here. For the events of September 1997, whilst they may have seemed momentous at the time, in truth changed nothing. As I write, another Royal Wedding has been dominating the headlines and we appear to be in danger of starting the new millennium with the same old story. The double valency of the closing moments of Branagh's *Hamlet* film, containing as they do a nostalgia for a former age alongside an inevitably thwarted attempt at political statement, may say more about the moral and ethical confusions of society in the late 1990s than even the director suspected.

Notes

1. The full text of the funeral tribute was published in *The Observer*, 7 September 1997, p. 2.
2. Elaine Showalter, 'Storming the Wintry Palace', *The Guardian*, 6 September 1997, p. 15.
3. *Hamlet*, ed. Harold Jenkins (London: Methuen, 1982), V.i.233–5. All further quotations appear in the text.

4. See, for example, *The Guardian*, 'Notes & Queries', 24 September 1997, p. 17.
5. The lyrics for the song were provided in newspapers on the day of the funeral; see, for example, *The Guardian*, 6 September 1997, p. 4. Taverner's piece is included on his 1995 album, *Innocence*.
6. Laurence Olivier's propagandistic version of *Henry V*, dedicated to the Allied Forces of World War II, is a case in point. See Anthony Davies, *Filming Shakespeare's Plays: The Adaptations of Laurence Olivier, Orson Welles, Peter Brook and Akiro Kurosawa* (Cambridge: Cambridge University Press, 1988), pp. 26–37.
7. See Frank Kermode, *The Sense of an Ending* (Oxford: Oxford University Press, 1967).
8. Deborah Cartmell has noted 'shades of *War and Peace*' in the film's setting in her 'Reading and Screening Ophelia, 1948–1996', *Shakespeare Yearbook*, 8 (1997), p. 38, and Samuel Crowl makes a related point in a forthcoming article in *Shakespeare Bulletin* (cited in H. R. Coursen, '"Words, Words, Words": Searching for *Hamlet*', *Shakespeare Yearbook*, 8 [1997], pp. 306–24).
9. The charge of schizophrenia and incoherence, however, has been levelled against other Shakespearean films by Branagh. See, for example, Derek Royal, 'Shakespeare's Kingly Mirror: Figuring the Chorus in Olivier's and Branagh's *Henry V*', *Literature/Film Quarterly*, 25 (1997), pp. 104–10, and Courtney Lehmann, 'Kenneth Branagh at the Quilting Point: Shakespearean Adaptation and the (Schizophrenic) Fabric of "Everyday" Life', *Post Script*, 17 (1997), pp. 6–27.
10. Kenneth Branagh, *'Hamlet' by William Shakespeare: Screenplay, Introduction and Film Diary* (London: Chatto and Windus, 1996), p. vii.
11. In his film diary, appended to Branagh's published screenplay, Russell Jackson's entry for Tuesday, 13 February, records: 'Cold wet morning in the grounds of Blenheim Palace. Our first set-up is outside the side gate of the extraordinary piece of English early eighteenth-century baroque that was the (enormously expensive) reward of a grateful nation for the military prowess of the first Duke of Marlborough' (Branagh, *'Hamlet'*, p. 192).
12. Mark Thornton Burnett, 'The 'very cunning of the scene': Kenneth Branagh's *Hamlet*', *Literature/Film Quarterly*, 25 (1997), p. 81.
13. Claudius is described as speaking with a 'Churchillian focus' (Branagh, *'Hamlet'*, p. 16). Elsewhere, allusions are made to US Gulf War General, Norman Schwarzkopf, as if to emphasize the twentieth-century applications of the scene (p. 12).
14. The point was made in 'The Making of *Hamlet*', an Open University production, BBC2, December 1997.
15. This phrase was used persistently in newspaper reports during the week after Diana's death.
16. Branagh was speaking in 'The Making of *Hamlet*'. Of course, the mirrored hall that provides such a striking context for the 'To be or not to be' soliloquy also conjures connections with absolutist European monarchies and their attendant architecture, not least the court of the Sun-King, Louis XIV, at Versailles.
17. Branagh, *'Hamlet'*, p. 193.
18. Harold Shukman (ed.), *The Blackwell Encyclopedia of the Russian Revolution*

(Oxford: Blackwell, 1988), pp. 357–9.

19. Francis Fukuyama, *The End of History and the Last Man* (London: Hamish Hamilton, 1992), p. xi.
20. Fukuyama, *The End of History*, p. xiii.
21. Percy Bysshe Shelley, *Poetical Works*, ed. Thomas Hutchinson (Oxford: Oxford University Press, 1935), p. 546, ll. 2–6.
22. Elaine Showalter, *Sexual Anarchy: Gender and Culture at the 'Fin de Siècle'* (London: Virago, 1992), p. 1.
23. Branagh, *'Hamlet'*, p. vi.
24. Elaine Showalter, 'Representing Ophelia: Women, Madness, and the Responsibilities of Feminist Criticism', in John Drakakis (ed.), *Shakespearean Tragedy* (London: Longman, 1992), p. 291.
25. Something similar can be seen in Branagh's *Henry V* where the anti-war ethos is overtaken by a militaristic romance. Curtis Breight has offered a persuasive reading of the film along these lines in his 'Branagh and the Prince, or a "Royal Fellowship of Death"', *Critical Quarterly*, 33 (1991), pp. 95–11, although Peter S. Donaldson's 'Taking on Shakespeare: Kenneth Branagh's *Henry V*', *Shakespeare Quarterly*, 42 (1991), pp. 60–71, gives more credence to the anti-war reading of the film.
26. Branagh, *'Hamlet'*, p. 23.
27. Clearly, Branagh's production company was aware of the competition. In 'The Making of *Hamlet*', Tim Harvey, production designer, observes, '[Ken] didn't want to do a castles and dungeons and sackcloth production', a pointed allusion to the *mise-en-scène* of Zeffirelli's film.
28. See Ace G. Pilkington, 'Zeffirelli's Shakespeare', in Anthony Davies and Stanley Wells (eds), *Shakespeare and the Moving Image: The Plays on Film and Television* (Cambridge: Cambridge University Press, 1994), pp. 163–79.
29. Elaine Showalter explores these in *The Female Malady: Women, Madness and English Culture, 1830–1980* (London: Virago, 1987). David Kennedy Sauer's '"Suiting the Word to the Action": Kenneth Branagh's Interpolations in *Hamlet*', *Shakespeare Yearbook*, 8 (1997), suggests that Branagh is directly influenced by Showalter's criticism (p. 332).
30. David Bordwell and Kristin Thompson, *Film Art: An Introduction* (New York: McGraw-Hill, 1997), p. 7.
31. See, for example, the introductory essay in Branagh, *'Hamlet'*.
32. Branagh, *'Hamlet'*, p. 211.
33. Other articles, however, have suggested filmic intertextual relevances for this choice; see, for example, Stephen M. Buhler, 'Double Takes: Branagh Gets to *Hamlet*', *Post Script*, 17 (1997), pp. 43–52.
34. Kenneth Branagh, *Beginning* (New York: St. Martin's Press, 1989), p. 244.

11
From the Horse's Mouth: Branagh on the Bard

Ramona Wray and Mark Thornton Burnett

In the space of an extraordinarily productive career, Kenneth Branagh has rapidly established himself as one of the twentieth century's foremost Shakespearean interpreters. His major directed cinematic productions span the whole range of the dramatist's *oeuvre*, from comedy to history and tragedy. *Henry V* (1989) offered itself as a seminal demythologization of a work traditionally read as a celebration of the English heroic endeavour; *Much Ado About Nothing* (1993) breathed new comic life into a 'problematic' representation of male–female rivalries; *Hamlet* (1997) served up the 'whole text' in a sumptuous widescreen format; and *Love's Labour's Lost* (2000) merged music from the 1930s and spectacular set-pieces in a bold revision of the play. As well as directing Shakespeare, Branagh has also been busy in being directed, chiefly in Oliver Parker's *Othello* (1995), in which he played Iago. These film versions of single plays can be supplemented by a body of related work which bears a Shakespearean theme. *In the Bleak Midwinter* (1995), the tale of a beleaguered repertory company struggling to mount a production of *Hamlet*, announced Branagh's continuing interest in the play from a simultaneously farcical and melancholic perpective.

This chapter takes the form of an interview with Kenneth Branagh, which took place on 23 January 1999, the eve of the production shoot for *Love's Labour's Lost*.

RW/MTB: *We'd like to begin by asking you about your Irish investment in Shakespeare. You've chosen to stage the European premières of all of your Shakespeare films in Belfast. How far has your Irish background inflected (and how far does it still inflect) your approach to Shakespeare?*

KB: The Irish heritage involves, I'm sure, at some subliminal level, a love of words, language and a story-telling tradition, which I was certainly very aware of when growing up in a large extended family who were forever gathering and telling stories. Both my parents, although not in a formal or a professional sense, were very good story-tellers. Both have a very keen sense of drama: whenever they told a story, albeit about family events or some local thing that had been memorable in their own colourful upbringing through the wars in Belfast, it was always done, as I look back on it anyway, with a strong sense of pace. They knew when to pause, they were implicitly quite dramatic and they loved a dramatic tale themselves.

There's also, I'd say in some part of the Irish heritage, a love of, and an acceptance of, melancholy, melancholy being a rather beautiful thing, and it's something that exists in Shakespeare, something that's sometimes harsh and sometimes realistic about what goes on in people's lives. Some [melancholic] bits I'm finding in particular in *Love's Labour's Lost*, a play that seems so deceptively light throughout and then turns on a sixpence in the last act: suddenly, this cool wind of realism blows into the play. I've always enjoyed that sort of dynamic: it's something that I think was probably influenced by an Irish background, which has a deeply silly strain and also a delight in the melancholic. The Irish find it a good and helpful thing to cry.

I was also aware of rituals in Irish life, particularly funerals. The attitude to funerals was very full-blown and full-hearted. There was a good deal of ritual about. There was quite a healthy attitude to the ways in which people allowed themselves, and encouraged each other, to react to death and to the ceremonies with which they marked the passing of people. I remember when doing *Romeo and Juliet* talking about Capulet's reaction to the death of Juliet. There's a whole sequence that goes between Capulet and Lady Capulet in which the language is structured as a shared choral wail. I felt some connection with that, which was allied to being Irish.

RW/MTB: *Was any of that, do you think, an influence on your filmic staging of Macmorris, in that he was played straight and not as a stereotypical Irishman, as he sometimes is in productions of* Henry V?

KB: It was partly a reaction to what, I thought, was a bold but an ineffective choice in the stage production I was in that played at Stratford and in London. [Macmorris] became quite broad and, to my mind, not very funny. I felt uncomfortable: I remember a rehearsal discussion when we played [*Henry V*] in London in the theatre, and many of us it was felt it was politically inappropriate and insensitive to [follow] the broad stage Irishman tradition, the [interpretation] that the part can produce [and sometimes] involves. That's why we went the other way.

   Small though that part of the play is, the issue of the four captains is one which it is quite possible to take seriously (I don't mean solemnly) from a dramatic point of view, as [the characters] all have things that they care about. They all have actions and drives, despite how little they say, and that seems to me to be more interesting as a dynamic and as another little colour in [Shakespeare's] depiction of an army. Seeing that insight into the kinds of tensions Henry must resolve by the end of the piece, or certainly before the battle of Agincourt, was, for our purposes anyway, better served by being a little straighter.

RW/MTB: *Your career has emerged as having a particular pattern. There is a series of non-Shakespearean films followed by a Shakespearean film every few years. (Prior to* Love's Labour's Lost, *for instance, there was* The Gingerbread Man *and* Wild, Wild West, *among others). How far is that because you wish to strike a balance between more mainstream commercial cinema and your Shakespearean interests?*

KB: As a cinema-goer, I'm quite eclectic in my tastes and watch a wide range of films. Part of the challenge with the Shakespeare films, which remain a sort of backbone to what I do, seems to be necessarily and healthily influenced by exposure to, as a performer and as a director, story-telling in other kinds of genres (with the idea being that one is constantly trying to challenge the ways in which Shakespeare can be offered up on film). Therefore, to be familiar with the ways in which popular cinema tells its stories is very important – to get some distance and to walk away from that subject for a while so as to allow the process (by which the development of one of these screenplays [is generated]) to have the appropriate time to marinate (which I find is a process that goes on over quite a long [period of] time). So time away from the subject matter, it seems to me, offers a little distance, a little objectivity, which can perhaps allow you to put together some of the lessons from the last time you did [a Shakespeare film]. The way in which to approach [a new Shakespeare film] continues then to develop. It's important each time to feel we're moving on and learn-ing from the mail-bag of critical reviews, from [the film's] life on video, from any sense of what received opinion may be settling into in terms of the view of the picture. You have to see if there's anything you can pick up from that to ask 'Where are we going?' or 'How can we make [Shakespeare] more available?' or 'How can we open up the plays more?' So being away from [Shakespeare] for a while helps me enormously.

RW/MTB: *What differences do you find between your Shakespearean direct-ing and being directed in Shakespeare? We're thinking of Oliver Parker's* Othello *in which you played Iago?*

KB: It was very good in that instance to be directed by someone I very much respected and admired, and I was drawn very strongly to what I felt was a passionate and intelligent response to the text itself. Oliver produced a screenplay which seemed to me to try and make the neces-sary translation from the stage to the screen, and he was already on the page very aware of how he wanted to use close-ups and how he wanted to treat the character of Iago. There was a clear sense of how he wanted to shape the piece in relation to the cuts he chose to make and [how he wanted] to focus on the domestic drama of that play. Not that he ignores the conflict and that the fact that the play travels from Venice to Cyprus, but the cuts definitely focused [the play] in a partic-ular way.

So what I began to think was a necessary thing, which was for Shakespeare on film to have a strong personal vision behind it. [This] was clear from [Oliver], and then I was grateful simply to be acting in a role which is a challenging one and which I hadn't played on the stage before. Having played [other] roles in [*Othello*] before on stage, it seemed to me, although not easy on film, that there was an ease that came from familiarity with the text that was enjoyable, so it certainly made the process of being directed less intimidating not having played Iago before and playing him in a condensed version. I was grateful just to have the challenge of that and my energies available just for that. I found [Oliver] a very good guide, and it was somewhat releasing actually. It was particularly enjoyable to do a Shakespearean role of such extraordinary quality without having to worry about where the caterers were.

RW/MTB: *From a theatrical background, you have now established yourself firmly as a cinematic presence. But there are points of contact between the two areas of acting activity. You acted in* Hamlet, Much Ado About

Nothing, Henry V *and* Love's Labour's Lost *earlier in your career (with the RSC or the Renaissance Theatre Company), and they're all now major productions on screen. Is there a link between your stage history and the films you go on to make in later life? Are there times when you feel you may want to return to your stage roots so as to find inspiration for future Shakespearean films?*

KB: I suppose that, even as I look back on it, I don't feel that there was any sort of conscious plan. My development into a film director was (and, in a sense, continues to be) something that surprised me. What each of those productions marked, and what marked my theatrical experience [of them], was a particular [encounter] with [a] kind of material which one can spend many lifetimes trying to consider. [Those productions were the] beginning of, or at least the first major stage in, considering [a] particular play, and beginning the struggle or the fascination or the tussle with that play – on some levels, with me, just to understand what was being said or to start experiencing (what then continued over a period of years) coming back to one of those plays, which I do regularly. With a play that is somehow in my blood, I'll come back to it and read it again, as one is inspired to do not as some conscious homework or preparation but just through interest in other productions, which suggest things or illuminate something (and you think, 'Gosh, I wish I'd realized that!', or 'Now I understand why that character is like that!', or 'Isn't that a fascinating way of realizing that relationship?', or 'What a terrific production idea that suddenly makes sense of that difficult time-jump or whatever it is that Shakespeare may be confusing you with!'). That stage work has been the beginning and in most places the beginning of something which, for instance in the case of *Love's Labour's Lost*, has every couple of years since made me try and consider how – with that particular play, with a play so caught up with the idea of how language is used and abused, and so politically connected to its time, with the kind of language that even in the context of Shakespeare production we don't hear that often – how can one make that into a film? That has been, and continues to be, a process which takes a long time, and the connection between now and the theatre is that all of that problem-solving began then. I walked into the [stage] production of *Love's Labour's Lost*, if you like, with a list of what, as far as I could under-stand them then, were the problems to be solved in production with that play, the problems of a comedy which revolves around Latin, the problems of clarity of story-telling when you have eight couples, [the problems of] the degree to which you present fantastical characters in what also requires a certain amount of naturalism in the setting. Indeed, with that play, what is a world in which we can accept a daft plot, with boys giving up women and studying for three years? What's the backdrop? What's the setting? And it's true of the basic question with all of these plays – what is the cinematic world, what's the setting that can release as many of the ideas in the play as possible? What is the idea that does not confine or reduce the play, but serves up as much dramatically of what's in there as possible? Those theatrical productions were the starting-point for that ongoing investigation; [they were] where the first information was assembled.

RW/MTB: *The essays collected together in this volume have as their unifying thematic thread Shakespeare on film at the end of the twentieth century. Many critics were struck by the sense you evoked in* Hamlet *of the end of one era (empire even) and the beginning of another – the toppling of the statue of Hamlet Senior, the associations of Blenheim Palace, etc. How far was that a conscious effect you were aiming for in the film's* mise-en-scène?

KB: I was certainly aiming to lay out what, it seemed to me, was in the play, which was to extend, in probably the most famous play in the world, the discussion of the internal struggle of one man to include, what Shakespeare also addresses, which is the impact on a country. And again it's rather like in the way you mentioned *à propos* of Macmorris, in *Hamlet*, in relatively minor characters, there is all this information and description and a sense of the emotional temperature and attitude towards life in the country as a whole – the worries of someone like Marcellus give us pictures of what's going on. Even the captain on the Norwegian plain with Fortinbras gives us a sense of the larger picture, so I did want to make the connection between the troubled lives of those in positions of power and privilege very directly having an impact not just on their immediate family and the court but on the nation at large. In fact, for me (and it's perhaps due to my age and being at the end of the twentieth century), Blenheim, rather than being a Gothic castle, you feel that the fates of nations can be decided in it. It's in there with power and surrounded by all this land – it's the kind of building that makes you wonder why there's never been a proper revolution in England. That sense of power was very important to convey and to show that it's not just the life of one man and one family that will change but the life of an entire nation. The world will never be the same again, the map of Europe will be redrawn, and the period in which we impressionistically set [the play] was also the case in a million European wars occurring in the latter part of the nineteenth century, often between sets of royal families. The actual borders were being redrawn as a result of these conflicts. We very directly wanted to make that point.

RW/MTB: *Like* Hamlet, *in some senses,* In the Bleak Midwinter *has nostalgic elements – the evocation of a previous period of theatrical play-making and playgoing. How far, for you, was the film a personal working-out of issues that you went on to explore in greater detail in* Hamlet, *which followed, as it were, hard upon?*

KB: I sometimes think that, in the way that Shakespeare occasionally used it and the Restoration dramatists definitely used it, in a way, *In the Bleak Midwinter* was an apology for or an excuse for what I was about to do. But, at the same time, somehow saying I don't mind this kind of apology, which was laying out how aware I was of the relative futility of attempting to produce a film of *Hamlet* with what we know to be the fullest amount of text at the end of the twentieth century, for a number of reasons. First, the relative futility with a play like that of the actual creative endeavour: it's impossible to be definitive with *Hamlet*, and just to include more lines is not to imply that the film will be better. Whoever it was – Garrick or Irving, or probably both – said you can never fully succeed in *Hamlet*. It's also true to say you can never fully fail, because there's usually something that the actor or the director can catch that connects with some feeling or emotion or illumination they have.

And then there was also the sense of the futility, if you like, of a four-hour film (that was obviously language-based) possibly finding an audience at the end of the twentieth century. And yet the love of the endeavour, the sort of, and not wishing to be immodest, mad heroism of the endeavour – which I think is also, *à propos* of your first question, an Irish thing – was something that *In the Bleak Midwinter* was trying to celebrate and also to evoke (a kind of theatrical inno-cence, that perhaps I had lost some sight of). But it was more to do with having fun, and in a way having fun at my own expense, and indeed cinematically, in a way I hoped was not going to be indulgent, because I hoped it was going to be funny – 'holding the mirror up to nature'. I thought that was a sort of Hamletian thing to do. In a strange way, I always thought because they were made in relative close proximity, they were companion films and that the artistic endeavour was somehow organically linked. The week before I delivered the first draft of *In the Bleak Midwinter*, I was on a location [reconnaissance] at Blenheim – a full year before we made the film [of *Hamlet*] – and the two things were constantly interlinked.

RW/MTB: *How far do you think Shakespeare's texts need to be cut or altered to suit late twentieth-century cinema tastes? Your* Henry V *and* Much Ado About Nothing *made textual changes;* Love's Labour's Lost *is a composite of the original text and interpolated songs. In contrast,* Hamlet *boasted the entire play and the text in its full format.*

KB: Well, for me it's been an experiment or an exploration, and with *Hamlet*, aside from feeling that it would be fascinating to see all of that text played out in a film, I also wanted to see how much an audience might be encouraged to take it or to sit through it – what reaction there would be to that amount of dialogue.

There are at least a couple of issues. One is the sort of thing brought up again by your orginal question about Macmorris where I think my attitude is born out of my time, partly out of my background, but partly culturally born out of my time. I'd say the same thing over the issue in *Henry V* of the way I deal with the King killing the prisoners, which I think I rather flunked and avoided, and although I make dramatic sense in the context of our picture, I could have possibly been braver about the way we presented it and not, as I feared we would, lose the sympathy of the audience for the central character. We definitely embraced the contradictions inside the role, but to make a point in relation to text (one of which is the cultural/political dimension in which an attitude to text in these films sits), there, I think I was probably cautious/nervous/cowardly about doing something that might provoke the wrong kind of reaction to the character.

So there is that sort of issue, and then there is the more direct issue of what, from project to project, you feel makes sense. With *Love's Labour's Lost*, I'm pretty sure I have cut as much, if not a little more, than was the case with *Much Ado About Nothing*, and there in a way it's a much more pragmatic view of what in this case is funny. And that's based on an experience of what was funny in the theatre and what [people] strained to [understand], and making a decision, in the case of *Love's Labour's Lost*, in cutting language which was very difficult to understand, trying to assess 'Well, what does that language do and what does its subject matter add, in as far as one can understand it, to Shakespeare's theme or essay here, and is there anything, in relation to our cinematic presentation, that we can replace it with that would be relevant or organic?' In this case, I've chosen to replace that element which I, for better or worse, deemed impossible to carry off in the cinema, with songs, and with songs from, arguably in twentieth-century terms anyway, equally witty writers – people like Cole Porter and Irving Berlin, who played with verbal conceit.

An attitude to text, I think, just has to be specific to the time, the place and your view of the piece. In [the] case [of *Love's Labour's Lost*], [I was] trying to find a world, as I mentioned earlier, where I could believe the themes in this play and the plot of this play could sit in a way that was pleasing for the audience, and then deciding to cut, for the modern ear and audience, excessively difficult language (which I think many people would concede about this play), replacing what it does thematically with music and with the wit and the invention of those twentieth-century writers in the musical world – Cole Porter, Irving Berlin – who have discussed all the essential subjects of love (which Shakespeare also does in the play). In that case, the cuts were dictated in that way. I didn't want to rob the play of what I suspect Shakespeare was trying to do in some part, but, in its cinematic trans-lation, decided to offer up some songs which often, even in terms of their lyrics, refer to what has just been spoken. I have no rule or philosophy about how much or what should be cut. I do think that there are some practical implications: it would be very tough to get a full-length version of *Love's Labour's Lost* made. It's been hard enough to get a cut version of it made!

In the case of *Love's Labour's Lost* and *Much Ado About Nothing*, one hopes that, without being bland or casual about it, that it is possible to trim the text for the cinema and still have a sense of the complete play. It was true in the reaction to *Much Ado About Nothing* that people who knew the play very very well, in the context of the whole of that film, and watching it in the cinema, failed to spot quite significant shifts and changes. There's a scene between Dogberry, Verges and Leonato, which, if one thought of it in three sections which follow the A, B and C [ordering] of Shakespeare's text, certainly in the film starts with section C, and then goes to section A and then B, because it seemed to offer a clearer cinematic logic. It was one of those things that was so rarely picked up on [that people thought] that they'd just been watching what Shakespeare had written anyway. So one's hoping that, from time to time, the attempt to address the issue of the move from stage to screen is determined by those things that don't stick out in the wrong way.

RW/MTB: *The linguistic wit of* Love's Labour's Lost, *then, is matched by musical wit in your interpretation?*

KB: The element that has been lost textually up to a point – [although] there's still plenty to enjoy as an essential characteristic of that play – is replaced by music and songs that reflect the subject matter with the same brilliance – in twentieth-century terms, with some significant brilliance (from people like Porter and Berlin and Jerome Kern and George Gershwin).

RW/MTB: *Does the fact that you are evoking in* Love's Labour's Lost *the style and mood of 1930s' musicals suggest that you are now moving into appropriating, even subverting, Shakespeare for the first time?*

KB: Who knows? I've resisted doing Shakespeare in the twentieth century. I've always been worried about offering up a world where you don't expect people to talk in a certain kind of way – it's makes me nervous. It's an entirely soluble problem, but it's not one I find easy to [adopt]. With *Love's Labour's Lost*, as I'm sure you know, the play disappears from the repertoire for a couple of hundred years (and then Harley Granville Barker described it as a 'fashionable play three hundred years out of fashion'). [It's a play] that seems to have responded to a very strong directorial hand, and the landmark productions of this century by Brook and Hall and Michael Langham have been ones that have been very strongly inflected, [with a] very strong sense of place, and my instinct in being in the play in the theatre was that it most certainly needed that – it needed a strong sense of reality, a strong sense of location, a strong sense of a world in which you were happy to accept or understand (a kind of implicit understanding) why the King might engage in this three-year plan. I've always been interested in the period between the wars – what it offered up, the sorts of regret and grief and tragic legacy of the First World War, with the political situation as it was, the threat of renewed violence, and what that seemed to do to the atmosphere of the time. The sense of perhaps one last idyll in the twentieth century before the world really would change for ever. That sense of a stolen, magical, idyllic time which nevertheless had a clock ticking: it's something which I think can work powerfully for *Love's Labour's Lost* and the world of film musicals – the sort of lightness of touch, which occasionally surprises you with the bitter-sweet qualities that they can also express, seems to be in tune with the mood of the play. So there was something about the pulse of the play, and the way in which that particular genre works in movies, that seemed to go together, and I said to myself, 'Well, this feels right, and this is a world, in cinematic terms, where I feel we can accept people speaking in heightened language.' I feel as though, in what again will be an impressionistic evocation of the period, that, in fact, Shakespeare will be very strongly alive in this one. I am thrilled with the way in which the film seems to be coming together.

RW/MTB: *You've always had a direct creative input (in collaboration with Patrick Doyle) to the music for your films. With* Love's Labour's Lost *being more of a musical production, and with Patrick Doyle again on board, how do you feel your creative input will manifest itself?*

KB: Certainly, it already has, in the selection of the songs, which are all very particular and specific to moments in the play. I'll give you one specific example. I've chosen to break up Berowne's wonderful speech at the end of the big scene with the four boys revealing that they're all in love, the speech beginning 'Have at you then, affection's men-at-arms!' It's true in some editions, I believe, that in fact the speech is broken up, so I decided to split it in the following way, which is to have [Berowne] finish geeing-up the boys up with 'And when Love speaks, the voice of all the gods / Make heaven drowsy with the harmony', at which point we go into 'Heaven, I'm in heaven' [KB sings], and then we have a fantasy sequence in which the boys dance with the girls, and give us some Fred and Ginger, and then [Berowne] comes back for the second part of the speech. But there's an endless number of times, actually, where the actual lyrics of the songs refer directly to and use words that are used [in the play], more than just a neat connection like that. So the songs were pre-chosen. What Patrick has inherited is how we arrange them, how we find a way to arrange them that is usually romantic, although not conventional: they won't sound as they have done before. He'll [Patrick Doyle] prob- ably write ten or fifteen minutes of actual score for the rest of the movie, for various moments that we believe might need that, and that will be something that we work on in the process of trying to fix arrangements. Patrick and I have an ongoing conversation which is really me continuing to express my view of the play, describing moments and how they'll be presented. We had a discussion about the end of the play and what we needed, and I talked both about the text and particular lines, and also about what the end of the piece needs cinematically, which I described in terms of *Casablanca* and *Brief*

Encounter. The *Casablanca* moment at the end is the girls leaving by airplane, so that kind of conversation – where there's a constant expression of where we are [and] what's developed from rehearsals – will develop much further with the input of the actors. We keep that up – we keep asking questions – and the score gets written quietly.

RW/MTB: *That connects with our next question which is about the cinematic moments of* Love's Labour's Lost, *or rather the moments in the play that might lend themselves well to cinematic treatment. We're thinking of Berowne's 'What's her name in the cap?' and the last lines, 'You that way; we this way'. Do such moments leap out at you when you are reading a play as having cinematic potential?*

KB: Over a period of time they do, and in this case we have a very big-screen moment for 'You that way; we this way'. We have a huge cinematic moment for the beginning of the pageant of the Nine Worthies, a big routine, and the arrival of the girls (by water, in this case). There is some link between it and the beginning of *Much Ado About Nothing* inasmuch as there is a kind of overture, and a visual montage of images and a laying-out of the energies we will use – the sweep and the energy that was shared by that opening sequence in *Much Ado About Nothing* with the boys coming and the girls getting ready and the boys arriving by horse. That will be a big cinematic moment. I think actually we've found many more ways to make this [play] more cinematic than *Much Ado About Nothing*, and that may just be experience.

RW/MTB: *We've been thinking about the whole glut of Shakespeare films in the 1990s, apart from your own – films like* Looking for Richard, Richard III, *two versions of* A Midsummer Night's Dream, *Baz Luhrmann's* William Shakespeare's 'Romeo + Juliet', *and also, of course, all the Shakespeare-inspired films, such as* Elizabeth, A Thousand Acres, Tromeo and Juliet *and* Shakespeare in Love. *Could you take a moment to reflect upon the popularity that such films are obviously generating?*

KB: Yeah, well it's something I enjoy, because it makes the process of trying to raise money for these films a little less unusual. I don't know if I can explain it – although God knows I've thought about it – but it seems to me that, in talking to filmmakers, it's just a chance to experiment (and explore) cinematically/technically/creatively with the presentation in each story, [and] that's given licence with the full understanding of the power of the stories themselves. [These films] have a terrific structure on which to rest and then be experimental. Baz Luhrmann can be as bold as he is with *Romeo and Juliet* [by] knowing that that's one of Shakespeare's hardiest plays, one of his sturdy plays, which allows him to be fantastically vivid and radical. In terms of cinema, there's a dearth of good writing, and, in the theatre, there's also a dearth of good writing, partly because it's so hard to make a living from writing for the theatre, and so people write for soap-operas, and that sends their writing in one particular way. So there are all sorts of factors at work. But the power of the stories – and here I'm recalling the remark you made earlier about the end of an era – the 1990s represented the end of an era in Shakespeare filmmaking. There was the end of, and a reaction to and a move away from Welles, Olivier, Kurosawa (a certain kind of Shakespearean filmmaking), which seems to have been reborn and freed up, so we might see a significant amount more.

RW/MTB: *How do you see your own Shakespearean future in the twenty-first century?* As You Like It *and* Macbeth *have both been mentioned as possible projects. How do you see the next ten/twenty years?*

KB: So much is related to the pragmatism of working in a cinema where box-office success and commercial success are linked to creative freedom inasmuch as, at some level, it seems possible that there are enough people interested in what I do to gather some money together for other Shakespeare films. But, of course, one doesn't necessarily want to make them all for 4 or 5 million dollars. *Hamlet* was 18 million dollars, and that was because the scale that we felt was required for our version of it needed that kind of money. So I would hope that we have sufficient commercial success to allow us to be free with how we wish to do the plays. I have been working for some time on *Macbeth* with another director: I would be in the film, but not directing, although I would do the screenplay, and *As You Like It* has been suggesting itself to me. Again, it's finding the world, finding a unifying concept. You have gut instincts about images or ways of doing it, and then you spend years with the play tripping you up, saying 'But that scene won't work!' and 'That scene won't work with that idea!', and then maybe you find a way around it. I'd like to think the next one we do, if we get through this one, would be *Macbeth*, and that would be some time next year, and then we try and do one every year or every two years.

RW/MTB: *Finally, in connection with the nature of this collection, how do you regard the relationship between yourself as a Shakespearean filmmaker and the academic Shakespeare establishment?*

KB: Well, as you probably know, a great friend of mine and a collaborator on the films, is Russell [Jackson], and I feel as though he's my link to what's going on. I'm interested in all things Shakespearean. I read quite a lot. I read the various newsletters and quarterlies, and find all that very interesting. I keep my distance a bit, and sometimes I'm amused and sometimes enraged by the passionate debates or heated arguments about certain moments or decisions we've chosen to take, but I've been very encouraged by the liveliness with which the academic Shakespeare community has responded to this last seven/eight years of Shakespearean filmmaking. It's a lively moment. It's an exciting moment. It's reinvented things a little, and, even if people have been against some of this work, they have been passionate, and there's been interesting new writing, I think. Certainly I always enjoy discussing it with academics. But I resist getting too drawn in. The practitioner in me says: 'Don't get too theoretical!' I'm an intuitive filmmaker, so a lot of times I'm just following my guts.

12
Virgin and Ape, Venetian and Infidel: Labellings of Otherness in Oliver Parker's *Othello*

Judith Buchanan

In February 1998, Kofi Anan, the Secretary General of the United Nations, arrived in Iraq to confront the threat posed by Saddam Hussein. Of all the things that were crucially relevant to Anan's high-profile embassy, colour was certainly not one of them. And yet, in the context of a world order which, in other respects, is anything but consistently equitable in its view of black and white, the symbolism of his 'ride to the rescue' of 'the civilized world' (as characterized in the *Wall Street Journal*) can carry a Shakespearean resonance: a black African was the commissioned representative of an organization, the majority of whose central power has traditionally lain in white communities, upholding *its* values against the dangerous infidel.[1] Seen in this light, Anan's mission to Iraq exposes the *degrees* of alterity that sometimes underpin cultural relations. In the face of a common foe explicitly defined in 'the civilized world' in terms of its absolute alterity, subsidiary categories of alien and insider – black and white, African and Euro-American – are pragmatically elided.

In *Othello*, white Venice's collective sense of what constitutes insider and outsider status is similarly, though more dramatically, challenged: Venice sends Othello, a Moor, to Cyprus as its commissioned representative in opposing its dangerous Other, the Turk. It is testimony to how thoroughly Othello is seen to have assimilated to a Venetian value-system that he, so visibly a non-Venetian, is chosen to serve as its strategic ambassador elsewhere.

Film productions of the play have depicted Othello in a variety of cultural relations to the city-state that employs him. In the first section of this essay, I survey the ways in which the balance of Othello's assimilation to Venetian culture, and resistance to it, has been signalled in different productions. Against this backdrop I then consider the cultural placement of Othello, and configurations of otherness, specifically in Oliver Parker's film. In the second section, I examine how the manipulation of the subjectivized gaze contributes to notions of belonging and alterity in the film. In the third section, I weigh the implications of a contemporary narrative by which the film was ambushed in its earliest reception context. And finally, I question the pertinence of our millennium moment in constructing a critical frame within which discussions of alterity may be conducted.

'Who albeit ... a More'

The Venice depicted in Shakespeare's play is acutely conscious of the particularity, and assumed rightness, of its own mores and beliefs. 'This is Venice: / My house is not a grange' (I.i.104–5), says Brabantio with smug indignation when awoken in the night.[2] The Venetians believe in the harmony and civilized order of their life, their rhetoric perpetuating this myth even when the evidence before them throws doubt upon it. To sustain its self-image as the epitome of well-regulated government and Christian virtue, Venice needs a foil, and the Turk – Venice's religious, economic and imperial rival – neatly provides one. In Shakespeare's Venice, as in the real Venice of the early modern period, the Turk is demonized as everything that is barbaric, untrustworthy and dangerous.[3] Thus in *Othello*, Venice's sense of its own worth is implicitly pitted against the Turks' supposed barbarism and indiscipline ('Are we turned Turks? ... For Christian shame, put by this barbarous brawl' [II.iii.166, 168]), deceitfulness ('Nay, it is true, or else I am a Turk' [II.i.114]) and damned condition (the Turks, unlike the Christians, 'shall [not] be saved' [IV.ii.88]). In being commissioned to represent Venice, Othello is being asked to oppose the very thing against which Venice defines itself most obviously. He must *be* Venice abroad, upholding its values in the face of its opposite.

We may assume that Shakespeare's depiction of Othello's Moorishness is intended to indicate a Muslim background. Indeed, sections of Othello's own life story as told to the Senate have parallels with that of a real Muslim-born North African of the period, Wazzân Al-Fasi. In 1550, Wazzân had published an account of the geography and customs of Africa under his Christianized name, John Leo. In 1600, John Pory translated this into English as *A Geographical Historie of Africa*, adding a prefatory address to the reader in which he recommended his author with this two-edged testimonial:

Who albeit by birth a More, and by religion for many yeeres a Mahumetan; yet if you consider his Parentage, Witte, Education, Learning, Emploiments, Travels, and his conuersion to Christianitie; you shall find him not altogether ... unwoorthy to be regarded.[4]

Some details of Wazzân's life (the North African origins, roaming the Mediterranean, being sold into slavery) may well have served as a pattern for Othello's own history.[5] Moreover, Shakespeare's depiction of *his* Muslim Moor-turned-Christian, and his depiction of Venice's conditional acceptance of him, turn on the same telling 'albeit' that underscores Pory's recommendation. Othello, 'albeit ... a More', is noble, courageous, dignified, experienced in battle, well-born and a convert to Chrisitianity, and so, *despite* his colour and culture, the Venetian Senate considers that he, too, on these terms, is 'not altogether ... unwoorthy to be regarded'.

Othello, like Wazzân, makes one of the expressions of his assimilation to his elected culture the adoption of its religion as his own. In advertisement of Othello's adopted Christianity, Laurence Olivier's Othello (filmed in 1965) wears a large cross around his neck to which he clings in moments of crisis. This symbol of his Christianizing, worn proudly on his chest, indicates his self-conscious and earnest desire to align himself with Venetian culture and beliefs. However, it sits oddly with his African robe, highly polished blacked-up appearance, African accent and bare, manacled feet. In a moment of torment on Cyprus, Olivier's Othello rips the cross violently from his neck, actively rejecting the value-system by which he now feels abused. His relationship with the symbol of his Venetian affiliation had from the first seemed strained. In ridding himself of it, he reclaims a cultural identity less riven by contradiction.

In Sam Mendes' 1998 National Theatre production, Othello (played for the first time at the National by a black actor, John Harewood) once again clutched a large gold cross at critical moments in the action. His obsessive fingering of this symbol of his adopted culture helped him sustain his affiliation. Indeed, Harewood's Othello clung to his cross almost as a talisman, a point of security in an increasingly tormenting world. Later, however, it became also, quite literally, the instrument of his destruction. Othello's secret weapon (produced at the end of the play to thwart those who would prevent him from taking his own life) emerged in this production from within the decorative cross that had been present throughout. Harewood's Othello unscrewed his crucifix and inserted the hidden blade contained therein into his jugular with surgical precision, appropriately declaring himself the slain 'turbanned Turk' (V.ii.351) as he died by the cross. At the last Othello had cast himself in the role of the dangerous infidel whom he had been sent by Christian Venice to oppose.

Oliver Parker's *Othello* (1995) aligns itself with the placement of Othello as a man willing to advertise his resistance to his environment more than with productions that present a man trying to minimize his distinction from it.[6] Laurence Fishburne, the first black actor to have played the role in a commercial cinema production, presents an Othello who is far from being a Venetian in all but skin colour.[7] Parker configures him as a fascinating and useful outsider in Venice, a man whose power carries hints of an eroticism, derived from his arresting physicality. Our first view of him is a close-up of his prominently scarred hand taking Desdemona's unblemished one during their clandestine marriage ceremony: a striking introductory image of black meeting white. The Othello who then leans in to claim a kiss from his bride is half-shrouded in a black hooded cloak. For Desdemona (Irene Jacob), as for the rest of Venice, his unapologetic otherness is undeniably part of his attraction. His Venetian garb does little to moderate the effect: his colour, stature, bearing, earrings, unfamiliar gestures and half-mocking atmosphere make him less the supreme exemplum of Venice than an exotic misfit within it.

In Janet Suzman's 1988 made-for-television production, one of the symbols by which John Kani's Othello powerfully signals his Otherness from his environment is his constantly visible African tribal necklace. Even in front of the Venetian Senate, this symbol of his non-alignment with white Christian Venice is worn with pride. The blue gem around Fishburne's neck is not worn as prominently as Kani's necklace. Nevertheless, having no equivalent among the Venetians, its presence marks him out as a man from a place governed by different cultural, aesthetic and trading norms and conventions. In the course of Parker's film, as Othello feels increasingly tormented by Venice and all that he takes it to represent, his symbols of non-assimilation – the blue gem, his loose African cape, a wooden staff – assume an increasing prominence. The necklace, in common with the one in Mendes' production, is more than mere decoration. At the end of Parker's film, in a self-dramatizing gesture, Othello pulls it tight round his own neck as he stabs himself. Whereas Harewood's Othello symbolically dies by the Venetian cross he has tried, but failed, to make his own, in the symbolic scheme of Parker's film, Othello dies from his refusal to break free of his old cultural attachments and make Venice's systems and beliefs fully his own.

In 1599, the English poet I. Ashley concluded his sonnet apostrophizing Venice with the line, 'Enamour'd like Narcissus thou shalt dye'.[8] Renaissance England perceived Venice as a place whose image had been constructed partly to gratify its desire to think well of itself. Parker's Venice, like Shakespeare's, is also in love with its own self-image: it believes the myths it has created about itself. In the opening scene of the film, a gondola skims quietly at night across the Grand Canal in Venice. The world to which we are immediately introduced is one of shimmering and beautiful reflections. It is a city whose very architecture dictates that it gaze unceasingly upon its own reflected image.

Shakespeare's Moor has a history as a mercenary ('an extravagant and wheeling stranger / Of here and everywhere' [I.i.134–5]). Fishburne's half-snarling, half-mocking, powerfully physical screen presence makes him credible in such a role. His Othello adjusts his character as he adjusts his allegiances. In Venice, even while standing clearly distinct from its inhabitants, he mirrors aspects of the character of the city. He is an Othello who, like Venice itself, is captivated by an image of himself which he fashions carefully for public consumption – a man not only taken with his own reflection but happy to encourage others also to gaze upon it.

Othello's self-dramatizing tendencies emerge early in Parker's film. His account of his life to the Senate is punctuated by flashback scenes which he conjures as pleonastic illustration to his words. He is quick to visualise how well received he was at Brabantio's house, and how irresistibly drawn to him Desdemona was. Othello is inspired and consoled by the graphic recollection of his own favourable impact on his world. As Parker's camera aligns itself intermittently with Desdemona's desirous gaze throughout the film, Othello's body is explicitly eroticized by its visual strategy. On the night of their arrival in Cyprus, it is, for example, his undressing, not hers, upon which the camera lingers with the most intimate and detailed appreciation. Moreover, the way in which Iago (Kenneth Branagh) looks at Othello, though more complex and full of contradictory impulses than Desdemona's gaze, is itself not free of a fascinated attraction. When Iago sits on the beach delivering his 'The Moor already changes with my poison' soliloquy, his line ('Look where he comes' [III.iii.333]), which in the text heralds Othello's entrance, is in the film reduced simply to 'Look'. Iago's instruction that we should 'look', delivered intimately straight to camera, immediately instructs it to swing around, following Iago's own turning gaze, until it lights upon Othello standing on a promontory. Parker's editing of the Shakespeare line here, and accompanying camera direction, is a defining moment for his film as its implicit visual strategy becomes momentarily explicit. The eroticized gaze is made central, and potential distractions from that concentration are minimized or excluded. Parker's interest in 'where he comes' (both cultural placement and historical context) is, by contrast, more limited. Rather, Parker attempts to spin the dramatic material into an erotic myth not finally determined by context or history. It is, moreover, impossible not to heed Iago's instruction that we 'look' upon Othello not only at this moment but throughout the film, since he is the privileged centre of its visual design.

Iago spends much of the time observing Othello with a complex mix of proprietorship, detestation and irresistible intimacy. Near the end of the temptation scene, Iago watches Othello looking at himself in a full-length mirror. The voyeuristic observation of self-observation is laden with significance, since it is the narcissism of Othello's self-obsessed gaze that Iago succeeds in warping. 'Why did I marry?' (III.iii.245) Othello is left to ask of his own reflection, seeing himself already as a man weakened and compromised. His admiration for himself as hero becomes in stages a contempt for himself as an idiotic aberration in a white world beyond his comprehension or control. Near the end of the film, the injured Iago climbs onto the bed to join its tragic loading, clinging like a needy, damaged child to his dead general's leg. Othello's body is thus fetishized as a point of fascination by the intradiegetic attentivenesses (voyeuristic and physical) of both Desdemona and Iago. And in tune with the self-indulgent dictates of Othello's own mind, it is also treated as an object of fascination and awe by the camera.

While still mirroring something of the self-dramatizing and narcissistic character of Venice, Fishburne's Othello, once on Cyprus, also then mirrors aspects of *its* cultural placement. Cyprus is a liminal territory. Both geographically and culturally it sits between worlds, looking both towards Christian Venice and towards the infidel Turk, having been conquered by each and unsure of its proper belonging.[9] In the action of Shakespeare's drama, the Turkish fleet is drowned in a sea-storm off the coast of Cyprus, and the Venetian forces posted there hold their subsequent night of revels in celebration of '*the mere perdition of the Turkish fleet*' (II.ii.3). In Parker's film, a stuffed effigy of a turbanned Turk with a crescent on his tunic is jeered at and ceremonially burned during these festivities. For a historically savvy audience, however, the 1570 date of the film's setting would ironize the implied triumphalism of this gesture. The months of that year were to be the island's last moments under Venetian rule: it was in the following year that the Turks were to rout the Venetians soundly from Cyprus in the name of the Islamic Ottoman Empire.[10]

An audience in the 1990s could not be expected to know of the imminent fall of Cyprus to the Turks in 1571 in the way that Shakespeare's first audiences may have done. Nevertheless, Parker's *Othello* does capture a sense of the precariousness of an outpost of empire that is not invulnerable to attack and whose complete collapse, though it does not yet know it, is imminent. A general sense of fragility in colonial Cyprus is evoked. Few things there may be relied upon as solid or dependable. Although the fortress, turrets and weaponry on Cyprus with their clear, hard edges present an appropriately defined front to a potentially threatening world, the dominant motifs in the film's visual scheme involve water and the billowing, diaphanous fabrics of curtains, drapes, dresses and a fluttering handkerchief. Elements in which one might drown or become impotently entangled define the psychological climate of Parker's Cyprus. With studied indifference, for example, Iago casually knocks two chess board figures – the black King and the white Queen – into a well where we see them sink in slow motion. This scene is then revisited at the end of the film in the burial at sea of Othello and Desdemona when their shrouded bodies are shown drifting towards the bottom of the ocean. Iago as director of his own fantasy drama has ensured that Othello's and Desdemona's black and white bodies eventually replace the corresponding chess figures which acted as substitutes for them in his earlier rehearsal of the scene.

Cyprus' cultural indeterminacy provides a disastrous pattern for Othello. As a man used to making a quick identification with each new territory he serves, he absorbs the cultural ambivalence of Cyprus into his own person and reproduces it for his final self-dramatizing speech. Here he casts himself simultaneously in the role of Venetian soldier of the cross and as the Turkish infidel, deliberately conflating a glorious incident from his past with his present situation:

> And say besides that in Aleppo once,
> Where a malignant and a turbanned Turk
> Beat a Venetian and traduced the state,
> I took by th' throat the circumcised dog

And smote him – thus!   *He stabs himself.*
(V.ii.350–4)

In slaying himself he feels himself to be both upholding his Venetian commission (smiting the infidel) *and* the obstacle to that commission (the malignant traducer of the state that must be smitten). He is both perpetrator and victim in his own death, ascribing not only different roles to the dichotomized self that emerges in the act, but also different cultures – Venetian and Turk. As Fishburne's Othello lies on his death bed strangled by his Moorish jewel, surrounded by all the personnel of his Venetian life, and identifying himself as the Turk, his unreconciled cultural identity echoes that of the island he had briefly and unsuccessfully attempted to govern.

Controlling the Look – Directors on Both Sides of the Camera

On arrival in Cyprus, Branagh's Iago peels a piece of fruit with a small knife. In its blade he watches the reflection of Cassio and Desdemona as they whisper together. The scene is directly reminiscent of the parallel scene in the 1955 Yutkevich *Othello* in which Iago (Andrei Popov) watches their innocent dalliance in blurred reflection in the hilt of his sword. However, the small neat knife wielded by Branagh's Iago, as he does precisely controlled violence to a piece of fruit, plays a more pivotal role in Parker's film than did the equivalent scene in the Russian *Othello*. In Parker's version, it becomes clear that it is Iago's observation of Cassio and Desdemona in distorted reflection in the blade of his knife that suggests his own future strategy to him: he must render the image of these two people blurred also to Othello by interposing himself as a distorting mirror through which Othello may observe the world.

Iago's desire to dictate the lens through which Othello is to perceive things identifies him as the film's internal cinematographer. It is Iago who explicitly instructs the spectator to 'look', and indeed how to 'look', at Othello when he is standing ruminatively by the shore. It is also Iago who determines how Othello should look both at others and at himself. In the carefully stage-managed encavement scene, Iago places Othello behind bars and theatrically blocks Cassio's mock-disclosure specifically to suit Othello's angle of vision. In a slightly heavy-handed metaphor for his emotional enslavement, the shadows of the bars fall on Othello's face. As our perceptions are then aligned with Othello's, we, too, are invited to see through the bars what Iago would have him see.

Envisaging Branagh's Iago as the man who determines who will see what, from what angle and in what clarity of focus, carries, of course, its own biographical resonance. Branagh, like the Iago he plays, is a man who likes to direct his own dramas. In having Branagh's character determine the ways in which others should look, Parker has incidentally alluded to the contained talent, the unacknowledged director, that he had on his set in the person of Kenneth Branagh. Rita Kempley in her review for the *Washington Post* speculated that Branagh's role in this production might have been more extensive than this: 'Kenneth Branagh doesn't just steal the show; one suspects he might have sat in the director's chair as well.'[11] In the penultimate scene of the production, however, Parker's camera finally makes clear its distance from Iago by rising above the bed to look down upon him as he lies injured and enfeebled. As the only rising, high-angle shot in the film, it is particularly striking, immediately and drastically redefining the camera's relationship with Iago. He looks up at the camera from his huddled position on the bed, but his look has changed. No longer is it the look of a man in control, a man whose intimate and knowing glances at the camera have encouraged the spectator into a complicity with his vicious designs. He has now been diminished and objectified. He is now denied the consoling illusion that he is constructing the pictures we see; rather, he is himself looked down upon as part of the composed patterning of the frame. As Parker's last-minute assertion of a superior angle upon a disempowered Iago cannily reminds us, the *Othello* picture that was finally created was, despite Kempley's speculations, not Branagh's but Parker's.[12]

Although Othello is the chief object of fascination and eroticism in the film, he is by no means always objectified by the film's gaze. By intermittently aligning the film's fluid subjectivities with Othello's own perceptions, Parker destabilizes a sense of his Moor's alterity. Of all Shakespeare's tragic heroes, Othello is perhaps the least intimate with an audience. He has fewer soliloquies than Hamlet, Macbeth or Lear, and those that he does have do not offer much honest disclosure, differing little in tone from his public speeches. He is, arguably, so accustomed to sculpting an image of himself for the benefit of an appreciative public that he never develops an honest inner life distinct from that. Parker, however, allows the spectator an unusual degree of intimacy with Othello, both through occasional voice-overs (a device often withheld from screen Othellos, although standard for screen Hamlets, for example), and by subjectivizing his perceptions. On both counts, Othello seems to be rendered a more private and knowable character than has been true of most Othellos. So strategic is the film's decision not to keep Othello simply as an objectified Other, viewed by the world and by the camera as an item of fascination, desire and horror, that he is even given a moment to parallel and parody Iago's imperious and directorial 'Look' that determines the subsequent camera angle and object. As Desdemona enters the bedchamber, in the second half of the film, Othello says, 'Look where she comes'. His instruction causes the camera to spin hastily through 180 degrees from objectifying him to subjectivizing his view of Desdemona's approach in the same shot. The camera work thus creates the illusion that he, too, like Iago, can control the spectatorial gaze. Othello's aspiration to subject status is, however, most obviously validated when Desdemona dances for him and the other guests after their victorious arrival on Cyprus. Her display is designed specifically to gratify his attentive observation of her, and the scene cuts between a shot of him as delighted voyeur and shots of her as self-styled object of his appreciative gaze. In his love scene with Desdemona, and in its many subsequent tormenting variations in his anxious fantasy, he is both voyeur and predator. At their first sexual encounter, she seems to back off a little nervously across the room before his semi-naked figure. He advances, the subjectivized camera alternating between seeing her retreating figure from his perspective and seeing his advancing one from hers. The impression generated both by point of view and editing is inescapably one of reluctance on her part and insistence on his – if only in a spirit of amorous play. Once she has slipped half-coyly, half-invitingly behind the curtains onto the bed, he parts the flimsy barrier purposefully and enters the bed, in order to claim the 'fruits' that he has just said were still 'to ensue' (II.iii.9). He has styled himself as the warrior-conqueror, she as the coyly vanquished. Parker has thus added a further slightly troubling, if titillating, opposition – that of desire and fear – to the array of more neutral contrasts (physical strength and physical fragility, a scarred body and an unblemished one, black skin and white, male and female) already inherent in the sexual union of Othello and Desdemona. Later, in a sequence from Othello's tormented fantasy, he once again advances naked towards the billowing bed curtains with clear sexual purpose to divide, see, enter and possess. With disturbing symbolism, however, in his fantasy he advances with his knife drawn. He parts the curtains with its blade and, still in his troubled fantasy, finds Desdemona and Cassio entwined naked there, mocking him. For Othello – a military man of action who feels increasingly adrift in a world of sexual intrigue – the knife which he grips in his fantasy is one of the few reliable and solid objects amidst the fluttering, shifting, insubstantial fabrics of his environment. From his perspective, it is also a symbol of his manhood in the face of bafflingly complex female charms and snares.

From a spectator's perspective, however, the presence of Othello's knife in his nightmare is also a reminder of the previous knife which had assumed some prominence in the film – that in which Iago had observed Desdemona's and Cassio's distorted reflection upon their first arrival in Cyprus. In triggering the recollection of the earlier scene, the knife in Othello's fantasy world serves as a reminder that his vision of Desdemona and Cassio has been deliberately rendered blurred by the interposing presence of Iago. The association punctures the impression of Othello's power as subject not object of the film's gaze by reminding the spectator of the strategic interference that now determines his observation of the world. Shortly afterwards, Othello watches from behind a muslin hanging as Desdemona searches for the missing handkerchief. Our spectatorial position is once again aligned with his so that we, too, see her only indistinctly through the distorting muslin filter. His stepping from behind this curtain in order to bring her into a clarity of focus has several parallel moments throughout the film. After his brief vigil sitting watching Desdemona sleep before he kills her, for example, Othello deliberately moves aside the flimsy curtain with his staff that he (and we with him) might see her more clearly. His several efforts to move aside the various obstructions that cloud his view of Desdmona are, however, futile. The flimsy fabrics that constantly interpose themselves between him and his wife are Parker's metaphors for a blurring of his vision that has taken place on a more fundamental emotional level. His attempts to manoeuvre his way around such *material* obstructions merely serve to emphasize his inability to lift the *emotional* filter that has been placed over his vision.

The irony of Othello's parodically directorial 'Look' moment is, therefore, that, far from being able to influence others' ways of looking, not even his own gaze is reliable, having been distorted by the interposing filter of Iago's vicious interpretative lens (itself a construct of the real director, Parker). Although the composition of the shot of Desdemona's approach here, and of Desdemona more generally at other moments in the film, is advertised as being part of Othello's perception, when *we* look upon Desdemona, what we are made most aware of is the discrepancy between the (innocent) woman whom we see and the (adulterous) woman whom Othello sees in the same figure. The fact that we are looking as it were *with* him serves only to emphasize the distinction between his and our reading of the image we have jointly received. Thus, being aligned with his point of view does not ultimately generate an unShakespearean kinship between audience and Othello, but rather reinforces a sense of the failings in his vision and, therefore, most commonly of the (wholly Shakespearean) gulf between him and us.

'Set you down this': The Black Man in White Public Space

Unlike many Shakespeare films of the past decade (most obviously Baz Lurhmann's *William Shakespeare's 'Romeo + Juliet'* and Christine Edzard's *As You Like It*), and many theatrical productions of *Othello* over the same period which have deliberately courted topical resonances, Parker's *Othello* does not update its source drama to modern times, nor does it explicitly draw out any contemporary parallels. In fact, although evidently *stylistically* of its moment, Parker's film shows every sign of attempting to abstract itself from topical allusions of all kinds through its firmly historical 1570 setting. Nevertheless, Shakespeare's play is so brimful of emotive triggers not exclusive to moment or context that it can scarcely escape chiming with contemporary narratives in a reception context.[13] Just as no contemporary production of *The Merchant of Venice* can duck the resonances of being played in a post-Holocaust world, so no contemporary production of *Othello* can be oblivious of how the interracial encounters in the play relate to those beyond its bounds. The increasingly multicultural nature of our world renders this necessary, and an ostensibly distant temporal setting for the production does nothing to circumscribe this.

The black man was, of course, notably absent from productions of *Othello* on the Jacobean stage, and has largely remained so since. When Othello is played by a blacked-up white actor, as he has so often been, the play may be a discourse *about* race, but at a discernible symbolic remove from the subject of its consideration. The 1920 silent Anson Dyer animated *Othello* contributes an apposite joke to the performance history of blacked-up Othellos. A cartoonist's hand appears in front of a line drawing and starts to colour in the figure of a man sitting in front of a dressing table mirror. As we watch, the bare figure is transformed in stages into a music-hall black minstrel, complete with banjo slung across his back. Mid-task, however, the cartoonist's hand places the burnt cork he has been using on the dressing table in front of his half-coloured creation and withdraws from the frame. Left to his own devices, the newly animated, but only half-coloured, Othello then himself picks up the cork and completes the task of blacking-up himself. The accompanying intertitles to this opening sequence make the joke yet more self-conscious. The opening intertitle, 'OTHELLO THE MOOR WAS BLACK', is immediately followed by a second, which puns on the dual significance of black (literal colour and synonym for wicked) to emphasize the constructed nature both of Othello's colour and of his degenerative reputation: 'BUT HE WAS NOT AS BLACK AS HE WAS PAINTED!' The fact that Dyer's Othello is made so obviously responsible for applying his own colour, and therefore for constructing his own racial self-projections, reflects back interestingly upon the play which it is parodying. The character of Shakespeare's Othello deliberately spins culturally evocative myths about himself and his history (by, for example, dwelling on the mystical origins of the handkerchief) in order to nurture a sense of his own exotic Otherness. Moreover, the actor of Shakespeare's Othello has indeed rarely been as 'black as he was painted', since he has almost always been a white man painted black. Both his reputation and his colour have been blackened by deliberate decision. In the final shot, Othello's girlfriend (known familiarly as Mona) becomes comically and exaggeratedly smeared with black as his artificially applied colour rubs off on her. Thus the Dyer cartoon ridicules by extravagant parody the contemporary practice of casting a white man as Othello who needs to turn himself into a comically grotesque sideshow in order to play the part.

Fishburne's performance as a black man playing the part of a black man reduces the gap between the player and the part played, and so renders the debates about skin colour and ethnicity more immediate and less stylized than they could have been on the Renaissance stage, and than they have been in earlier film adaptations with a blacked-up Jannings, Welles, Olivier or Hopkins. In the opening scene of Parker's film, another Venetian black man is seen floating by on a gondola with another white woman, covering his face with a white mask – as if to adopt a pretence of belonging, of 'being' a white man in ways similar to those in which Jannings, Olivier, Welles, Hopkins and even Dyer's minstrel have, conversely, covered their faces in order to 'be' black men. And in an ironic reversal of this opening, Branagh's Iago deliberately blackens his own hand with charcoal – a gesture simultaneously of mock-derision and of intimate identification with the black

Other whom he professes to hate. In sudden acknowledgement of the fact that he is himself being watched, Branagh's Iago then puts this freshly blackened hand over the lens of the camera as he declares his intention to construct a 'net / That shall enmesh them all' (II.iii.356–7). The conjunction of word and gesture here is doubly eloquent in the terms of the film. The camera in this production *is* that enmeshing net. It is the camera's characterization of the subjectivized gaze, and a failure to acknowledge the limits of one's own subjectivity, that enmeshes them all. Iago makes the spectator inescapably conscious of the camera's crucial role in the process of the drama by manually obscuring it here as he unfolds the detail of his plot. The conscious irony of the gesture is that, in putting it out of commission, he alerts us to its multiple functions. But it is also, as Branagh's Iago's artificially blackened hand attests, a man pretending to be black that brings about the downfall of the central characters. Iago's obvious pretence of blackening is a literalized metaphor for the way in which he has urged Othello to live. At the opening of the film, Fishburne's Othello is a black man who defies many of Venice's expectations about black men. He is noble, dignified, articulate, restrained. As the Duke says of him, in value-laden terminology, he is 'far more fair than black' (I.iii.291). He does not live out the stereotype of a black man – passionate, irrational, brutal, jealous, barbaric, libidinous, inarticulate.[14] However, the racist propaganda of the dramatic milieu, championed most obviously and most crudely by Iago, eventually has its effect on Othello, who begins to live down to the prevalent expectations of his environment, becoming the thing he had been claimed to be. Thus Othello's emerging 'blackness' as a set of stereotypical behavioural patterns is the force tapped by Iago that eventually 'enmesh[es] them all'. In Parker's production, the complementary moments of assuming whiteness (literally, with a hand-held mask) and assuming blackness (literally, with charcoal by Iago, and metaphorically, with passionate jealousy and violence by Othello) appropriately point to the complexity of the constructions of cultural identity in the world of the play.

Despite the film's eschewing of any obvious topical engagement, contemporary parallels presented themselves irresistibly after the film's release. Played in the movie theatres of the United States in late 1995 and early 1996, for example, a Shakespearean story about a successful, high-profile black man living in a predominantly white world, married to a white woman, made sexually jealous, driven to violent extremes and finally accused of her murder, could not but take on a particular topical resonance. Another story composed of the same essential narrative ingredients had until very recently enthralled the United States as it played out on every television in the country (and many more around the world). Parker's *Othello* was released in the United States shortly after the height of the media hysteria surrounding the trial of the black American football player, sports commentator and actor, O. J. Simpson, accused of murdering his white ex-wife. The political and emotional fall-out from what became known as 'the trial of the century' was still being felt.[15] In both *Othello*'s and O. J. Simpson's story, the central protagonist was a black man who had been celebrated by white society for his heroic performances in a masculine, combative endeavour (soldiery/football) and who had refused to allow himself to be confined by restrictive definitions of his colour, in each case marrying a white woman (Desdemona/Nicole Brown), attracting a blaze of publicity in the process and, rightly or wrongly, suspecting her of having a sexual relationship with a white man (Cassio/Ronald Goldman). After the murder, each displayed self-dramatizing suicidal tendencies: Othello delivered a self-exonerating obituary for himself before his public suicide, and Simpson memorably held a gun to his own head in the glare of the television cameras on a Los Angeles freeway. Each confined his expression of personal remorse to an accusation of having loved his wife 'too well' or 'so much'. Simpson wrote a suicide note, addressed 'To Whom It May Concern'. In an uncanny echo of Othello's self-portrait as 'one that loved not wisely, but too well' (V.ii.342), Simpson wrote: 'I loved her. I always have and I always will. If we had a problem, it's because I loved her so much.' Later in the letter he reiterated the sentiment: 'I loved her; make that clear to everyone.'[16] His 'make that clear to everyone' exhibits the same concern for how he will be remembered after his death that motivates Othello's comparably insistent 'set you down this'. Each invests his energies in trying to script his own obituary. Othello's initial plea for truthfulness in the account:

> I pray you, in your letters,
> When you shall these unlucky deeds relate,
> Speak of me as I am. Nothing extenuate,
> Nor set down aught in malice ...
>   (V.ii.338–41)

is immediately followed by his dictation of exactly what he would like that 'unextenuated' truth to be:

> Then must you speak
> Of one that loved not wisely, but too well;
> Of one not easily jealous ...
>
> (V.ii.341–3)

Othello's attempts at self-exoneration and self-ennoblement in trying to ensure that the dimensions of his love for Desdemona are mythologized after his death carry the same hollow ring that accompanies O. J.'s 'I loved her; make that clear to everyone'. Under pressure, each reaches for words of self-consolation.

The several parallels and uncanny echoes ensured that, in its American reception, Parker's *Othello* was overwritten by the O. J. story. The film became a palimpsest on which were inscribed both its own intended Shakespearean story and a closely related, though accidentally acquired, contemporary narrative. The O. J.-saturated cultural backdrop for the early exhibition of Parker's *Othello* ensured that the film offered itself as a site on which the host of fears and prejudices unleashed by the O. J. affair could be remediated and examined at a useful symbolic remove through the distancing filter of a Shakespearean narrative. Roger Ebert in the *Chicago Sun-Times* saw 'the fates of O. J. and Nicole Simpson projected like a scrim on top of the screen' when he watched Parker's *Othello*, and John Dargie in the *L.A. Weekly* asked 'Why ... is there something so creepy and so very O. J. in the intial love scene between Othello and Desdemona?'[17]

The O. J. Simpson trial received an astonishing, unremitting level of press coverage, keeping the television ratings high and selling newspapers. There was something inherent in the material that fascinated, and the fascination ran deeper than simply seeing a famous and successful man brought to account. The story played to a firmly entrenched set of cultural anxieties about the dangerous libido of the black man and the concomitant vulnerability of the white woman before his lascivious and violent clasps. It is an image whose disturbing and erotic inflection has found repeated narrative representation. The stories that are told most frequently, and which resurface in new guises in successive generations, are the ones that explore and assuage deep-rooted human anxieties, fears and repressed desires. The frequency with which the central image of the *Othello*/O. J. story finds narrative expression suggests that there is something latent in its texture that both troubles and appeals to us considerably. In his poem, 'Goats and Monkeys' (1969), which was inspired by his reading of *Othello*, the Caribbean poet Derek Walcott provided a cartooned and exaggerated image of the union of Desdemona and Othello as 'Virgin and ape, maid and malevolent Moor'.[18] The dichotomized imaging of 'virgin and ape' tips the story quickly towards the same fascinating grotesque that has given stories such as *Beauty and the Beast* (and, by extension, *King Kong*) a central place among our narrative myths.[19] The extremity of contrast in an image of female helplessness juxtaposed with a powerful male monstrosity has the power to trouble and to titillate. Introducing also a black-white colour contrast to the formula adds an additional layer of sensationalism.

Within a few years, the parallels between the O. J. story and *Othello* will have become part of the critical orthodoxy about the play in general and perhaps about Parker's production, with its successful African-American in the central role, in particular. As a telling of Shakespeare's *Othello*, Parker's film certainly plays to the same primal prejudices about the black man and black male sexuality that the O. J. affair drew to the surface of white American society. In its representation of an interracial sexuality, it is alive to the emotive power and visual appeal of the exaggerated dichotomy in the aggressive black ram/defiled white ewe image. In fact, the film even flirts with the suggestion of an aggression in Othello's sexual relations with Desdemona from their first scene of love-making, and, in more pronounced fashion, in his subsequent fantasy. Thus for the film marketed as an 'erotic thriller', and whose advertising poster played up the eroticism of the sexual union of Othello and Desdemona, Parker exploited some of the disturbing eroticism lurking in the deep-rooted white prejudice about the danger that attaches to black male sexuality.[20]

Early in cinema's development, a black–white violent sexual clasp was made a subject of grotesque fascination. In D. W. Griffith's seminal feature film, *The Birth of a Nation* (1915), for example, the Ku Klux Klan arrive on horseback (to the triumphant accompaniment of 'The Ride of the Valkyries') to save Elsie Stoneman (Lillian Gish) from the lascivious and violent clutches of Silas Lynch (played in black face by Griffith's assistant, George Siegmann).[21] Although there were plenty of black actors in minor roles in the film, it was considered unthinkable to subject a white actress to the trauma of being manhandled by a real black man, even in pretence; Lynch therefore had to be played by a blacked-up white man.[22] *The Birth of a Nation* established or confirmed many filmic conventions, both technical and thematic, that were to influence later filmmakers. One of these conventions, much emulated since, was a corrosive sexual-racial pattern. A subliminal message of the film was that black men's desire of white women is animal, ignoble and predatory. The message was not new, but Griffith's insistence upon it in one of the most influential films of the first quarter century of cinema helped to suggest it as a fertile subject for later film treatment.

The intensity of emotional responses to such images ensures that they are constantly recycled, providing the opportunity for the horror and the primal appeal of this particular taboo to be felt anew.[23] In a predominantly white interpretative community in which racist fears still have an almost inexhumably deep hold, the story of a passionate and violent black man doing violence to a defenceless white woman can lend itself to being read as a narrative on a continuum at the most extreme end of which is the 'virgin and ape' myth. Parker's particular contribution to the corpus of *Othello* films nudges the material further in that direction.

Othello's Resistance to Christian Appropriations

In Othello's dignified and eloquent speech to the Senate in Act I, he seems to out-Venice Venice in exemplifying the virtues for which it would like to believe it stands. So amenable is he to being absorbed into Christendom that he even accepts a commission to fight for its interests. In aligning himself with Venice's values and cultural systems, he implicitly turns his back on those of his past. Even his view of the black man, and of the negatively charged connotations of the word black, seem to have been inherited wholesale from a culture overtly antagonistic to all that is not white. 'Her name, that was as fresh / As Dian's visage, is now begrimed and black / As mine own face' (III.iii.389–91), he says of Desdemona, poignantly illustrating how Venice's value-laden views of colour have infiltrated his own perceptions.

Once on Cyprus, however, the Venetian veneer is pared away from him in stages, suggesting that, although he had learned Venice's forms and manners, its identity had never been organically *his*. His marriage to Venetian ideals, like his marriage to one of its most eligible maidens, unravels in the course of the play. As if living down to the prevalent expectations of his cultural environment, Othello finally starts to resemble Christian Venice's stereotypical image of an infidel Moor – superstitious, inarticulate, crude, irrational, dangerous: the very things that Venice had initially been at pains to reassure itself that Othello, *despite* his Moorish origins, was not.

Although Norman Rabkin thinks him 'the most emphatically Christian' of 'all the tragic heroes', Othello ultimately resists Christianizing.[24] In slaying himself, he both voices and enacts his resistance to it, 'turning Turk' in his act of suicide. His final speech (in which he casts himself simultaneously as champion of, and emblem of absolute alterity to, Christian Venice) demonstrates his sense of a riven identity: in his own person, as in the culturally ambivalent territory of Cyprus, the conflict between competing worlds, Christian and infidel, is played out.

The focus of this collection is to read these Shakespeare films, made on the cusp of the new millennium, in the light of anxieties attendant upon a moment of historical transition. Although the specifically Christian apocalyptic myth about the year 2000 AD had some purchase on the intellectual climate in the period in which Shakespeare was writing, it is no longer a feature of Christian consciousness.[25] Its emotional legacy (associating significant temporal end markers with momentous events on a material or metaphysical level) now finds its most obvious focus in direful prophecies about the possible consequences of the 'Millennium Bug'. That apart, little serious eschatological significance is now attached to the fact of calendrical juncture. Rather than heralding metaphysical crisis, the millennium is, more mundanely, now taken to refer simply to a system for counting time. That counting system is not, however, culturally neutral, and its heritage is significant.

At midnight on 31 December 1999 (or 2000, to be calendrically pedantic), it will be 2000 years since the date (erroneously) taken as the birth of Christ. In the midst of the millennial mania, it is easy, in an historically Christian culture, to be seduced into believing that the turn of the millennium is of moment to the whole of humanity. Rather, of course, it is only according to the Gregorian calendar of Christianity that this *is* a *fin de siècle*, and a new millennium. Other religions and other cultures have employed, and many still do employ, other calendars.[26] The Christocentric assumption that the millennium is a *universal* phenomenon carries traces of an anachronistic cultural imperialism. Where this calendar now holds sway, it is due to the economic and militaristic expansionist successes of Christian Europe. As much as anything, therefore, the millennium serves as a reminder that European Christians have been empire-builders. It is, after all, only by a Christian dating system (devised by Dionysius Exiguus, a sixth-century monk) that this moment receives the specific temporal labels that identify it as the end of a century and of a millennium.

Parcelling up history into temporal units – decades, centuries, millennia – helps us to organize and focus our sense of things. 'Teach us to number our days, that we may apply our hearts unto wisdom' writes the Psalmist (Psalms 90:12), implying a close association between counting time and understanding its import. In this same endeavour, we not only identify discrete temporal units but retrospectively assign a character to them too – the roaring twenties, swinging sixties, selfish eighties. If we are to ask what characterizes the drift tendencies of thought specifically at the *end* of this century and millennium, however, we encounter a paradox. One of the characteristics of the tide of thought in our own time springs from an increasing awareness of, and sensitivity to, cultural diversity. Alongside this has emerged a desire to challenge systems of cultural norm-referencing that automatically interpret difference from ourselves as either inferior or threatening. So one aspect of the spirit of the age at the end of this millennium – the aspiration to live multiculturally – sits in tension with the label applied to the moment, whose unexamined provenance is so specifically Christian.

Parker's film explores the locations and labellings of Otherness and, through its troubling and shifting subjectivities, the means by which notions of Otherness are constructed. It depicts a Venetian world trying to conceive of itself as a multicultural place – a place that can embrace the exoticism of another and even employ that Other on useful service in the pursuit of its own interests. Its 'embracing' of that exoticism, however, succeeds in extinguishing it. The story of *Othello* acknowledges that squeezing cultural others into the mould of the dominant power of the moment is unlikely to yield healthy results. Othello's response is finally to exaggerate his alterity in Venetian terms by aligning himself dramatically with the infidel Turk.

C. L. Barber has argued that Shakespeare's tragedies 'present a post-Christian situation where, with some of the expectations and values of Christianity, we do not have God'. Their 'extraordinary relevance to the modern age', he writes, derives from their refusal to accommodate themselves to a specifically Christian world view.[27] Not only Othello, but the tragic world of the play as a whole resists Christianizing. Reading this particular dramatic material (which both narrates and illustrates the resistance to a process of Christianizing) in millennial terms (whose heritage is so institutionally Christian) is, perhaps, a symbolically fraught project. Its implied Christocentric assumption about hegemony and cultural dominance even perhaps mimics Christian Venice's attempt, dramatized in the play, to subsume Othello into the heart of its values and systems.

Notes

1. 'Editorial', *The Wall Street Journal*, 24 February 1998.
2. *Othello*, ed. E. A. J. Honigmann (Walton-on-Thames: Nelson, 1997). All further references appear in the text.
3. See particularly Lazaro Soranzo, *The Ottoman of Lazaro Soranzo*, trans. Abraham Hartwell (London: J. Windet, 1603).
4. John Leo (Wazzân Al-Fasi/Leo Africanus), *A Geographical Historie of Africa*, trans. John Pory (London: George Bishop, 1600). The quotation is from Pory's introductory epistle 'To the Reader', sig. A3ᵛ.
5. See Rosalind Johnson, 'African Presence in Shakespearean Drama: Parallels Between Othello and the Historical Leo Africanus', *Journal of African Civilizations*, 7 (1985), pp. 276–87.
6. Jonathan Miller's 1981 BBC production, for example, boasts a very pale-skinned Othello (Anthony Hopkins), who obfuscates his cultural heritage in both appearance and behaviour – a thorough-going Venetian in his self-projections.
7. Liz White's filmed *Othello* (1980) had a black Othello and other black cast members. However, it was never commercially released. For a discussion of the distinction between the exhibition of black people and the mimesis of blackness in relation to *Othello*, see Dympna Callaghan, '"Othello was a white man": Properties of race on Shakespeare's stage', in Terence Hawkes (ed.), *Alternative Shakespeares*, Volume 2 (London: Routledge, 1996), pp. 192–215.
8. One of the dedicatory English verses to Lewes Lewkenor's translation of Cardinal Gaspar Contarini, *The Commonwealth and Government of Venice* (London: John Windet, 1599), sig. A3ᵛ.
9. Venice had annexed Cyprus in 1489 and ruled it as an outpost of empire, strategically placed to facilitate trade with the East. After sieges at Nicosia and Famagusta in 1570-1, Cyprus finally fell to the Turkish invasion fleet, led by Mustapha Bassa, on 1 August 1571. Cyprus had, therefore, been both Venetian and Turkish within living memory of 1604, the probable year of *Othello*'s composition.
10. Sections of a 1604 London audience familiar with the newly published English translation of Richard Knolles' *Generall Historie of the Turkes* (London: A. Islip, 1603) would have known that Cyprus had recently been lost to the Turks and was still a Turkish possession. This would have introduced a filter of cynicism through which Venice's pride in the face of the Turkish threat was viewed by the first audiences for *Othello*.
11. Rita Kempley, *Washington Post*, 29 December 1995.
12. For the UK release, Branagh insisted that his image be removed from the advertising posters. It was not his production, and he clearly wished to distance himself from it lest others should speculate as Kempley had.
13. In this century, for example, Paul Robeson has written that American audiences found the play 'strikingly contemporary in its overtones of a clash of cultures, of the partial acceptance of and consequent effect upon one of a minority group' (Paul Robeson, 'Some Reflections on *Othello* and the Nature of Our Time', *American Scholar*, 14.4 [1995], p. 391), and Janet Suzman, a South African, that '[t]he overtones, undercurrents and reverberations for

our country [were] hauntingly evident' (Janet Suzman, about the 1987 Market Theatre production in Johannesburg, *Washington Post*, 6 September 1987). David Harewood said that he had found part of his inspiration for his role as a black man in a white world (in Sam Mendes' 1998 production of *Othello* at the National) by attending during the rehearsal period to the case of the murdered black London teenager, Stephen Lawrence (David Harewood, interviewed on Radio 4's *Midweek*, 27 May 1998).

14. A selection of these stereotypes about Moors is peddled in Leo, *A Geographical Historie*.

15. The verdict at the O. J. Simpson trial was delivered on 3 October 1995 after almost nine months of testimony. Parker's *Othello* was released in the United States on 15 December 1995.

16. The letter was read at a news conference on behalf of Simpson on 17 June 1994 and reprinted the following day in the American dailies. See, for example, *New York Times*, 18 June 1994, late edition.

17. Roger Ebert, *Chicago Sun-Times*, 29 December 1995. John Dargie, review in *L.A. Weekly*, 27 December 1995. Dargie is quoted in Lynda E. Boose and Richard Burt, 'Totally Clueless?: Shakespeare Goes Hollywood in the 1990s', in Lynda E. Boose and Richard Burt (eds), *Shakespeare, the Movie: Popularizing the Plays on Film, TV, and Video* (London and New York: Routledge, 1997), p. 15. A Dutch production entitled 'O. J. Othello' had its UK *première* in the Observer Assembly Ballroom at the 1998 Edinburgh Fringe. Barbara Hodgdon, in her wonderfully rich essay, 'Race-ing *Othello*, Re-engendering White-Out', in Boose and Burt (eds), *Shakespeare, the Movie*, pp. 23–44, has enumerated some of the parallels that may be drawn between Shakespeare's Othello and O. J. Simpson as part of her consideration of representations of blackness in productions of *Othello*. She does not, however, make it her brief to weigh the significance of these parallels specifically to readings of Parker's *Othello* (whose moment of release and casting of an African-American successful black actor in the central role perhaps makes them particularly pertinent).

18. Derek Walcott, *Collected Poems, 1948-1984* (New York: Noonday, 1986), pp. 83–4.

19. Even in *King Kong*, the primitive, sexually insistent, oversized gorilla who wants as his 'bride' 'The Golden Woman' (Fay Wray in a blond wig) is associated with the sexuality of the black man. The men from the African village even dress up as Kong in gorilla fur as part of a ceremonial dance.

20. It is difficult to identify from where in our social or psychological make-up such deep-rooted myths emerge. It is, however, tempting to speculate that this particular one may have sprung from an unconscious desire by insecure white men to 'blacken' that rival male sexuality that has also taken on other, intimidatingly desirable, proportions in the popular imagination.

21. In the costume tests for the film, the character of Lynch is even more sexually threatening to Elsie than he is in the finished film. The costume tests were shown in the first part of the Thames Television and Thirteen/WNET 1993 co-produced three-part documentary, 'D. W. Griffith: Father of Film'.

22. In 1920, for the filming of *Way Down East*, Griffith had Gish lie on real ice-floes while wearing only a thin cotton dress. Griffith considered that risking the health of his leading lady (who did indeed suffer from the expo-

sure to the cold) was an acceptable nuisance in the pursuit of the filmic moment; nevertheless, allowing her to be grabbed by a black man would have been an indignity too far. This relative discrimination is revealing about attitudes of the time, and about Griffith's in particular.

23. In Emil Jannings' 1922 silent film adaptation of the play, the potential horror of this taboo must have been felt so keenly that it was considered advisable to mollify its effects by diluting the 'Africanness' of Othello's pedigree. In his moment of formal self-annunciation, Jannings' Othello declares himself (by intertitle) the 'son of an Egyptian Prince and a Spanish Princess'. It is his half-European royal lineage that enables him then to make the claim, 'My blood is fair, like hers, my wife's'. This suggestion of 'fairness' makes it the more likely that his mother is not intended to be thought a Spanish Moor. The decision to temper Othello's alterity (and explain his nobility) by giving him a Spanish mother is illuminating about the anxieties that surrounded even the fictional representation of a black and white sexual union in 1922.

24. Norman Rabkin, *Shakespeare and the Common Understanding* (New York: The Free Press, 1967), p. 63. See also Stanley Cavell, *Disowning Knowledge* (Cambridge: Cambridge University Press, 1987), p. 129.

25. Christian thinking about the apocalypse had often taken the Genesis account of Creation as an allegory for the life of the world, which would toil for six days and then rest for one day. Since in 2 Peter 3:8 it is written 'one day is with the Lord as a thousand years, and a thousand years as one day', this was taken literally to signify that one day in God-speak meant a thousand years in human-speak. Thus the Creation would endure for 6,000 years before being brought to account and entering the 1,000-year reign of Christ (the Millennium). Since it was thought to have endured 4,000 years already at the moment when Christ was born, it therefore had 2,000 years left to run before the second coming and the beginning of the millennium. These anxieties were certainly characteristic of the period in which Shakespeare was writing. In 1593, for example, John Napier published *The Plaine Discoverie of the Whole Revelation of St. John* (Edinburgh: Robert Waldegrave). In it he calculated that the 'latter daies' of Creation had already arrived and the Day of Judgement was at hand, since the allotted span of 2,000 years 'appeareth to be shortnd' (Proposition 14, p. 19). Napier was well respected as a mathematician and scientist, and his *Plaine Discoverie* sold so well that by 1700 (the last date to which he calculated the world could endure) it had run to more than twenty editions. Despite the minor flurry of millenarianism in his intellectual environment, however, Shakespeare demonstrated little interest in it.

26. Let us for a moment pursue a batty line of enquiry. If we were to construct out of Shakespeare's Othello a full person with a history, we would deduce that he would not have grown up within a Christian dating system. As a Moor, he would, more probably, have known the Muslim calendar which counts as *its* year 0 the Christian year 622 AD (the year in which Mohammed fled from Mecca) and which works to a 354-day year. One of his gestures of assimilation to Christian Venice is, therefore, to transform his way of thinking about time and its passing. Thus, to locate him now within an explicitly Christian system of time-keeping is akin to Venice's

attempt to subsume him into the heart of their values and beliefs.

27. C. L. Barber, 'The Family in Shakespeare's Development: Tragedy and Sacredness', in Coppélia Kahn and Murray M. Schwartz (eds), *Representing Shakespeare: New Psychoanalytic Essays* (Baltimore: Johns Hopkins University Press, 1980), pp. 196, 188.

13

Shakespeare in Love and the End of the Shakespearean: Academic and Mass Culture Constructions of Literary Authorship

Richard Burt

In *Shakespeare in Love*, a Harvard professor is said to have played a tiny, but critical part. Marc Norman, one of the screenwriters, said he consulted Stephen Greenblatt, a Shakespeare scholar, to make sure that at least the framework of his story followed what was known about Shakespeare's life. 'I needed some sort of firm ground, some sort of confidence,' Mr Norman said. 'The great thing about writing about Shakespeare is that everyone in the world knows him and there are about five facts.'

James Sterngold, New York Times reporter[1]

The point about Shakespeare's life is that nobody knows anything. All we know is that [Shakespeare] paid 50 pounds to join the Chamberlain's Men and that in his will he left his second best bed to his wife – that's about the sum of it.

John Madden, director of Shakespeare in Love[2]

Some readers might take these epigraphs to be yet more instances of a screenwriter's and journalist's typically low regard for academic knowledge: in the first epigraph, the college professor plays a 'tiny' role, 'critical' only in the sense that he frees the screenwriter to disregard academic authority over a film about Shakespeare's early life as a lover and writer in the theatre.[3] Like Norman, the director John Madden wanted to make a film about this part of Shakespeare's life, the so-called 'lost years' and, according to him, as the second epigraph makes clear, there are only two, not five, things we know about the dramatist.[4] Moreover, the film was marketed so that knowledge of Shakespeare among moviegoers was irrelevant: 'Mr Madden is at pains to make it clear that knowing about Shakespeare and his time are not necessary for enjoying the film.'[5] The academic may be the one who knows about Shakespeare, and thus, according to the screenwriter, has to be consulted, but the academic is also the one whose knowledge does not matter much at all.[6]

Some academic readers who like the film, telling the story of how Shakespeare came to turn an idea for a play called *Romeo and Ethel, the Pirate's Daughter* into *Romeo and Juliet* after he fell in love with a fictional character named Viola de Lesseps, might nevertheless want to dismiss it as so much fluff on the grounds that it has next to nothing to do with Shakespeare or Elizabethan England. Alternatively, some academic readers might want to laud the screenwriters and director for disregarding academic knowledge about Shakespeare on the grounds that this disregard has a politically progressive potential, especially for feminism. At the present historical moment (I write as President Clinton's impeachment trial is ending), I am less and less clear about what a progressive feminist position regarding mass culture might be. But an academic fantasy about the progressive is perhaps clearer, and might run as follows: feminist mass culture versions of Shakespeare's life would open new kinds of female authority over high culture writing and performance. Correspondingly, canonical male writers and performers would have their authority reduced, their masculinity revised, some might say feminized, a process signalled by gender trouble, ambiguity about sexual orientation, sexual/literary impotence, and so on.[7] One could argue that *Shakespeare in Love* feminizes Shakespeare along these very lines, particularly his love life and his writing process.[8] Indeed, in order to put the brakes on a perceived feminization (which, of course, is by no means inevitable or inherent in the process of turning Shakespeare into a character), historical accuracy may sometimes be sacrificed to mainstream notions of what now counts as masculine for some film producers. As Sandy Powell, the costume designer for *Shakespeare in Love*, says: 'On *Shakespeare in Love*, the studio was very worried about the pants. It's a difficult period for men not to look stupid, so the exec types kept asking, "Will there be tights?" So we made the jackets a little longer, the pants a little longer. You want to have believable clothes for the period, but you don't want your actors to look silly.'[9] The screenwriters and director of *Shakespeare in Love* might be thought to be working against the 'exec types' in writing a love story about a man whose clothes make him look all too feminine (read 'silly').[10]

In this essay, I focus on Shakespeare's appearance as a fictional character in a single genre of mass culture, namely, the romance, using three examples: in addition to *Shakespeare in Love*, I discuss two mass-market paperback novels, Erica Jong's *Shylock's Daughter* and Julie Beard's *Romance of the Rose*.[11] In Jong's novel, the narrator and heroine, Jessica, an over-the-hill, ageing movie star, is in Venice for a film festival. She ends up going back in time to the late 1580s, where she encounters Shakespeare and Henry Wriothesley, the Earl of Southampton. After having a passionate affair with Shakespeare, Jessica returns to the present. Beard's *Romance of the Rose* is written very much as a generic harlequin romance, and Shakespeare plays a marginal role as a character. The heroine, Lady Rosalind Carbery, is a virgin who longs to enjoy both sex (as a member of a committed and passionate loving couple) and writing plays. She grew up with a man named Drake Rothwell whose father lost his fortune to some unknown, malevolent agent at court. As an adult, Drake is a pirate, adventurer and spy in Elizabeth's service. Both Rosalind and Drake fight over who should inherit her father's property, and the Queen intervenes and resolves the conflict by forcing them to marry. The couple eventually declare their love for each other and get married. The plot in some respects resembles *Much Ado About Nothing* in that the two lovers, like Beatrice and Benedick, have to be forced into wedlock. (Beatrice's response in the garden to Hero and Ursula's deceiving her into thinking Benedick loves her is quoted [p. 145], and the play's title is twice cited [p. 145].) Shakespeare is a friend of Rosalind's who, among other things, performs plays for her at her house, and helps produce one of her own plays on the London stage.

My purpose in discussing these romance narratives about Shakespeare as a character is not merely to dismiss or to celebrate them but to explore the relation between criticism and feminism in both academia and mass culture. I want to ask not only whether academics have much, if anything, to tell the producers of mass culture films and novels about Shakespeare, but also whether these same mass culture films and novels have anything to tell academic critics about Shakespeare and mass culture. The romance genre is particularly significant for academic feminist critics, many of whom regard the mass-market romance novel as offering women, both straight and lesbian, liberating possibilities, primarily in terms of emotionally satisfying sexual experiences.[12] While the romance narratives I examine in this essay arguably open up feminist possibilities for their audiences, particularly regarding male sexuality, female acting and female authorship, they fail, I will argue, to tell a substantially different story about Shakespeare, about his plays, about how to read them and about the relation between his life and his works: despite filmic and novelistic protestations of disinterest in academic credentials, the narratives reinscribe an older Romantic theory of literary authorship, a familiar view of Shakespeare the author whose life is a mystery and whom we cannot know except through his works. These narratives similarly rely on older, academic interpretative strategies, such as biographical readings of the plays and sonnets.

Whatever the limits of these narratives in rewriting Shakespeare for feminist purposes, however, it would be a mistake simply to conclude that academics, not mass culture (screen)writers and film directors, are in an authoritative position to judge what is and is not really Shakespeare, what is or is not historically accurate and authentic. I focus on novels, not just on film, in this essay in order to counter a tendency in Shakespeare studies to accord film a signal privilege as the form of mass culture closest to Shakespeare and therefore the most legitimate as an object of criticism. This tendency blinds us to the way the present interpenetration of mass media and academic discourses about Shakespeare has produced an enabling (and often disabling) dialectic between academic and mass culture versions not only of the plays but of Shakespeare's authorship and life. Both *Shakespeare in Love* and *Shylock's Daughter* rely on academic authority in order to offer a critique of Hollywood film production (enormous egos of actors and producers interfering with undervalued writers and so on), positioned as a low mass culture, from the vantage of 'high' literary and theatrical culture. Just as screenwriters and novelists feel compelled to consult academic authority (even if they also undercut it or disregard it in a number of ways), academics, whatever their politics, require mass culture to legitimate their authority as critics (that is presumably why academics work as consultants, why they agree to be interviewed on camera in films like Al Pacino's *Looking for Richard* [1996] or in the television A&E biography of Shakespeare, and why they write on mass culture films like *Shakespeare in Love*).[13]

While avowedly political critics who want to undermine Shakespeare's authority for progressive purposes might see in mass culture versions of Shakespeare's life an occasion to demystify Shakespeare's cultural authority, what they take to be a difference between a conservative notion of Shakespeare as the great author (the genius whose works are timeless and universal) and a progressive notion of 'Shakespeare' as an author-function (whose works are appropriable and revisable for hegemonic and counter-hegemonic purposes) is, I will suggest in the conclusion of this essay, really no difference at all. For the Romantic theory of literary authorship, with Shakespeare as the icon of the Author, is now alive and well in the mass media versions of Shakespeare. What I find even more striking is that the present mass mediatization of academia works in the opposite direction: as mass culture and academia have become more and more interdependent, the very identity of Shakespeare as author/ author-function has also been called into question.[14] One consequence of this interdependence is what I am calling the end of the Shakespearean, the signature effect within the writings themselves, which separates the Shakespeare canon from the Shakespeare apocrypha.[15]

I

In all three narratives I discuss, the screenwriter, director or novelist is interested in viewing Shakespeare's life as basically shrouded in mystery.[16] In *Romance of the Rose*, for example, when Shakespeare is first introduced, the heroine raises questions about his personal life she cannot answer:

> Rosalind ... [wished] as she always had that [Shakespeare] would speak of the woman who had inspired passionate volumes. Was she a dark-skinned beauty? An exotic lover? Or a dark-skinned widow who had first shown him love? Was she an apparition? Or was she a he? What went on in the mind of someone so brilliant, and so humble? But she said nothing. She knew the limits of their friendship. Shakespeare was always discreet. (p. 38)

Like director John Madden, Jong focuses her novel on the so-called 'lost years'. Near the beginning of *Shylock's Daughter*, Jong's heroine, then in Venice, asks:

> Was Shakespeare here? Remember those 'lost years' in his life – the years no one can account for, the years after he marries Anne Hathaway and has three babes, but before 1592, when an envious Robert Greene mentions him as an 'upstart crow'? ... What was he doing then? Apprentice player? Schoolmaster in the country? *No one knows*. Then there were the plague years, 1592 and 1593 ... when the theatres in London were closed and players had to tour the countryside to earn their bread – or might he instead have voyaged to Italy with Henry Wriothesley, the Earl of Southampton, his patron and (some say) lover? *Who knew?* (pp. 10–11, my emphases)

In Jong's view, academia is clearly not the place where serious questions about Shakespeare's writings or his life may be definitively answered. Quite the contrary. Jessica continues:

> Shakespeare scholarship was rife with empty academic rivalries, outrageous suppositions, the mad hypotheses of good brains gone bad in college libraries, eaten by the maggots of paranoia and thwarted literary ambitions. Stratfordians said 'the Bard' (How I hate that orotund, pretentious epithet!) was a simple glover's son; anti-Stratfordians made him an earl of this or that, because in their snobbery they could not believe that our greatest poet could lack a title. Piffle. (p. 11)

Jong engages the debate between Oxfordians and Stratfordians over Shakespeare's authorship not to take sides but in order to dismiss it as essentially worthless, the product of damaged academic brains. While obviously siding with the Stratfordians, she pointedly asserts that no academic really knows what Shakespeare did or where he was during his 'lost years'. Similarly, Beard puts an 'Author's Note' before her novel proper, stating:

> Avid Shakespeare readers will note that I've taken a few liberties with the Bard, including having the audacity to include ... Shakespeare as a character. I simply couldn't resist. I've also rearranged the order in which Shakespeare is believed to have written his plays. (p. xi)

(In Beard's chronology, *Hamlet* comes before *The Taming of the Shrew*.) Historical accuracy does not limit the author.

One consequence of this disregard for academic authority and historical accuracy is that it opens up a feminist account of literary patronage and literary authorship in general, though not of Shakespearean authorship in particular. It is worth noting that all three of the narratives are set during Elizabeth's reign and that she is a character with an interest in the theatre in two of them. In Beard's novel, Elizabeth is a well-informed, judicious monarch who knows of Shakespeare's plays (particularly *Richard II*). In *Shakespeare in Love*, Elizabeth exerts an enormous power over the theatre and the genre of plays produced there. The first performance of a play by Shakespeare we see is one which she commands and which she presides over, with her assembled courtiers also present. We see her laugh at the comic

Lance and his dog, Crab, while she nods off in boredom at Valentine's serious speech in praise of Silvia from *The Two* (here retitled *One*) *Gentlemen of Verona*. (This is the main reason that Henslowe wants Shakespeare to write a new comedy – to please the Queen.) Similarly, Elizabeth appears almost magically near the end of the film, after the *première* of *Romeo and Juliet*, in order to prevent the actors from going to jail for letting a woman act on the stage (without whom the play would have failed utterly). Elizabeth sides with Viola, pretending that she is really a boy, partly out of a sisterly impulse: she knows what it is like 'to be a woman in a man's profession'. At the end of *Shakespeare in Love*, Shakespeare has discarded his male collaborators, Christopher Marlowe and Edward Alleyn, but his women collaborators remain firmly in place: Queen Elizabeth supplies the title of *Twelfth Night*, and Viola gives him the plot as well as the characters, Orsino and Viola. (The film even rewrites *Twelfth Night*: as we see Shakespeare begin to write it, he writes down 'Viola', giving her, not Orsino, the play's opening speech.) Jong's heroine similarly inspires what is understood to be authentically Shakespearean writing.

In addition to providing women characters with opportunities for patronage and collaboration, these narratives accord women the freedom to perform on a variety of stages. In *Shakespeare in Love*, Viola breaks 'the law of the land' that prohibits women from acting on stage. Similarly, Beard's heroine appears in a masque of her devising quite scantily dressed, much to the horror of the ladies present, and she also occasionally cross-dresses as a spy to foil plots against Elizabeth, including the Essex rebellion. Jong's heroine laments the fact that feminism has had no impact on the movie industry as far as roles for middle-aged women are concerned, and she celebrates Elizabeth I as a feminist.[17] All these narratives involve the heroine cross-dressing and acting on stage or film, thereby allowing these characters at least sometimes to 'wear the pants' in the relationship and gain knowledge of important public affairs on their own (Rosalind works as a spy).

Recalling the central character of *As You Like It*, Beard's heroine, Rosalind, is not only an actress but a pioneer playwright who ignores the custom of her time, which forbids women from writing. Rosalind initially thinks she cannot both write and marry. As she says to Shakespeare: 'I do not plan to marry. A husband would expect me to see him as my lord, my life, and my keeper' (p. 41). Shakespeare replies 'A right supremacy, some would say' (p. 41), picking up the allusion to *The Taming of the Shrew*. Drake is initially opposed to her being a writer, seeing her plays as an impediment to their marriage; he insists that she resists having her plays staged or published. He gives in, at the end, and accompanies her to the first performance of her play, *The Taming of the Shrew*, though this moment also can be construed in very different terms, as I shall make clear momentarily.

These romance narratives also feminize Shakespeare's sexuality. According to Ann Snitow, who maintains that romance novels are a laudable form of soft-core porn for women, the genre of romance reconstructs heterosexual men in ways that make them more desirable as lovers and partners to heterosexual women: they remain hard, but not too hard.[18] In all of the examples under discussion here, Shakespeare is a reconstructed male, no longer the macho guy who is concerned only with satisfying his sexual drives, but the man who is sensitive to his lover's needs and desires and who wants to get her off as much he wants her to get him off. In *Shakespeare in Love*, Shakespeare is initially inept and impotent. His bed in Stratford has grown 'cold', and he finds his mistress having sex with the Master of the Revels. Once he falls in love with Viola de Lesseps, his juices, literary and otherwise, begin to flow, and an analogy between Romeo and Juliet and Shakespeare and Viola quickly falls into place. Much of the film's comedy comes from making Shakespeare a rather doltish, callow cad rather than a traditionally masculine romantic hero: he falls from the balcony after seeing Viola's nurse when expecting to see Viola, and runs off to escape the guards of the Lesseps house; he lies to Wessex that he is Marlowe (twice) in order to escape being assaulted or killed by Wessex; he uses what turns out to be a fake sword during a sword fight with Wessex (Viola counsels Shakespeare that Wessex, a powerful man and a trained swordsman, will kill the inexperienced and weaker Shakespeare if they ever fight); and he steals lines and ideas from others. In somewhat different but equally conventional terms, Jong makes Shakespeare a deep, suffering, soulful lover. And in Beard's novel, Shakespeare's romantic feelings are so intense that they have to remain private. In a variety of ways, then, what I am calling a process of feminization in these narratives may be regarded as feminist (admittedly of a rather essentialist sort) in so far as it expands discursive access and opportunities for women and reconstructs male authorship and subjectivity along female lines.

II

Although it would be possible to claim these romance narratives for feminism, it would be just as possible to argue the reverse – namely, that they end up subverting their potentially feminist fantasies about women, about men and about romance. Consider, for example, the question of female agency as these narratives take it up in the arenas of literary patronage, theatrical performance and literary authorship. In *Shakespeare in Love*, Queen Elizabeth is less powerful, if more humane, than is usually the case in mass culture films about her. In contrast to other films such as *Fire Over England* and *The Private Lives of Elizabeth and Essex*, where Elizabeth makes decisions about sending men to war or executing princes and rebellious aristocrats, the theatrical arena of these romance narratives has the effect of significantly shrinking what kinds of effect female agency can have: the most difficult conflicts Elizabeth resolves in *Shakespeare in Love* are whether Viola can go to Virginia and who won a wager over whether a play can truly represent romantic love.[19] Similarly, Queen Elizabeth is in control only of the love lives of her courtiers in Beard's novel.

Female authorship in Beard's novel similarly turns out to be considerably less feminist than first appears. Indeed, some readers might criticize the novel for opening up a feminist perspective on writing, knowledge and sex, only to draw back from it. Not only does Rosalind decide to stop writing for the stage by the end of the novel, but her best achievement turns out to be *The Taming of the Shrew*, perhaps the hardest of all Shakespeare's comedies to recuperate for feminist purposes. The novel's plot is somewhat incoherent. While having Rosalind cite a line from *The Taming of the Shrew* early on (p. 41) to show that her opposition to marriage is based on feminist reasoning, having her author the play does not exactly amount to feminism for several reasons. First of all, she does not take over Petruchio's role, becoming the tamer of Drake. (How much more coherent the novel would have been had Shakespeare performed *The Taming of the Shrew* for Rosalind and then had her rewrite it as the much less obviously patriarchal *Much Ado About Nothing*.) Second, the novel ends before the play is performed, so we never get a new interpretation of the play, one that might allow us to see the play as feminist. Third, domestic conflict between the newly married couple is avoided by having Rosalind decide not to write anymore and, moreover, to have her last play performed without her being credited. While this scenario could, of course, be told as tragedy for a woman writer, Beard's version is not tragic at all. Rosalind happily defers to Shakespeare, who suggests that, in any case, getting credit as the author doesn't really matter:

> Her play ... was being staged in its entirety, but Rosalind would
> not be listed as its author. She did not care. She was simply
> honoured that Shakespeare thought enough of her skills as a
> dramatist to present it. (p. 378)

Later Rosalind comments, 'What a pity no one will ever know I wrote
it.' But Beard immediately dissolves this question by having
Shakespeare modestly suggest that his plays may not be remembered
and, making an ironic allusion to the various attempts since the nineteenth century to ascribe authorship of the canon to someone else,
that he may not be credited as author eventually:

> Shakespeare shrugged. 'Does it matter? Who knows? Perhaps one
> day my plays will be lost. Or if they survive, perhaps my name will
> be long forgotten. Or, Heaven forbid, perhaps future generations
> will give credit to someone else for my labour.' (p. 379)

Ironically, Shakespeare ends up describing Rosalind's fate: she has
written a play, and Shakespeare has been given the credit for her
efforts. Finally, Rosalind even lets Shakespeare take control over her
play. The novel concludes with the following passage:

> 'William, what did you decide to name my play?' ...
> 'Read for yourself.' He winked and was gone.
>   Rosalind righted the playbill in her hands and read the title aloud.
> '*The Taming of the Shrew*'. She beamed up at Drake [now her
> husband], treasuring his proud smile. 'I think I like it.' (p. 380)

To be sure, the ridiculousness of Shakespeare's language here challenges those who privilege the signature, and the conceit of Rosalind
being the real writer, Shakespeare the pretender, does grant a woman
a significant status.

Yet Beard, like her heroine, shows a tremendous deference to male
authority, winning her husband's and the playwright's approval. (And
her claim for authorship is radically limited, after all, to one play.)
Shakespeare, the male author, entitles her play (and, of course, takes
credit for it as its author, as if it were unlady-like to get angry at this,
since a truly modest author wouldn't care about fame). Jong and
Beard, in short, are what some feminists would caustically refer to as
'male-identified' writers.[20]

In the same way, Shakespeare's feminization, however progressive from the point of view of heterosexual romance, necessarily stops short of making him bisexual or homosexual, if Shakespeare is a lover at all, so that he can appeal to the presumptively heterosexual woman reader or moviegoer. In Beard's novel, for example, it's not quite clear whether Shakespeare can really stay hard enough to satisfy the women characters and readers. Shakespeare is not romantically involved with anyone, and the heroine speculates that he may be gay. Moreover, masculinity remains rather traditionally defined. Drake is the hero of the novel precisely because he is in many ways Shakespeare's opposite number: he is sexually active and verbally assertive, and he opposes Rosalind's desire to act and to write for the stage (he does change his mind, but only after she has quite conveniently decided to stop writing on her own). Similarly, Shakespeare is discredited as insufficiently masculine by implying that his plays are romantically appealing only to boyish, romantically inept youngsters. One of Rosalind's unwanted suitors is shown to be romantically inept by virtue of the fact that he constantly quotes (and often misquotes) love poetry from *Romeo and Juliet*.

Jong goes a step further than Beard in making Shakespeare the love-slave of the bisexual Henry Wriothesley, Earl of Southampton (whose mother pays Shakespeare to write sonnets to the Earl). Whereas Shakespeare is asexual in Beard's novel, he is often tied to gay and bisexual signifiers in Jong's *Shylock's Daughter*, particularly when he is linked to Romeo.[21] For example, early on in the story, Jong sees a man kissing another and cannot decide if he is Shakespeare or a modern-day Romeo:

> Suddenly I look up, and in a window on the second floor an auburn-haired man with an earring glinting in one ear is kissing the same blond courtier I saw before. It is a kiss of such lingering passion and longing that I can almost feel it there on the street where I stand ... If I ... climb[ed] that stair right now ... would I encounter Will Shakespeare and his beautiful boy lover or merely an Italian punk Romeo and his American bimbo? (pp. 80–1)

Similarly, Shakespeare is aligned with both Romeo and Juliet: just before Shakespeare cites a line of Romeo – 'Will laughs derisively. "Marry, come up, you jest of scars that never felt a wound"' (p. 127) – Jong has Shakespeare cite two lines of Juliet's: 'Rosaline, Jessica, Emilia – what's in a name? A rose by any other name [*sic*] would smell as sweet' (p. 126). And Jong also has Shakespeare repeatedly cite with intense admiration the line 'Who ever loved, who loved not at first sight?' from Marlowe's homoerotic narrative poem, *Hero and Leander*, especially right after Jessica and Shakespeare first have sex (p. 192). But when Jessica sleeps with Shakespeare, we are assured that he is indeed heterosexual and interested in monogamous, true love with a woman.[22] (Shakespeare is coerced by Southampton into various bisexual threesomes and orgies.)

While Shakespeare is more clearly a functioning heterosexual in *Shakespeare in Love*, some gender confusion is also introduced here as well. The film complicates its own equation of Shakespeare and Viola with Romeo and Juliet by introducing a great deal of what I have elsewhere called 'Shakesqueer' material into their romance.[23] Viola, like her *Twelfth Night* namesake, is given to cross-dressing, thereby disturbing the film's equation of literary creativity and well-oiled heterosexual desire.[24] We see her silently mouthing Valentine's lines, for example, during the performance of *Two Gentlemen*. When Viola auditions for the part of Romeo, she fools even Shakespeare into believing she is a boy. In the first sequence discussed above, Viola reads Romeo's lines and Shakespeare reads Juliet's, and the second sequence wonderfully implies an equation of same-sex desire and heterosexual desire, as we see a series of shots of a very short-haired Juliet as Romeo, complete with moustache, beard and bean-bag penile prosthesis, kissing Shakespeare while the two are alone in the theatre rehearsing the final scene of the play. Moreover, Shakespeare himself cross-dresses as Viola's laundry woman in order to accompany her – undetected by Wessex – to her first appearance before the Queen.

Yet the film does not really go very far at all with any kind of gender trouble when it comes to Shakespeare's sexuality. Moreover, gender confusion is 'straightened' out in many respects. It is never in doubt that Shakespeare is attracted to the woman underneath the boy. Even when speaking to Viola disguised as Thomas of Kent in a boat, and when kissed by her/him, he does not realize her/his dual identity, and responds with shock and astonishment. And when Viola rehearses with the boy actor, Shakespeare interrupts them before they can kiss (only we know his motive for doing so). Similarly, the mouthing of Valentine's lines does not produce significant cross-gender ambiguity. Viola could have mouthed lines from the play by the crossed-dressed heroine, Julia. Moreover, Shakespeare writes Viola Sonnet 18, addressing her, not the young man, Thomas of Kent, and sends it to her via Thomas (to be sure, she reads it aloud passionately while still dressed as a boy, but later replies to it in a letter while dressed as Viola). Most strikingly, in the film's conclusion, when the play is performed on stage, Shakespeare appears as Romeo and Viola as Juliet.[25] Shakespeare can remain heterosexual in this film only by repressing any notion that he may have been bisexual.

Of course, in trying to encapsulate these points under a central rubric, one could simply argue that the romance narratives under discussion are contradictory, both feminist and anti-feminist.[26] My interest is less in establishing the feminist credentials of these narratives or lack thereof, however, than in examining their failure to imagine an alternative to traditional accounts of Shakespeare as author. These narratives do not really alter anything we know, and instead fall back on the more common romantic view of Shakespeare's life as a mystery. Another way to put this point is that the mass culture narratives rely on dated scholarship: they view the writings as timeless monuments, as literary texts in which Shakespeare was working toward a final draft, rather than as thriving, continuing sites of cultural production and revision.[27] And, to make a larger point, these narratives cannot dispense with academic accounts of Shakespeare even though they try to do so.

The mystification of Shakespeare's life and his writing process is writ large in *Shakespeare in Love*, where the line 'It's a mystery' gets repeated throughout the film, as if suggesting that there is some providential guide to theatre's success.[28] Similarly, though Jong's heroine will kiss Shakespeare, she will not tell. Jong provides (relatively) explicit sex scenes with Shakespeare, the Earl and a woman or women, but she stops short of going in a fully pornographic direction when it comes to sex between Shakespeare and the heroine, Jessica. When the heroine does actually have sex with Shakespeare the man, Jong refuses to narrate the sex scene:

> And here I confess I am torn – whether to break off … or whether, indeed, to describe our carnal amour as he himself, that most carnal of poets, would have done. Shall we pause and let the readers vote? … To detail organs, motions, sheets, wet spots, would be too gross, too literal, too finally deflating! It is quite one thing to imagine the poet abed with his convent Juliet or his bisexual earl – but for a mere player like myself to go back in time, bed him, and then tell tales out of school? Fie on't! Was Will Shakespeare good in bed? Let the reader judge! (p. 191)

Similarly, Jong's heroine does not share with her readers what

Shakespeare tells her about himelf:

> The poet told me much about himself, save where he got the child.
> He told me of his noble friend and his noble friend's proclivities.
> He told me of his struggles to establish himself as poet and player.
> He told me of his wife and children, his parents, Stratford country
> life. I could reveal all this here – but what purpose to my tale,
> which longs to rush onward? (p. 176)

She could reveal, but she doesn't.

As far as Shakespeare as a character goes, we get the same old story.
Here is Jong's description:

> Then all at once I see him. He has soft wisps of auburn hair worn
> loose about his nape and flowing into a wispy auburn beard, which
> he continually twists into a point. One small gold hoop gleams in
> his left ear, catching what light there is. Over his pinked, white silk
> doublet he wears a tattered velvet mandilion that gives little protec-
> tion against the wicked night. His velvet breeches, which at one
> time seem to have been trimmed with braid to match the mandil-
> ion, are travel-worn and rubbed. His pale flesh-coloured stockings
> are mud-stained, his pale shoe leather muddy and worn. He appears
> to be in his late twenties, but who can tell? This man has a sadness
> and pensiveness well past his years. I know at once who this brave
> stranger who ventures into the locked ghetto is. (pp. 125–6)

Jong's description of Shakespeare is clearly based on the Chandos
portrait.

This romantic view of Shakespeare enables a critique of contemporary mass media; that is, these narratives paradoxically turn against
their own respective media, using Shakespeare and high culture to
position themselves as the true critics of trashy, dehumanized mass
culture, whether the film or the harlequin romance. Jong's feminist
critique, for example, is also a critique of Hollywood. As Jessica
comments: 'Actresses kill themselves in LaLa Land because they are
trapped in a world that pronounces them finished, over the hill,
washed up, just when they are beginning to command their powers'
(p. 110). Similarly, she observes: 'I have paid for my passion for
Shakespeare with movie and television roles so silly that I sometimes
wanted to giggle (or weep) when I first read the script. I have been
murdered again and again, seduced and abandoned again and again,

and now that I am in my "middle years" ... I sometimes play the mother of the girl who gets murdered or seduced ... The whole women's movement came and went without murder and seduction ceasing to be the principal fate of woman on film' (p. 25). By contrasting the theatrical and poetic past with the cinematic present, Jong is able to use Shakespeare as the standard against which contemporary trash may be judged. The film festival is significantly disrupted by a rioting public, and the academy assembled in Venice fails to show the value of 'art' films to a wider audience.

Shakespeare in Love develops a similar critique of contemporary mass culture by ingeniously projecting contemporary aspects of film production back onto Shakespeare's theatre, making the latter a rather transparent allegory for the former. Thus, we get the various in-jokes about Ben Affleck as a pompous, self-regarding actor like the Elizabethan actor he plays, about the insignificance of the screenwriter, about egomaniacal and star-struck producers, as well as a critique of the way Shakespeare has become a mass culture icon (for example, the use of Shakespeare's teacup, a contemporary commodity, inscribed with the words 'Memento of Stratford-upon-Avon' on it, and the confessor as psychic, who pokes fun at pop, pseudo-Freudian therapy). This critique of mass culture depends, however, on a very conventional way of representing literary authorship: Shakespeare's composition process is privatized, and the sonnets and plays about love are granted a privileged generic status precisely because they are to be read as autobiographical documents (the history plays are generally left unmentioned). Though the film disavows the need for academic knowledge of Shakespeare, or even familiarity with his plays, in order for moviegoers to enjoy *Shakespeare in Love*, the film's critique of mass culture also depends on constructing the audience as those who are 'in the know': through a variety of framing devices, we are positioned as an audience who get the in-jokes and who voyeuristically have access to Shakespeare's private life, such that we can read the true, hidden meanings of the dramatist's works.

More crucially, the turn against the mass media involves representing Shakespeare as a solitary, suffering, lonely author. Instead of working in a pub at night in order to save the expense of candlelight, as scholars tend to think he did, Shakespeare in the film works during the day in his own study, alone.[29] Furthermore, though the inspiration for much of the plot and some famous lines of *Romeo and Juliet* come from things Shakespeare hears said by strangers on the street or friends in a pub, his real creative breakthrough has to do with the play's love scenes, and these are first performed while Shakespeare and Viola are alone: the aubade scene, for example, is conducted as an undress rehearsal, as it were, while the two have sex in bed. The film suggests that Shakespeare matures psychologically and artistically as he sheds outside influences such as Christopher Marlowe and Edward Alleyn and relies either on himself or on the private influence of Viola. As he matures, he moves out of mere theatrical posturing into writing something that supposedly has never been performed on stage before: the representation of true love.[30] This maturation is marked by a development from Shakespeare being a Hamlet-like neurotic who sees a confessor/therapist/psychic (Shakespeare cites Hamlet's line, 'Words, words, words') to the romantic Romeo (Shakespeare cites 'I am fortune's fool').

A specifically Shakespearean composition process is represented, then, as an individuated rather than collaborative process. This privatization serves to help authenticate both Shakespeare in particular and the author as origin of meaning in general, dividing off the author from the theatrical producers in terms of an opposition between pure, romantic inspiration and base, financial transactions. The critique of contemporary mass culture production noted above involves comically denigrating Shakespeare's importance as an author, for example. Marlowe is consistently regarded by characters in the film as Shakespeare's vast theatrical superior, and, when Shakespeare gives a pep talk to the actors as they begin to work on *Romeo and Juliet*, the producer Fennyman pulls Henslowe aside and, *sotto voce*, asks him who Shakespeare is. Henslowe replies disdainfully, 'Nobody. He's the author.' This joke is picked up later in the film when the camera pans down the handbill for the *première* of *Romeo and Juliet* and we see, not author Shakespeare's name, but producer Fennyman's.

The interiority of Shakespeare's composition process is marked in a number of ways, including the medium of publication, the author's signature and theatrical performance. The film opens with a shot above the Curtain Theatre, which turns out to be empty, and, after panning down into the theatre, the camera stops to focus on a quarto edition of a play lying there, called *The Moneylender's Revenge*.[31] A contrast is immediately constructed by the film between Shakespeare's method of literary production as 'a private activity' and anonymous bound editions of plays set in type. Just after the opening scene involving a confrontation between a moneylender, his two thugs and Philip Henslowe, the owner of the Rose, we first see Shakespeare writing furiously with ink and quill on paper as the title *Shakespeare in*

Love appears on the screen as if written in by hand. When Shakespeare is later inspired to write acts for *Romeo and Juliet* at successive moments, we tend to see him writing alone in his studio, his pages blotted with revisions and corrections, and his fingers covered in ink.[32] He rushes to give Rosaline a copy of the handwritten pages of *Romeo and Rosaline*, for example, and, when he gives Viola a copy of the completed *Romeo and Juliet*, it is handwritten, copied by a scribe and loosely bound with a string.[33]

Shakespeare's ability to sign his name as Shakespeare privatizes his writing in a similar way. Though Shakespeare spelled his name in various ways during his life, and though his named appeared on the printed page with various spellings, in a quite funny scene in the film, Shakespeare learns to spell his name as we now spell it. When we first see him writing, it turns out that he is throwing away page after page with nothing written on them but his name, (mis)spelled in various ways. After being inspired by a kiss from Rosaline, however, he signs his name 'William Shakespeare' and, folding up the paper on which he wrote his name, puts the paper in a bracelet to give to Rosaline, on the advice of his confessor/therapist/psychic. Though the film enacts the process whereby Shakespeare has become a cultural icon, it presents that process not as an historical one constructed in the present, but as the inside story of Shakespeare's growing up into an adult lover and playwright.

The performance of these lines is also represented in terms of their privatization, either as their internalization by memorization or by a coded interpretation of the lines' true meaning. Viola's love of the theatre is marked by the fact that she has learned lines from Shakespeare's play by heart. The first time we see her, Viola is distinguished from the Queen by her response to Valentine's speech about Silvia. During the performance of *Two Gentlemen* I noted earlier, Viola's authentic love of the theatre and of Shakespeare in particular is established by a sense of the play's interiority in her psyche: in a close-up, she silently mouths the words, obviously having memorized them. Later in the film, she can play Juliet at the last minute's notice, a part she knows 'entirely' even though she has rehearsed only Romeo's part.

The staged performance of *Romeo and Juliet* is similarly privatized. When Shakespeare and Viola rehearse the aubade scene in bed, it seems as if they are making up the lines as they go, as if they really were Romeo and Juliet. Similarly, these narratives commit the biographical fallacy when it comes to the interpretative strategies they adopt when reading the works in relation to Shakespeare, the man. The film sets up several analogies between the lovers' lives and the play: the Capulet ball is anticipated by a ball where Shakespeare dances with Viola before being thrown out by Wessex (who is like Paris, except that here he wins Juliet). It later redoes the balcony scene from the play with Shakespeare wooing Viola, calling to her from below as she says, from the balcony, 'Romeo, Romeo, a young man from Verona'. And the aubade scene is also anticipated by a scene in which the lovers awake in bed at morning. Similarly, Shakespeare first recites Romeo's line, 'I am fortune's fool', at Viola's balcony, then in the staged performance of the play and then again behind the scenes just to Viola during this same performance.

The effect of these analogies is to position the audience as insiders: our access to the lovers' private scenes also gives us access to a series of coded interpretations of works such as Sonnet 18 or *Romeo and Juliet*. The writings are recontextualized by the film's back-formation of Shakespeare the filmic character's authorship, an effect which naturalizes the film's character as the historical truth of the work's genesis even as it also cleverly exposes that character as just another fiction (refusing ever to pass itself off as the 'true' story of Shakespeare's 'lost years').[34] In the staged performance of the end of the aubade scene, for example, Romeo and Juliet's lines are meant to be read by us as those of Shakespeare and Viola, who both know they are about to be parted because Viola has just married Wessex and will shortly have to return to him:

> *Juliet.* Art thou gone so, love, lord, my husband, friend?
> I must hear from thee every day in the hour,
> For in a minute there are many days.
> O, by this count I shall be much in years
> Ere I again behold my Romeo.
> *Romeo.* Farewell.
> I will omit no opportunity
> That may convey my greetings, love, to thee.
> *Juliet.* O, think'st thou we shall ever meet again?
> *Romeo.* I doubt it not, and all these woes shall serve
> For sweet discourses in our times to come.[35]

Positioned by the film on the side of the actors rather than the audience in the theatre viewing the play, we hear these lines as if spoken by the two lovers. It is the lovers' pathos, not that of the characters

Romeo and Juliet, that is supposed to concern and move us, just as we earlier laughed at Shakespeare when he struggles to learn how to spell his name correctly.

Academics are positioned along similar lines as insiders within the insider audience. They are not only able to spot the line references but the icons by which Shakespeare or his characters have come to be known. For example, when Shakespeare crumples a piece of paper in the first sequence where we see him writing, the crumpled paper lands on a shelf next to a skull, linking Shakespeare to Hamlet. Academic knowledge of Shakespeare, reduced to the ability to identify an allusion or recognize a quotation, makes academic viewers that much more in the know as the film defines knowledge.

Though the various framing devices also produce externalizing and distancing effects (or what I would call meta-cinematic moments), I would argue that the film's self-reflexivity in making one fiction the basis for another enables not so much a critique of the Romantic account of literary authorship but instead enables its reinvention. Thus, the scene in which Shakespeare learns to spell his name 'correctly' reproduces rather than departs from the scene in which we see the teacup bought from a Stratford tourist shop: it enacts Shakespeare's construction in this very film as a mass culture icon. *Shakespeare in Love*'s turn against the mass media enables the film paradoxically to install the dominant mass culture account of literary authorship served up as high cultural achievement.

In the process of disavowing academic knowledge about Shakespeare, the romance narratives I am discussing thus make strong claims for their own knowledge about Shakespeare as a literary author. By giving us an insider track on the mass culture production industry and on the characters' private lives, narratives like *Shylock's Daughter* and *Shakespeare in Love* assert their authority over the production process: the screenwriter/actress/novelist knows better than anyone else, they imply, what it took for Shakespeare to write his plays and what his cultural achievement and legacy are.[36]

III

Whatever the politics of these romance narratives, feminist, anti-feminist or some combination of the two, then, they cannot break with academia altogether. As we have seen, screenwriter Norman consults Professor Greenblatt; mass market novelist Beard defers to scholarly authorities in *Romance of the Rose*; and, in Jong's *Shylock's Daughter*, amateur Shakespearean Jessica tells us that her 'footlocker is fairly bursting with Shakespeare ... Shakespeare biographies, Shakespeare criticism' (p. 16). Moreover, the chief reason she gives for not revealing all about Shakespeare's performance in bed in the passage I cited earlier is that doing so would adversely affect academia:

> if I told these things about this man of Stratford, what pleasure would I take away from how many book-bound scholars, whose greatest joy is to speculate upon this mythical man, providing him with professions he never followed, ancestries he never traced, even names he was never called! I'll not have that on my conscience. Let the Shakespeare industry flourish! I speak not of the 'the Bard', whoever that may be, but only of a lost and homesick young Englishman named Will who travelled a little way with me on time's continuum. (p. 176)

In a comparable fashion, the Miramax press kit for *Shakespeare in Love* provides a brief biography of Shakespeare (giving his birth year as 1554!), cites a dated 'Shakespearean scholar', whose name is incorrectly spelled Arthur Aches (it's Acheson) and who reads the sonnets and *Romeo and Juliet* in terms of Shakespeare's personal life, and then puts the label either 'fact' or 'fiction' in front of each of the characters in a section introducing them.[37] And in her mass market novel, *Acts of Passion*, which makes use of *Hamlet*, Deanna James even takes over the role of teacher (or teacher as game show host), commenting on her use of Shakespeare: 'I further thought to allow you the fun of seeing how well you remembered your Shakespeare. Have you tested yourself thus far? Four points for each correct answer. Ninety-six is a perfect score.'[38]

When engaging the authorship controversy between Stratfordians and Oxfordians, for example, all side with the Stratfordians. This is predictable enough. Though an Oxfordian website set up a page entitled 'Shakespeare in Love: the True Story', I doubt that we can expect a film entitled *Oxford in Love* to be released anytime in the near future.[39] (I do find it ironic, however, that we now have the *Oxford Shakespeare*.)[40] More significant is the fact that, in coming down on the Stratfordian side, these romance narratives end up replaying the Romantic view of Shakespeare as an unknowable and indeterminate author and person, someone whose life is to be read only in terms of his plays, someone who has no personality outside them. Mass culture narratives like those under discussion here (and generally) cannot dispense with academic authority either.

Nor does their reliance on academic authority effect a critique of mass culture that breaks with mass culture. Indeed, the plot of *Shakespeare in Love* is not new. The plots and thematic elements of two novels written by women, *No Bed for Bacon* and *Shakespeare's Sweetheart*, are very close to the film, and one critic has suggested that the screenwriters have plagiarized from *No Bed for Bacon*.[41] These novels are, of course, not originary either, relying on early Shakespeare myths such as Shakespeare leaving Stratford because he was caught poaching.[42]

One way of theorizing both the blunted critique of literary authorship, and the way the mass culture romances about Shakespeare under discussion here rely on academic authority and on outmoded academic scholarship, would be to adopt Raymond Williams' distinctions between dominant, subordinate and residual forms of cultural production: while it is in some respects dominant (money spent on production, promotion, distribution and so on), mass culture also relies on residual elements of scholarship (such as work by the obscure scholar Arthur Acheson), not the latest.[43] These romances could then be read as part of what Graham Holderness has called 'the Shakespeare myth', regarded as yet more examples of the various ways in which Shakespeare's construction as a timeless monument serves hegemonic interests in the present.[44] Instead of being shown how Shakespeare's cultural authority might be dismantled or constructed otherwise, the audience of *Shakespeare in Love*, for example, are given the pleasure of knowing in advance of the characters in the film what the audience already know to be true – namely, that Shakespeare will write *Romeo and Juliet* and that it will be loved by its audience.[45]

The problem with this way of reading the failure of the romance narratives about Shakespeare to break with academia, or to use it to produce a more trenchant critique of literary authorship and Shakespeare's status as mass culture icon, is that it assumes that the academic production of knowledge is wholly unified, as if there were no debates or divisions among critics. But mass culture accounts of Shakespeare indirectly call this assumption into question. For example, one effect of the use of 'the Shakespeare myth' in these narratives is to expose the way academics, particularly Stratfordians (of which I count myself one, I hasten to add), themselves rely on a version of the same myth. In his generally quite kooky book, *Alias Shakespeare* (1997), James Sobran has his own account of what he calls 'the Origin of the Shakespeare Myth', and he convincingly shows that

Stratfordians have had to legitimate Shakespeare's authorship not only by pointing to historical documents about Shakespeare and his relatives but by suturing to them a Romantic theory of Shakespeare's universal genius (and typically ascribing a democratic politics to his writings).[46] Moreover, some prominent Shakespeare scholars themselves are suggesting narratives about Shakespeare to film producers that seem to be as much conspiracy theories as do Oxfordian conspiracy theories about Oxford's authorship.[47]

Moreover, academia is not necessarily a site for exclusively up-to-date knowledge either, and not simply because more traditional and more innovative critics differ in their critical methods (as if traditional critics could simply be consigned to the dustbin of the residual). For example, in her romance novel, *Miss Grimsley's Oxford Career*, Carla Kelly tells the story of a woman writing Shakespeare criticism and not getting credit for it (since she is a woman, she cannot attend Oxford and cannot get her work published in her own name).[48] Her dunce of a brother gets the credit instead. Unlike Beard's heroine, Kelly's is not reconciled to her loss of recognition as a critic. As Laurie Osborne suggests, Kelly's novel resonates with Virginia Woolf's account of her own exclusion from that same university.[49] Yet Woolf's account of Shakespeare in a celebrated passage of *A Room of One's Own* itself reproduces the Romantic version of Shakespeare's composition process:

> The reason perhaps why we know so little of Shakespeare ... is that his grudges and spites and antipathies are hidden from us ... All desire to protest, to preach, to proclaim an injury, to pay off a score ... was fired out of him and consumed. Therefore his poetry flows from him free and unimpeded. If ever a human being got his work expressed completely, it was Shakespeare. If ever a mind was incandescent, unimpeded ... it was Shakespeare's mind.[50]

Shakespeare is Shakespeare, in this view, because we know nothing of his mind (whatever we know about his life is irrelevant, since his works transcend their biographical origins). Moreover, Woolf's retro-feminism (given the dialogical status of all discourses and subjectivities, is it possible to say that anyone has a room of her own in which to write?) hardly seems a solid foundation on which to build a feminist critique of contemporary mass culture. And, despite the contemporary Foucauldian turn from authors to author-functions, academics continue to read Shakespeare's plays in relation to his life, regularly linking, for example, the years in which he produced his greatest tragedies (1601 to 1607) to the death of his father, John, in 1601. In his introduction to the *Norton Shakespeare*, for example, Stephen Greenblatt indulges in several 'biographical daydreams that have supposedly been made obsolete by modern criticism' (p. 46).[51]

In addition to having its own residual elements, academia's claim to provide a base for alternative Shakespeares is further limited by the fact that even the most up-to-date, fully theorized critical practice has increasingly come to depend on the mass media for its cultural legitimation. Just as mass culture is concerned with academia, so too academia is concerned with mass media, especially film (which seems to be closer to the plays and more of a 'high art' form than romance novels). As academia is being mediatized and becoming virtual (editions coming out on CD-ROMs, internet websites constructed for Shakespeare, the reconstructed Globe, the museum for the Rose theatre and new films of the plays), the appearance of Shakespeare outside of academia becomes an important – perhaps the most important – way of validating academic work on Shakespeare. The recognition of academic work in mass culture is the chief way in which academic criticism can claim to have had a significant socially transformative effect beyond the captive audience of university students in classrooms.

Moreover, the boundary between mass culture and academia is also breaking down. The present proliferation of mass media biographies of Shakespeare and citations and revisions of his works is occurring at the same time that we witness the proliferation of entirely new and entirely different editions of Shakespeare, in old and modernized spellings, some of which include what was formerly regarded as belonging to what Tucker Brooke called the Shakespeare apocrypha, such as *Edward III* in the second Riverside edition.[52] This proliferation is the result not only of new academic research but of new markets for editions (in which the point is to show that the latest new edition is more valuable than the others by virtue of its difference from them). In my view, while the proliferation of mass culture representations, as well as the present proliferation of academic editions of Shakespeare, might seem to affirm the authority of Shakespeare (leaving Oxfordians behind as kooks), it is loosening the grip academics have over what we have until recently taken to be the canonically Shakespearean. It marks what I am calling the end of the Shakespearean.

IV

At the end of the 1990s, a decade which has seen not only an unprecedented number of Shakespeare's plays made or remade as films or made
into film (and then released on video), but also Shakespeare's citation
across all mass media ranging from advertising to popular music to
fiction and comic books, it might seem perverse to speak of the end of
the Shakespearean. In doing so, I mean to suggest that what might be
termed mass culture's current romance with Shakespeare does not actually reaffirm Shakespeare's cultural authority either as author-function
or cultural icon, as might be argued both by critics who regard
Shakespeare's plays as universal (the foundation of the western canon
if not the Western canon itself), and by critics who quite differently
regard Shakespeare's plays as theatrical revisions and the product of
collaboration, later mass culture citations and replays viewed as historically specific appropriations. This account of Shakespeare's authority
and authorship depends on the assumption that current reproductions
of Shakespeare are essentially hermeneutic; that is, there is some interpretative and dialogical relation between the Shakespearean 'original'
and later replays. The potentially feminist process I discussed earlier
whereby literary authorship, patronage and performance are feminized
likewise depends on the assumption that mass culture appropriations
remain in some hermeneutic relation to Shakespeare's works.

When analysing Shakespeare's presence in mass culture, it is not
surprising that academics focus on film and, to a lesser extent, other mass
culture citations and revisions of the plays rather than on mass culture
constructions of Shakespeare's biography, since the more extensive the
relation between mass media and Shakespeare's works – revision as
opposed to mere citation – the more valid the study of Shakespeare in
mass culture will be considered to be by other academics. Less significant
relations between the 'original' Shakespeare text and mass culture citations and spin-offs of it will mean, it is widely assumed, that a given
example is trivial, that the academic, whether feminist or not, will have
little, if anything, to say about it. It is not surprising that many examples
of Shakespeare in mass culture have yet to be archived.

As I have argued elsewhere, however, many mass culture spin-offs
have a post-hermeneutic relation to Shakespeare's plays: that is, they
are so far from the original as not to be interpretable as Shakespearean
at all.[53] By speaking of the end of the Shakespearean, I mean to
suggest that this distinction between the hermeneutic and the post-
hermeneutic is now in the process of breaking down, that the

reception of Shakespeare as a biographical author or as an author-function, which serves to establish what is and is not canonically written by Shakespeare, involves distancing Shakespeare as character and author from anything that might be said to be characteristically 'Shakespearean' about his writings. The very proliferation of Shakespeare editions and Shakespeare in mass culture might then be read as a symptom of this psychotic breakdown of authority rather than an expansion of it (to be used, in the dominant critical fantasy, for ennobling, civilizing ends, whether those ends are conceived as the carrying on of a tradition or the dismantling of it, the policing of the boundary between high and mass culture or the transgression of it).[54] This is what I take to be, in effect, the breakdown not so much of Shakespeare's cultural authority as an author but of the specifically Shakespearean – that is, those characteristics that can be said to define his writings as *his* writings. The character of Shakespeare produced inside of mass culture in which realism rules, to put the point another way, is displaced by the character of Shakespeare understood as the letters, the authorial signature *in* the works themselves. Mass culture screenwriters, directors and costume designers cannot dispense with academics just as academics cannot dispense with mass culture productions of Shakespeare in order to legitimate their (some might say 'merely') academic authority. As the distinction between the Shakespeare canon and the Shakespeare apocrypha dissolves before us, it may soon be time to speak of the Shakespeare apocalypse.

Notes

1. See James Sterngold, 'Just Like Real Life? Well, Maybe a Little More Exciting: Scholars Get Cameo Roles as Film Consultants', *New York Times*, Saturday, 26 December 1998, section A23, p. 25.
2. See the Miramax press kit for *Shakespeare in Love*.
3. On the way the academic is positioned as a loser in films citing Shakespeare in particular and in mass culture generally, see Richard Burt, *Unspeakable ShaXXXspeares: Queer Theory and American Kiddie Culture* (New York: St. Martin's Press, 1998), pp. 1–28, 203–46.
4. For a rather different account of the more extensive role Stephen Greenblatt played, see his 'About That Romantic Sonnet', *New York Times*, Saturday, 6 February 1999, section A29. Greenblatt suggested that Norman turn to the 'lost years', since what we know of Shakespeare's life does not present the screenwriter with very promising dramatic material.
5. Sarah Lyall, 'The Muse of Shakespeare Imagined as a Blonde', *New York Times*, Sunday, 12 December 1998, p. 25.
6. One suspects that the movie's popularity, extensive coverage, and acclaim – nominated for thirteen academy awards – has to do with the way its

marketing made clear that one doesn't have to know (about) Shakespeare to enjoy the film. Richard Wilson tells me a film is in the works by screenwriter Tom O'Connor about Thomas Campion based on his work on Shakespeare and Campion, the story retold through the sixteen-year-old eyes of Shakespeare. Whether this film turns out to be a counter-example in so far as the screenwriter relies on an authority like Wilson will be seen once the film is released. For a personal account of academic consultation on films involving Shakespeare, see Russell Jackson, 'Working with Shakespeare: Confessions of an Adviser', *Cineaste*, 24:1 (1998), pp. 42–4.

7. See, for example, Kaja Silverman, *Male Subjectivity at the Margins* (New York and London: Routledge, 1992).

8. In representing Shakespeare as a lover, *Shakespeare in Love* departs from the representation of him as non-sexual in hardcore pornographic films and videos. See Burt, *Unspeakable ShaXXXspeares*, pp. 77–126.

9. See Lynn Hirschberg, 'A Dresser for the Ages', *New York Times Sunday Magazine*, Sunday, 20 December 1998, pp. 60–1.

10. Of course, tights on men do not in themselves involve feminization. Witness Errol Flynn's prominent package in *Robin Hood* (directed by Michael Curtiz and William Keighley, 1938) or Carey Elwes in *The Princess Bride* (directed by Rob Reiner, 1987). But, at least in the present moment, the period is ripe for parody. See the reprisal of Robin Hood's romantic role in Mel Brooks' burlesque, *Robin Hood: Men in Tights* (1993).

11. See Julie Beard, *Romance of the Rose* (New York: Berkeley Books, 1998); Erica Jong, *Shylock's Daughter: A Novel of Love in Venice* (New York: Harper Paperbacks, 1995), first published as *Serenissima* in 1986; John Madden's *Shakespeare in Love* (1998). All citations from the novels are to these editions and appear in the text.

12. The politics of the romance has been a matter of longstanding debate among feminists. See Ann Douglas, 'Soft Porn Culture', *New Republic*, 30 August 1980, pp. 25–9; Tania Modleski, *Loving With a Vengeance: Mass-Produced Fantasies for Women* (Hamden, CT: Archon Books, 1983); Ann Barr Snitow, 'Mass Market Romance: Pornography for Women is Different', in Ann Barr Snitow and others (eds), *Powers of Desire* (New York: Monthly Review Press, 1983), pp. 245–63; Jan Cohn, *Romance and the Erotics of Property: Mass-Marketed Fiction for Women* (Durham and London: Duke University Press, 1988); Tania Modleski, 'Questioning Scholars' Torrid Romance with Popular Culture', *Chronicle of Higher Education*, 65:12, 13 November 1998, sections B8–9; Tania Modleski, *Old Wives' Tales and Other Women's Stories* (New York: New York University Press, 1998), pp. 47–79. On lesbian cross-gender identification, see Modleski, *Old Wives' Tales*. See also Paul Burston and Colin Richardson (eds), *A Queer Romance: Lesbians, Gay Men, and Popular Culture* (New York and London: Routledge, 1995). For fascinating accounts of Shakespeare's citation in romance novels, see Laurie Osborne, 'Romancing the Bard', unpublished paper circulated in the Shakespeare Association of America Seminar, 'Citing Shakespeare in American Popular Culture', directed by Richard Burt and Lynda Boose, Cleveland (1998) and Laurie Osborne, 'Sweet, Savage Shakespeare', forthcoming in Don Hedrick and Bryan Reynolds (eds), *Shakespeare Without Class* (New York: St. Martin's Press).

13. *Looking for Richard* (directed by Al Pacino, 1996) offers another instance of mass culture's ambivalent relationship to academic knowledge. See also the A&E Television production, *William Shakespeare: Life of Drama* (directed by Bill Harris, 1996).

14. On the mass mediatization of academia, see Samuel Weber, *Mass Mediauras: Form, Technics, Media*, ed. Alan Cholodenko (Stanford: Stanford University Press, 1996).

15. On Shakespeare's character as a literal character or letter in Shakespeare's writings, see Joel Fineman's essay on *The Rape of Lucrece* in his book, *The Subjectivity Effect in Western Literary Tradition: Essays Towards the Release of Shakespeare's Will* (Cambridge, Mass.: MIT Press, 1991).

16. This seems to be generally true of fiction about Shakespeare, in which the story generally focuses on his early years in Stratford and in London. See, for examples, Sara Hawks Sterling, *Shakespeare's Sweetheart* (Philadelphia: George W. Jacobs, 1905), Anthony Burgess, *Nothing Like the Sun: A Novel of Shakespeare's Love Life* (New York: W. W. Norton & Co., 1975) and Stephanie Cowell, *The Players: A Novel of the Young Shakespeare* (New York: W. W. Norton & Co, 1997).

17. For a representative passage from Jong's novel, see p. 42.

18. See Snitow, 'Mass Market Romance', pp. 245–63.

19. See *The Private Lives of Elizabeth and Essex* (directed by Michael Curtiz, 1939) and *Fire Over England* (directed by William K. Howard, 1937).

20. In her defence, Jong does identify Shakespeare as a 'maternal' figure.

21. For a fuller analysis of gay and lesbian versions of *Romeo and Juliet* in various mass media, see Richard Burt, 'Masked Balls: Homonormativity and the Gay and Lesbian Romance with *Romeo and Juliet*', forthcoming in Hedrick and Reynolds (eds), *Shakespeare Without Class*.

22. Even this moment is somewhat ambiguous, as Jessica refuses to tell what Shakespeare was like in bed. For more on this novel's queerness, see Burt, 'Masked Balls'.

23. See Burt, *Unspeakable ShaXXXspeares*, pp. 29–76.

24. On Stoppard's inclusion of gay material in the theatrical and film versions of his earlier *Rosencrantz and Guildenstern*, see Burt, *Unspeakable ShaXXXspeares*, p. 30. See also Mel Gussow, 'Tom Stoppard in Love, With Shakespeare', *New York Times*, 12 January 1999, sections B1–2.

25. For a fuller account of the queer aspects of this film, see Burt, 'Masked Balls'.

26. This seems to be the usual feminist take on the romance. See, for example, Modleski, *Old Wives' Tales And Other Women's Stories*, pp. 47–79.

27. They indirectly confirm Harold Bloom's knowingly retro-theory of Shakespeare's creation as advanced in *Shakespeare: The Invention of the Human* (New York: Riverhead Books, 1998). The irony to consider here is why this traditional view of Shakespeare should thrive in a mass medium whose mode of production so thoroughly contradicts it.

28. Similarly, the Miramax press kit for the film opens with the following account of Shakespeare's life: 'Although he wrote some of the world's most reknown [*sic*] romances and comedies, William Shakespeare's personal life remains a great mystery. Little is known about the writer and what is *thought* to be known is hotly debated by scholars. Conspiracy theories and suggestions of hoaxes and false identities abound, but have resisted proof

for centuries.'

29. For an example of the scholarly view, see the film documentary, *William Shakespeare: Life of Drama*.

30. Marlowe gives him the plot, the Italian setting and the character of Mercutio. Alleyn gives him the play's title.

31. The handbills for the play are similarly set in type and linked to the production process, which is regarded as at best an interference in Shakespeare's authentic composition process. The producer Fennyman eventually browbeats Henslowe into dropping his request that Shakespeare write a comedy.

32. The book, *Shakespeare in Love: The Love Poetry of William Shakespeare* (New York: Miramax Books/Hyperion, 1998), released along with the movie, also matches typeface to handwriting, establishing the latter as archaic and original by making the blurred and sepia handwriting larger than the black typeface. The handwriting is also linked to the stills in the book, all of which have blurred edges and sepia tones, recalling 'old' photos (from the late nineteenth century). The archaic and less than fully legible and accessible are thus mystified as more authentic.

33. Of course, the fact that Shakespeare wrote on paper with ink is historically accurate, but the film nevertheless personalizes this medium. No one in the film but Shakespeare uses it.

34. In *Shylock's Daughter*, Jong similarly offers biographical readings of Shakespeare's works. Jessica writes: 'Looking into [Shakespeare's] sad eyes last night, I felt I knew him. And I have read his poems – even those he thinks he has not yet conceived – anyone who truly reads another's poems knows his soul' (p. 136).

35. All quotations are from Stephen Greenblatt and others (eds), *The Norton Shakespeare* (New York: W. W. Norton & Co, 1997), III.v.43–53.

36. Jong in particular enlarges Jessica's authority by virtue of the fact that she knows what is to come while Shakespeare does not. Thus, she warns Shakespeare not to wish Marlowe dead after identifying a quotation by Shakespeare from his rival. See p. 193.

37. The kit doesn't give the reference. It's Arthur Acheson, *Shakespeare's Lost Years in London, 1586–1592* (New York: Haskell House, 1970). The book was first published in 1920.

38. Deanna James, *Acts of Passion* (New York: Zebra Books, 1992), p. 477.

39. On the other hand, the Oxfordian account is getting new press. See, for example, Howard Chua-Eoan, 'The Bard's Beard', *Time*, 15 February 1999, pp. 74–5. For a Stratfordian site, see the Shakespeare Authorship Page (maintained by David Kathman and Terry Ross) at http:www.bcpl.lib.md.us/~tross/ws/will.html. On the authorship controversy, see Marjorie Garber, *Shakespeare's Ghost Writers* (New York: Methuen, 1987).

40. The website address is http://home.earthlink.net/~mark_alex/.

41. See Caryl Brahms and Simon Jasha Skidolsky, *No Bed for Bacon* (New York: Crowell, 1950) and Sterling, *Shakespeare's Sweetheart*. On Sterling, see my essay, 'Masked Balls'. I thank Professor Stanley Wells for pointing out to me the many parallels between *Shakespeare in Love* and *No Bed for Bacon* in a short unpublished piece he sent me. The screenwriters deny they plagia-

rized from the novel. See Daniel Fierman, 'Reelworld', *Entertainment Weekly*, 12 February 1999, p. 55.

42. On this and other legends about Shakespeare, see Samuel Schoenbaum, *Shakespeare's Lives* (New York: Oxford University Press, 1970).

43. Raymond Williams, *Marxism and Literature* (Oxford: Oxford University Press, 1977).

44. See Graham Holderness (ed.), *The Shakespeare Myth* (Manchester: Manchester University Press, 1988). For a more recent version of this kind of critique, see Barbara Hodgdon, *The Shakespeare Trade: Performances and Appropriations* (Philadelphia: University of Pennsylvania Press, 1998).

45. One could add to this a full-scale analysis, not yet conducted to my knowledge, of Shakespeare as a character in literature. For a collection of some of the raw materials for such a project, see Maurice J. O'Sullivan, *Shakespeare's Other Lives: An Anthology of Fictional Depictions of the Bard* (Jefferson: McFarland, 1997).

46. See James Sobran, *Alias Shakespeare: Solving the Greatest Literary History of All Time* (New York: Free Press, 1997).

47. In his discussion with Marc Norman, for example, Greenblatt invited him to script a conspiracy scenario: 'I first suggested he might invent a Shakespearean involvement in the murky, dangerous world of religious struggle. (After all, [in] 1588, when Shakespeare was 24 ... there are hints that Shakespeare was involved in or at least knew ... secret Catholics; he could have witnessed exorcisms, thwarted plots against the queen's life, watched the execution of Jesuits).' See Greenblatt, 'About That Romantic Sonnet', A29. Richard Wilson's view of Shakespeare as a conspiring Catholic goes even further.

48. See Carla Kelly, *Miss Grimsley's Oxford Career* (New York: Signet, 1992).

49. I would like to thank Professor Osborne for generously lending me a copy of the novel.

50. Virginia Woolf, *A Room of One's Own* (New York: Harcourt, Brace & World, 1959), pp. 56–7.

51. See also Walter Cohen's introduction to the sonnets in the Norton edition of Shakespeare's works: 'The intensity of these feelings ... encourages a biographical reading of the sonnets' (p. 1919). This biographical mode of reading the sonnets, in particular, has its origins in German Romanticism. See Schoenbaum, *Shakespeare's Lives*, for a discussion of August Wilhelm Schlegel's view that the sonnets were inspired by 'an actual friendship and love' (p. 252).

52. See C. F. Tucker Brooke (ed.), *The Shakespeare Apocrypha* (Oxford: Clarendon Press, 1908) and G. Blakemore Evans and others (eds), *The Riverside Shakespeare: Second Edition* (Boston and New York: Houghton Mifflin, 1997). See also the new Cambridge edition edited by Giorgio Melchiori, *King Edward III* (Cambridge: Cambridge University Press, 1998).

53. Burt, *Unspeakable ShaXXXspeares*, pp. xiv–xv.

54. It is worth noting that the proliferation marks a kind of academic imperialism: the new editions all add new material, though what they add differs. No edition – and does this not seem the legacy of capitalist marketing strategies? – offers less or excludes anything previously thought to be written by Shakespeare.

Index